Hu...
and Paula

Praise for *Hughie & Paula*:

'As one of Hughie's early discoveries, I was totally absorbed by Chris Green's page-turning investigation of his father's dark secrets.'

Amanda Barrie
(A hostess on *Double Your Money*)

'A shocking, tragic, and heart-rending account of the consequences of the cycle of abuse.'

Tony Holland
(TV's original musical muscle man on *Opportunity Knocks*)

'An interesting insight into a valued friend and remembered colleague.'

Berni Flint
(*Opportunity Knocks* winner, 1977)

Hughie
and Paula

The Tangled Lives of Hughie Green
and Paula yates

CHRISTOPHER GREEN
WITH CAROL CLERK

ROBSON BOOKS

First published in paperback in Great Britain in 2004 by Robson Books, The Chrysalis Building, Bramley Road, London W10 6SP

An imprint of Chrysalis Books Group Plc

British Library Cataloguing in Publication Data
A catalogue record for this book is available from the British Library.

ISBN 1 86105 749 0

Typeset by SX Composing DTP, Rayleigh, Essex
Printed by Creative Print & Design (Wales), Ebbw Vale

To Nannie

Contents

Acknowledgements

I would like to thank:

My wife Lynne and my stepdaughters, Kristin, Keely and Kady for their gracious patience and love.

My 'Uncle' Victor Hallums, a fine gentleman who always treated me as a son. I love you and thank you for having been a true friend of my family.

My new-found kith and kin, Margaret Hulme, Father's cousin, whom I totally adore for her love, wonderful sense of humour and, above all, compassion.

Janet Moat and her colleague, Pam Rostron, of the British Film Institute, for their absolutely tremendous and heartfelt support for both Lynne and me.

Janice Robinson, my London-based researcher, who not only did brilliant work in penetrating the shadows of the past but, along with her delightful husband, Desmond, was so very gracious to me.

Melissa Brooks, David May, Tan Ashraf and Julian Henson of A&H Associates, London, who tirelessly supported my 'must-have-it-now' requests for research documents.

Emma Worth, a true and loving friend of Paula Yates and her family.

The late Kell Hutchence, a thoroughly decent man who suffered greatly but strove with grace to 'do the right thing'.

Kirsten and her son Ben Stuckey of The Orchard, Meopham, for sharing with me so kindly their memories of Papa.

Liz Turner who worked as a secretary in my former bedroom/ train room and who wrote beautifully and from her heart of the Hughie Green that she knew.

Margaret Pow, Mrs Carr's daughter. My thanks for sharing memories with me of your mum, Agnes. Papa was blessed to know her.

Charles Cochand, who defines what a family friend is all about and who tirelessly helped me to see the way back into the early years of my Papa – thank you so very much.

Father Peter Harding and Mark Graddon, two remarkably kind and caring souls who will always be in my heart. You afforded me more than you know.

John Heyman and Pip Wedge, who both knew Papa so very well and who generously allowed me their time to share their memory and thoughts about the man they knew who was 'an icon of British light entertainment'.

Joseph, Jenny and the entire wonderful staff of the Moat House Hotel, Sloane Square, who became my 'extended family' during the many long weeks away from home researching in London.

Robert Smith, my literary agent, who has great patience and who has always treated me well as 'a person with a story to tell' rather than 'a client'. . . a gentleman I am fortunate to have met.

Carol Clerk, my very talented co-author, who, with her understanding husband, Nigel, and lovely daughter, Eve, has 'gone the distance'. My heartfelt thanks for having been with me, all along the way, to realise our book.

And there were so many more who gave me their appreciated attention and help in many different ways. I thank Andrew Hersey, Arthur Teulon, Barry Breckon, the late Betty Raymond, Dr David Jenkins, Dr Eric Lever, Elizabeth Kerins-McManus, Elizabeth Silverthorne, Ella Wilson, Jenny Read, Louise Cox, Mark Stephens, Michael Ingram, Nicholas Allen, Nicola Solomon, Peter Pollard, Pierre and Roger Vacher, Rojina Coghill, Susan Westhorpe . . . and all of those supportive others whom I will think of later – and kindly.

Christopher Green

I would like to thank Christopher Green warmly for his co-operation, patience, painstaking research and willingness to share so completely his turbulent and often harrowing story. Much appreciation goes to Lynne Green for her valuable and perceptive insights, and to Kristin, Keely and Kady for their generosity of spirit. Special mention is due to our fearless leader, Robert Smith, and the proofreader, Alison Leach. Stephanie Jones – take a bow for the diversional reading! Big thanks, too, to my mother, Doreen Clerk, and to Patricia Mitchell, Maria Jefferis and Scott Mckenzie for their unswerving moral support. I am grateful to Choccy for the sanity. And to my husband and daughter, Nigel and Eve O'Brien, all the love in the world for their endless understanding, devotion and help at every turn and twist of the way.

Carol Clerk

The following books yielded crucial information in the preparation of this manuscript: *Ocean Bridge: The History of RAF Ferry Command* by Carl A Christie; *The Canadians* by Patrick Watson; *Opportunity Knocked* by Hughie Green; *The Autobiography* by Paula Yates; *Is That It?* by Bob Geldof; *Just A Man* by Patricia Glassop and Tina Hutchence; *Steve Race: Musician At Large* by Steve Race; and *The Complete Book of the British Charts, Singles and Albums* by Tony Brown, Jon Kutner and Neil Warwick.

A wealth of knowledge was provided by various British magazines, including *Hello!* and *OK,* but three articles were particularly illuminating: 'The Perils of Paula' by Steven Daly in *Vanity Fair*, February 2001; 'The Bizarre Legacy of Hughie Green' by Robert Chalmers in the *Mail on Sunday Review*, June 29, 1997; and 'Daughter of Darkness' by David James Smith in the *Sunday Times Magazine*, February 11, 2001.

Historical accuracy and a wide understanding of events was made possible by personal family papers as well as archive news and features cuttings from all of the UK's daily and Sunday newspapers, the local and regional press, and publications in Canada, the USA and Australia.

Christopher Green and Carol Clerk would like, finally, to recognise the abundant help provided by these websites: www.ananova.com; www.britmovie.co.uk; www.theboomtownrats.com; www.cnn.com; www.cunardline.com; www.frapa.org; www.gamesbiz.net; www.gordondadds.com; www.users.zetnet.co.uk; www.world-productions.com; www.munster-express.ie; www.mynottinghill.co.uk; www.nftsfilm-tv.ac.uk; www.michaelhutchenceinfo.com; www.whirligig-tv.co.uk; www.scriptwritermagazine.com; www.sixtiescity.com; www.britishpictures.com; www.theage.com.au; www.bbc.co.uk; www.chu.cam.ac.uk; www.georgeformby.co.uk; www.guardian.co.uk; www.independent.co.uk; www.memorabletv.com; www.mirror.co.uk; www.archives.ca; www.observer.co.uk; www.pads.ahds.ac.uk; www.thestage.co.uk; www.telegraph.co.uk; www.timesonline.co.uk; www.fiftiesweb.com; www.ukgameshows.com; www.televisionheaven.co.uk; www.whatthepaperssay.co.uk; www.skool-days.co.uk

Foreword

In December 1997, at the age of fifty, I discovered that I had another sister. DNA testing had proved that my late father, Hughie Green, had also sired the controversial TV star Paula Yates.

My father was an icon of British television, but his avuncular charm and generous humour onscreen could not have been more at odds with the person he became after the credits rolled. His audiences would have been shocked to know that their friendly, faithful TV host, in his private life, was a serial womaniser, a pathological liar and a supreme manipulator of other people.

One of his guilty secrets exploded into the public arena when he was sensationally exposed at his own funeral, by his supposed friend Noel Botham, as the father of a secret lovechild – who, it transpired, was Paula.

Living in Canada, I had never heard of Paula Yates, but later I would come to know everything about my new sister: her glamour, wit and audacity as a co-presenter of *The Tube* with Jools Holland; her marriage to Bob Geldof; the star interviews she conducted naughtily on a bed for Channel 4's *The Big Breakfast*; her vivacity as a presenter and her eloquence as an author; her contradictory homeliness and capacity for outrage; her abandonment of Bob Geldof and her tragic love affair with INXS singer Michael Hutchence; and her devotion to her children.

The revelation of her true parentage shattered me and my sister Linda as completely as it devastated Paula. It changed our lives. And it came as the closing chapter of a feud which had seen

Hughie Green set out to ruin the reputation and career of his former friend and fellow-broadcaster Jess Yates – the man whom Paula had believed, for almost all of her life, to be her natural dad.

When I came face to face with Paula some months later, she was haunted, reeling under the weight of the shock disclosure. She asked me why Hughie had hated Jess Yates so viciously. She wanted and needed to know the whole truth about her biological father, and there was much that I myself did not understand.

Consequently, I set about searching for the answers. I embarked on a four-year voyage of discovery, travelling the world to speak to relatives, friends and associates of our father from every period of his life. As my journey continued, I was drawn not only into the darkly troubled, rock'n'roll world of Paula Yates but also into the deep and murky waters of our father's secret life.

Some of the things that I have discovered about Hughie Green have been traumatising, upsetting beyond words. In retracing his footsteps, I have followed a trail of misery, deception, spite, retribution, blackmail, violence and suicide.

And I have learnt a great deal about Paula's significance in his life. She was one of five illegitimate children who were fathered by him, but she obsessed him from the moment of her arrival. Indeed, the sudden death of his own father was directly linked to Hughie and to a baby called Paula.

She grew up into a beautiful star, quite unaware that her birth had propelled Hughie Green into a spiral of duplicity, revenge and catastrophe which would last his lifetime, and longer.

Here, finally, are the answers to Paula's questions, the ones that she was desperate to know – but, tragically, didn't live to hear.

1

Me and My Sisters: A Day in the Sun

'Chris, you know I'm not well, don't you?' Paula Yates was talking to me in a clear and measured tone.

I replied, 'Yes, Paula, I can see you are not well. I'm so sorry.'

My sister Linda came into the room at this moment.

'Oh, but you will be all right,' she assured Paula. 'Yes, you'll be all right.'

Paula looked me directly in the eyes, as if I, and not Linda, had been the one trying to reassure her, and said, firmly, 'No, Chris, I really do not think I'll be well again.'

I had only just met Paula for the first time. I had travelled from Canada with my wife and stepchildren especially for this day, and I had not known what to expect. But from the first glimpse of my waif-like sister, I knew that she was suffering terribly – and it was a lot more than nerves at coming face to face with her new family.

Later that evening, when Paula had left, I said to Linda, 'I don't think we'll ever see Paula again. She's desperately ill and she will not receive the medical treatment she needs.' Tragically, I was right.

Two and a half years later, Paula died from a heroin overdose, alone on her bed in a London mews house. Now I would never have the chance to make up for lost time, to forge a closer bond with the sister that, for most of my life, I never knew I had.

1

Our trip to England had started out badly. BA flight 94 to London Heathrow was cancelled at the last minute due to engine trouble, and we were stranded overnight at the Montreal Airport Hilton Hotel. This was frustrating enough for my wife Lynne and me, but especially tiresome for Lynne's girls, my stepchildren Kristin, Keely and Kady. We were additionally concerned for Kady, the youngest at nine, who was developing a streaming cold.

We had expected to spend the next day enjoying a private, family gathering. I had fondly pictured all eleven daughters – Paula's, Linda's and Lynne's – chatting and laughing as they got to know each other. We would now arrive 24 hours late, on a day that had been set aside for an interview and photo session with the *Sun*. Paula had arranged it. The newspaper wanted to cover the story of all of us meeting for the first time, and had paid our way over to England. The day we had hoped to have with Paula and her children was now lost, and I was dismayed at the thought that I'd be saying hello to my new sister over a photographer's lens.

We finally arrived at London's Heathrow Airport at 8.15 a.m. on Tuesday, March 17, 1998 – which gave us less than two hours to get to my sister Linda's home in Mayfield, East Sussex, for our appointment with the *Sun*. On disembarking, I received a terse message telling me that Linda's friend and regular driver, Margaret, who was to pick us up, would not be coming. We'd been stranded in Montreal and now we were stranded at Heathrow with three relatively young children, one of whom was not feeling well; we'd travelled thousands of miles across international time zones; and we were suffering from sleep deprivation. Dispiritedly, we dragged our ton of baggage to the cab rank.

I had £200 on me in cash, and Keely lent me another £60 from her London shopping money, given to her by her grandmother Frankie, to pay the taxi fare. My abiding memory of that ride to Mayfield, apart from the anxiety of our race against time, is of wanting to commit a capital crime upon the driver. He was a little shit. He got hopelessly lost en route and left the meter running as he stopped to ask for directions every other mile. We were grossly overcharged, and he had the temerity to demand a £20 tip when, finally, we did arrive. He was out of luck.

We checked into the Middle House Inn, situated on the high street of sleepy, bucolic, little Mayfield. Lynne and I were delighted to be allocated the honeymoon suite, with its large, four-poster bed. The room looked out across the high street towards the church and the graveyard where my mother and David Langton, her second husband, are now at rest.

Built eons ago, the Inn is a wonderful place; the owners, the staff and the food are all exceptional. The downside is the plumbing. It is truly antiquated, and the water drips rather than flows out of taps and showerheads. On that particular March morning, it was a monumental pain. While I was trying to wash myself and my hair under the drip in the shower, Lynne was hurriedly ironing the creases out of one of my sports jackets and a pair of conservative slacks.

Linda's third eldest child, my niece Stephanie, was on her way to pick me up. Lynne and the children would be collected later. When Stephanie arrived, I was just about ready to make the final dash to Linda's country farmhouse for my joyous, first meeting with Paula and the *Sun* newspaper. Stephanie, then a beautiful and intelligent 20-year-old, said, 'Oh, Uncle Chrissy, I am so glad you are here. It is all simply crazy back at the house and Mummy is in a terrible tizzy.'

Her deliberate use of such theatrical, stylised language per-fectly conveyed her mother's sense of agitation, which had been increasing as today approached. Linda's emotions had been in chaos from the moment that Paula was named as being our flesh and blood, and I felt her anxiety like no one else could. I imme-diately began to worry that her 'tizzy' would blow up into a bigger ball of confusion and upset if everything did not now go well.

It was a five-minute drive to the house and there wasn't much time for talk, but I did ask Stephanie who was with Linda. She said Paula and Tiger were there with Belinda Brewin, Paula's right-hand woman or, as I usually describe her, road-warrior and bodyguard.

And what had happened to Margaret? 'Oh, Mother told her to go to Wadhurst station to pick up Paula – something about secrecy and protecting the *Sun*'s exclusive story. Crazy, isn't it?'

Yes, it was crazy and totally surreal. I was embarking on one of the most bizarre days of my life, and in these early moments, my heart was sinking. This was simply not how you should meet your half-sister for the first time. If nothing else, I knew that the day ahead was going to be a long one, and I prayed for a charge of adrenalin to save me from my jetlag and general exhaustion.

Stephanie suggested I get out of the Honda before she parked it between two other cars at the top of the long, uphill drive to the house. As I opened the door, I turned to her and asked, 'If Margaret picked up Paula, Tiger and Belinda . . . where are Paula's other children?' 'Uncle Chrissy, I really don't know,' she replied. 'It's all just rather weird.'

While Stephanie was parking the car, I looked down at the paving bricks with some interest and pleasure, and picked out 'my brick'. Linda's husband Rainer and I had worked a little on these bricks, one of his improvement projects at their charmingly restored farmhouse, the previous August. In the pale sunlight of that spring day, they looked good.

The air was fresh but not cold; it was invigorating to take a deep breath of it. My feet started moving across the bricks, towards the front door. In an instant, I had the uncanny feeling of being watched. I looked up at the kitchen's small bay window on the side of the house facing me and saw a person I immediately recognised to be Belinda, dressed in black, sitting with her knees up and her hands resting on them. Framed in the window in that position, she looked cat-like, rigid, to me and even a little spooky at first glimpse.

The unexpected sight of her startled me. Then she raised a hand and gave a single, slow wave of greeting. Her face was not at all animated; it was like a mannequin mask with a thin smile painted on it, a smile I would see again in *Hello!* magazine. She passed a hand across her forehead and pointed towards the front door. It was around the corner at the front of the house, and my view was blocked by my angle of approach.

Belinda's gesture said to me, 'Heads up! Be prepared!' It was intended, possibly, to signal that Linda was on her way out to greet me. But the 'look' and gesture together I found ominous. They suggested that inside the house all was stressed – and it was.

I responded with a slight nod of recognition, and then, suddenly, Linda appeared in front of me. Stephanie had vanished, probably to avoid intruding upon the scenes that would follow. Linda was wearing a navy-blue skirt with an attractive, flower-patterned shirt. Her hair looked freshly styled. She immediately raised her clasped hands to her chest in a gesture I knew well from our childhood; she was very nervous. She visibly quivered, and as we got closer, I saw her eyes were watering with emotion. She stretched out her hands, took my shoulders, pulled me towards her and said in an almost supplicating whisper, 'Chris, please, be very, very gentle with her. She is so nervous to meet you and she is on her very best behaviour.'

'Best behaviour'? The words sounded incongruous, but then, everything was. It all seemed so far removed from reality.

Linda lightly pushed me back and with her hands still on my shoulders, looked across towards the front door. Tears started rolling down her cheeks. Instinctively, I turned slowly, the way you do when a small bird has lit on a branch nearby and you don't wish to scare it away. Paula was standing, barefoot, against the door, which was slightly ajar. When our eyes met, she lowered hers for an instant, and then looked up again with a wan little smile. Nothing was said. I was looking at a sister of mine, and the familial similarity was astonishing.

During the preceding months of pain and doubt and questions tumbling out into the void, I had not allowed myself to rehearse mentally for this, our first meeting, and I thanked God for that. Nothing could have prepared me for the moment. Closing the gap between myself and Paula, I heard my voice say in a calm but slightly animated manner, 'I hear that you're nervous to meet me. Well, truth to tell, I have butterflies in my tummy enough for both of us.'

Paula put her hand on my right shoulder but remained silent. Out of the corner of my eye, I saw something moving, down to my left. Tiger had arrived. All of twenty months old, she was shyly looking up at me with enormous brown eyes, her face framed by thick, dark, curly hair and her arms wrapped around Paula's right ankle. I fell in love with that tiny person and with that image; it will follow me for a very long time. I looked into Paula's full gaze and said, 'Shall we all go inside?' Paula replied, 'Thank you . . . yes, please,' and gave me a tender hug that lingered for a second and ended with a little squeeze.

She was wearing a cotton frock that harked back to the sixties – pretty, summery, floral. We'd seen her dressed in others like it in magazine photos. Her short, blonde hair was tousled, and if she was wearing any make-up, it wasn't apparent to me. There was no hint of perfume, body lotion or any other feminine scent. Her skin was pale, her face drawn. She was much smaller than I'd imagined, and she looked vulnerable, tired, melancholic.

Paula scooped up Tiger and I ushered them and Linda, who had been standing behind us, over the threshold. Linda then steered us through the first door on the right into the country kitchen and told us, 'I'll give you a few moments alone to chat. Remember, though, the *Sun* people will be here any minute.' Belinda was nowhere to be seen. She had left for some other place in the house.

Paula, with Tiger on her chest, walked to the bay window and asked, 'Don't you find this all to be so very surreal?'

It was uncanny, as if she'd read my own thoughts by using the same word to describe our situation: surreal. I agreed, and added my sadness that we'd missed our 'personal day' together due to the flight delay. We heard a car arrive in the driveway. Paula said, 'Not much time. This really is a ghastly shame.' Picking up on her sentiment, I replied, 'Yes, but there is time ahead, and I hope we may contact you directly now as opposed to communicating through Belinda. I know she is your close friend and manager, but . . .' Paula cut me short, 'Belinda isn't my friend. I don't really know what Belinda is to me. She just sort of does things for me. Jo Fairley is my friend. And well, yes, I hope Emma Worth still is too.'

This was the first I'd heard of Paula's best pal, Jo, although Lynne and I had come to know and like Emma – Paula's former representative and link to the world at large. Emma had recently been sacked in favour of the omnipresent Belinda, with whom Paula was frequently photographed and seemed joined at the hip.

I was taken aback by Paula's outburst. Of course, I understood her words literally, but their actual meaning and her apparent need to say them to me at that moment perplexed me. 'I don't know how to describe Belinda,' Paula carried on, trying unsuccessfully to offer me some sort of clarification. 'She isn't really my manager or anything.' Then she became more upbeat, urging, 'Remember, now, we are related, so you and Linda can call me directly at any time.'

Instinctively, I felt I had to apologise. 'Paula,' I ventured, 'this must really have been awful for you and I'm so sorry about it all. Finding out you have a half-brother and half-sister in such an unexpected and unkind manner must . . .'

She interrupted.

'Chris, do me a favour, please?'

'Yes, of course.'

'Please call me "sister",' insisted Paula. 'I really don't like the sound of *half*-sister. Do you mind?'

'Not at all,' I replied. 'I would personally prefer that.'

We heard more activity outside, and it was then that Paula made the extraordinary statement that she was unwell and did not expect to recover. I assumed that she was talking about a psychological illness, a problem she did not believe she would be able to overcome. This slip of a woman in front of me was not the glamorous, front-cover gal of the magazines, nor was she any drop-dead gorgeous, sexy vamp-bitch. She looked haggard. She was visibly an exhausted, washed-out person under more stress than was good for her. Her pain was of the mind. I was sure it was excruciating, and that frightened me.

Possibly, she felt able to confide in me because of our mutual reading of the current events as 'surreal'. Paula was fully aware of the strange world she had somehow entered, and was scared that she would not find the door back out to a gentler reality.

On a more practical level, I believe that Paula, in her own way, was trying to say a 'thank you' to Linda and me while warning us,

apologetically, Don't expect too much from me – 'I'm not well . . .
I really do not think I'll be well again.'

I saw in that instant that she was telling the simple truth. There
was nothing histrionic about her tone or delivery. She spoke from
the depths of her being. She didn't see any happiness or hope
ahead. Linda, I have no doubt, believed that Paula was referring
to the anguish of losing her lover and Tiger's father, rock star
Michael Hutchence; that she was grieving bitterly for Michael but
would eventually recover from that state of mourning.

Paula's central misery was, of course, Michael's death, but it
was not her only demon. She was struggling to make sense of the
cruel discovery that she was not who she thought she was; that
Hughie Green, my father and Linda's father, was also hers. As
one writer commented, 'In the space of three weeks, she lost her
future and her past.'

And as if this wasn't enough for one human being to bear, Paula
had a ton-load of other problems. Bob Geldof was only three
months away from gaining primary custody of Fifi Trixibelle,
Peaches and Pixie, the daughters Paula adored, and, as I later
discovered, she was scared to death of losing Tiger too. She was
facing problems with the Hutchence family. She was broke. She
believed she had only one real ally in Jo Fairley, and, clearly, she
felt guilty about firing Emma, whose friendship she still desired.

Paula's life was in one hell of a mess. To try to escape it, she
was retreating into a world of booze and dope – which served only
to exacerbate her mental trauma, to threaten her physical well-
being and to unbalance her sense of responsibility to herself and
others. Her relationship with drink and drugs was definitely not
any part of what she was communicating to me when she spoke of
being 'not well'. She was referring to her severe depression.

In no way, then, did I connect either alcohol or illicit substances
to Paula at that moment. But the realisation would hit me later in
the day. . .

The *Sun* crew were waiting, and Paula was called out to meet
Amanda Cable, the journalist and person in charge. Belinda
popped her head around the kitchen door and said hello. Camera

equipment and lights were being brought in, and I had a nicotine craving, so Belinda and I stepped outside and we had our first chat while I smoked a cigarette.

She was wearing a tight, black jumpsuit with a zipper down the front and a white shirt underneath. Her hair was a filthy-looking mess, and her looks and manner were as hard as nails. Lynne later remarked that as the frontwoman for a celebrity, she could have put a little more effort into her appearance.

I quickly discovered that Belinda cannot talk if she is not, literally, in your face. She was constantly twitching about, and she hovered a foot closer to me than was normal or necessary. She told me immediately about the tandoori takeaway Paula had eaten the night before. It had given Paula food poisoning, she declared, and she had been up for most of the night being violently ill. Belinda was clearly protesting something, and she was scrutinising my face, as if to make certain that I was buying the story. Circuitously, she came to the point about the poisonous tandoori: it explained Paula's pallor and bedraggled appearance. She then abruptly remarked that Paula was on her best behaviour.

There it was again – 'best behaviour'. It was as if Paula were a child, a known brat, who had that day promised to be, indeed, on her best behaviour. I moved on. 'Where are Paula's other children?' With that, Belinda launched into a tirade about Bob Geldof, forcefully explaining that he had prevented his girls from coming to the family meeting. Geldof, she raged, was a total bastard who was capable of making Paula's life miserable. Her contempt was consummate, vitriolic. Within a couple of minutes, she had blamed him for all that ailed Paula. Belinda, in full, verbal flight for no apparent reason, then turned her wrath upon her ex-husband, declaring him, too, to be a bastard.

I was shell-shocked. Belinda's unsolicited attacks on Bob Geldof and her ex-husband in front of me, a stranger, were neither expected nor appreciated. I had no axe to grind with Bob Geldof, but I was overcome with an intense dislike for Belinda Brewin, and it would increase as the day wore on.

Paula, meanwhile, was on autopilot, switched on to working mode for Amanda Cable – a truly impressive woman aged around thirty. Towering six feet tall, with an attractive face and figure and driving a black BMW Z-series sports car, she reminded me of Diana Rigg and her famous *Avengers* character of the sixties, Emma Peel. Amanda was a no-nonsense professional who handled all of us, and the story, capably.

Dave Hogan was the photographer. A well-known freelance and a member of the dreaded *paparazzi*, he has enjoyed a colourful career but is obviously sensitive to circumstance. I found him unobtrusive and relaxing, and our kids were charmed by him and his sweet assistant Lotti. Dave promised Kristin, Keely and Kady that he would send some of his shots of Madonna to them in Canada, and he kept his word.

But when Paula saw Dave, she showed a glimpse of temperament. For a second, Linda and I feared she was about to storm out in a huff. We were in the main sitting room when it happened. I was on the sofa with Paula, and Linda was seated across from us in a high-back, single chair. Dave, outside in the front garden, was passing by the French patio doors when Paula spotted him. She stiffened, announcing that Dave had been one of the *paparazzi* photographers who had caused trouble for her in the past. Sensing a possible upset or worse, Linda asked, 'Oh dear, are you sure?' Paula replied, 'Yes, almost positive. I am sure it was his fat ass up the tree with his bloody telephoto lens.'

'Up a tree, with *his* fat ass?' queried Linda.

I couldn't help chiming in, 'Yes, Linda, I'm sure he took his fat ass with him up that tree.' One, two, three seconds of silence . . . and then gales of laughter from all of us, including Paula. The spark of tension evaporated.

Later, Paula asked Dave if he had ever taken pictures of her or Tiger. He said, 'Oh, no, Paula, you would know if I'd photographed you.' He gave me a wink when Paula looked away. Paula was pacified but not altogether convinced. In any case, Dave, his fat ass and his camera became the day's running joke.

The first hour at Linda's house had been extremely emotional and confusing, but oddly relaxing. If there was any awkwardness to begin with, it soon wore off. There were tense, flashpoint moments such as Paula's first sighting of Dave Hogan, but they resolved themselves as quickly as they surfaced. For the most part, the atmosphere was dream-like – it was all happening, but it wasn't. It wasn't a pleasant dream, really, but it certainly wasn't a nightmare. It was Lewis Carroll. It was a moment of holding Alice's hand. Was Belinda the Cheshire Cat?

There were no outpourings of joy or angst from Paula, no proclamations of intent for the future. She had not come to terms, emotionally, with the idea that she had a new family, and I believe that she just didn't know what her feelings were about us.

I had never actually thought about whether or not I was going to like Paula, and it has taken me a long time to collect my thoughts about her. I did wonder, over and over, if she could ever possibly like *me* after what Hughie Green had done to her and to Jess Yates, the man she had believed to be her father. My worries were compounded by the fact that I'm physically similar to Hughie. Would she look at me and loathe me? To my relief, I saw no indications of that.

Fleetingly, her legendary sparkle would burst into life, but such moments were rare. Overall, she was subdued, and her body language was neutral or limpid. I was surprised, almost startled, when she suddenly started throwing lively poses on the sitting room sofa for the benefit of the camera.

That memory would haunt me over the worrying months ahead as she twinkled out of one magazine cover after another. I'd imagine each photo session and wonder, how had she really been feeling that day? Had she told someone else she was ill and didn't believe she would get better? One conversation more than any other showed me the extremes of Paula's personality at that time.

We were in the sitting room – Paula, Linda, Amanda and I – waiting for the activity to begin. Linda was telling Paula about our bankruptcy years, living in Baker Street, London. She talked about the day the bailiffs arrived and removed everything they legally could towards recovering Father's debts. Paula appeared to be engrossed in the story.

Linda ended her description of the stripped-down flat by saying, with quite a dramatic flourish, 'They took it all except for

a few things such as the beds and the chandeliers over them.'
Without any hesitation, Paula remarked, 'Pity they didn't take the
chandeliers too; it might have saved us this situation.'

There was silence. It took us about five seconds to appreciate
the incredibly funny line that Paula had just drily delivered and
then we all roared with laughter, appreciating the meaning and the
mental images she had conjured up.

Linda carried on with another story, mainly for Amanda's
benefit since Paula had already heard it, about her husband,
Rainer, and his reaction to the news that Paula Yates had been
named as Hughie Green's love child. Measured, reflective and
with resignation, he responded, 'Yes, of course, my love. With
our luck it couldn't have been Emma Thompson, could it?' Again,
this brought the house down, and for a brief moment I had hope
that the rest of the day would be as light-hearted. But a question
from Amanda broke the mood, 'If you don't mind, Paula, why
didn't your mum just tell you what had happened? Wouldn't that
have made it all somewhat easier?'

Paula's voice became cold, angry and hurt as she spoke of the
disregard and disloyalty she had received from her mother. Her
outpouring sent a chill around the room. Linda felt awful, Amanda
felt awful, I felt awful. Within a couple of minutes, I had seen
Paula's wit, flair, brilliance and warmth. And then her sadness.

The whole press operation was grinding into gear. Tiger had been
put to bed for a nap, and Stephanie and Belinda had driven to the
village to pick up Lynne and our girls. Paula had combed her hair
down flatly to her head, and changed her outfit for the cameras.
So had Linda.

Lynne walked into the lobby of the Inn to find Belinda
sprawled on a loveseat, looking like death warmed over. Now
regaling Lynne with the story of the bad food that Paula had eaten
the night before and how she'd been sick, she swore like a trucker,
even though the children were present. Lynne thought that odd,
since Belinda has kids of her own. Later, Lynne confided to me,
'Belinda disgusted me, and I really didn't want her around my
children. I couldn't understand why she was allowed to spend so

much time with Tiger.' We had just endured the trip from hell to Mayfield, but we still found a few minutes on the run from the hotel to wash our hair and put on fresh clothing.

By the time my family arrived at the house, Paula, Linda and I were being interviewed together by Amanda Cable, so Lynne and the girls were ushered into the den where they chatted with Dave Hogan and Lotti. The kids were eventually invited to go upstairs to Linda's room to watch TV. It wasn't until much later, when Paula's entourage was leaving, that my wife and stepdaughters finally met Paula and Tiger. Even then, they didn't get the chance to exchange more than a few words.

Arriving at Heathrow, we had been under the impression that all of the children would be photographed together for the first time on Linda's expansive, front lawn. This would form part of the 'big, happy family' story that the media was determined to present to the public. We were surprised, then, to find that Paula's daughters by Bob Geldof would be absent. All four of Linda's children were meant to be at Mayfield that day, but only Stephanie turned up. Rainer, Linda's husband, wasn't there either. He was in London at his office, and didn't come home that night until the shoot was over. The concept had obviously been scrubbed, and no one had thought to inform us.

As a result, Kristin, Keely and Kady became secondary to the main event, along with Lynne. Their parts had been written out of the script. Although I was really upset over this, I kept my silence so as not to create a situation during a day that was already complex enough.

Paula didn't show any real interest in Lynne and her children, although she knew that we had all come from Canada to meet her, as her new relatives. She never said a word to me about my loved ones. I felt really lousy about their day. It wasn't what it was meant to be nor was it much fun for them.

By contrast, I was kept very busy. The farmhouse at Mayfield became the scene of an efficient, military operation as Amanda interviewed Paula, Linda and me separately and in combinations of two or more, and we grouped and regrouped similarly for Dave's camera.

Finger food, delicious stuff in a great variety, arrived at around 11.30 a.m. from the Middle House Inn. It would not require formal plates or interrupt the flow of what was going on. Coffee, tea and soft drinks were on hand at all times. I cannot remember all of the food on offer – smoked salmon comes to mind – but Paula did eat, and she didn't once refer to the tandoori takeaway that had so dominated Belinda's conversation. Paula did not seem to have the tummy cramps one normally experiences after such an ordeal.

As for me, my 'personal clock' was completely out of whack, but my earlier prayers had been answered; my adrenalin had kicked in, my energy was up, and my mind was clear and functioning. I was feeling relaxed, alert and very much myself. That said, a decent belt of whisky – a large Johnnie Walker Red in a short glass with a little ice – was just the ticket.

Reflexively, I turned to Paula and asked if she would like one too, not realizing that, for years, she had been famously teetotal, or that rumours connecting her to drinking had been circulating since Michael's funeral. Paula hurriedly glanced at Linda and said, 'Oh, no . . . no, thank you.' Linda shot me a look that could only mean I had said something inappropriate, and, of course, I had. Shortly afterwards, Linda gave my arm a discreet squeeze and said, 'Paula isn't to be offered alcohol. She doesn't drink.'

My instincts told me that this had something to do with the incongruous 'best behaviour' statements made by both Linda, from the very first, and Belinda within twenty minutes of my arrival. At that same moment, Belinda's graphic tandoori tales came rushing back to mind.

Linda's phrasing and intonation gave the game away; they lacked the candour we normally enjoyed with one another. Possibly, Linda had been cautioned not to offer drinks to Paula, especially with the press about, but she was definitely aware that alcohol and Paula should not be mixed.

As for me, I suddenly saw the tainted takeaway for what it was: a cover-up. Flashing back to my university days in the sixties, I remembered how often we resorted to 'bad food' to explain our hangovers – a classic excuse and a bunch of crap, then and now.

Little by little, I was starting to piece things together. But a niggling whisper in my ear kept trying to tell me that there was more, that my sister Paula had another, unspoken secret. At the end of the day, something happened which gave a name to that secret, and I heard my whisper clearly say 'drugs'.

As the interviews and photographs continued, the day became more and more like a bedroom farce – out of one room, into another room, change partners, into the garden and then the kitchen.

Paula, Linda and I did not have the luxury of sitting down privately to discuss the chain of events that had brought us together in Linda's farmhouse, to seek out common ground and to try to establish some way in which our new relationships could work.

Two things were happening. Firstly, we were giving a story to the *Sun*, which had already decided on its theme. There was to be no insight into the whole, cloudy mess that had, apparently, ended with a shimmering, silver lining and a rainbow. The story was not going to be a 'downer'. It was not going to dwell on Hughie Green, Jess Yates, Paula's mother, Hélène Thornton-Bosment, or Bob Geldof. And the subject of Michael Hutchence was strictly taboo, even among ourselves.

Secondly, there were only opportunities for private moments between two people when the third was being separately interviewed or photographed. This gave me the chance to be alone with Paula for periods of half an hour to forty-five minutes, and we did have some very meaningful exchanges.

What went on the record for the *Sun* and what I talked about with Paula were two completely different things. Privately, she told me something of herself and her life – and asked some searching questions. She wanted to know: Why did Hughie Green hate Jess Yates so deeply? Having secretly sired Paula, Hughie had achieved the ultimate revenge upon Jess – so why, then, did he take his vendetta further still by ruining Jess' career and reputation? What was it all about? Why didn't Hughie tell Paula about his paternity of her when he was still alive, since he knew it could one day emerge from Noel Botham?

Hélène had obviously told Hughie that he was Paula's real
father. What was really going on between them?

I vividly recall Paula sitting beside me on the sofa, desperate to
know the truth. How I wish that she were still with us, now that I
have unravelled the mysteries and unlocked the sometimes
appalling secrets of our shared kinship. Back then on the sofa in
Linda's sitting room, I simply did not have the answers and we left
the uncertainty hanging in the air as we were called back to work.

Later, in the mid-afternoon, Dave hurried Paula and me outside
to do some garden shots, since the natural light, bright as it was,
wouldn't last too much longer. We walked from the sitting room
out through the patio doors and on to the terrace. It faced a long
expanse of lawn and field, stretching downwards towards the
country road. Dave wanted to look up the incline at us, shooting
from below. He told us where to stand and set off down the slope.
Finding his spot, about 60 or 70 feet away from us, he started
fiddling with his telephoto lens.

I said to Paula, who was arm-in-arm with me, 'Do you think
Dave really enjoys playing with that big, long lens of his, or is he
possibly compensating for a lack somewhere else?' Paula loved
this naughty remark; she nearly bent double laughing. Teasingly,
I followed on, 'Now, now, do behave nicely as your pal Dave is
trying to photograph us,' which cracked Paula up even more.

Sensing that we were, finally, having a 'light personal moment'
together, I called out to Dave, 'Just a couple of feet back and you
will have the perfect shot. Couple of steps backwards, please . . .'
This was a visual joke – Dave was now only a few feet away from
the duck pond behind him. He was aware of the pond, he wasn't
going to fall in, but it really looked as if he might, and it was very
funny to watch and imagine. Paula was, again, convulsed with
laughter. I think those were her happiest moments of the day. She
really appeared to have forgotten herself and her problems.

Then she straightened up, squeezed my left arm tightly and,
still trying to catch her breath after all the hilarity, mock-
admonished me, 'Now, steady on here, I'm the one who is meant
to make the jokes and be funny.' After a second's pause, she
added, 'Oh, do you think that this is the start of a sibling rivalry?'

We both laughed at her repartee. It was spontaneous, witty and beautifully delivered, and I will treasure the memory of it for a very long time. The finale of this round of verbal jousting came with me saying in feigned horror, 'Rivalry? Paula, never! As your wonderful, older brother, you will just follow my lead and everything will be simply marvellous.'

Paula, interviewed later, described me as 'a very funny man'. I guess she came to that conclusion because of the interlude on the patio terrace. For my part, it gave me a glimmer of hope, within my deep doubt, that we would eventually be able to enjoy a proper, brother-and-sister relationship.

My head was spinning with all the things that had happened over the course of the morning – but I had heard nothing yet. There would be more outbursts of abusive opinion, with Geldof cast as chief villain but Kell Hutchence, father of Michael, also coming in for a drubbing. And the afternoon would take on even stranger shapes as Paula underwent the most jarring and bewildering transformation.

2

Childhood Demons

Hughie Green's mother never wanted him. Indeed, she tried to abort her baby, and when he insisted on being born anyway, she packed him off to be brought up by relatives and nannies. Hughie did not share a home with his mother and father until he was fourteen years old and a child star. Major Hugh Aitchison Green and his wife, the former Violet Eleanor Price, might kindly be described as unconventional parents. As their grandson, I can vouch for that, and more: they were positively satanic.

The Major cut an extremely handsome figure in wartime London. With his rank, privilege, money and position, he was one of the city's most eligible bachelors. Home, to him, was the Piccadilly Hotel, or the fabulous house he owned in Meopham, Kent, picturesquely named 'The Orchard' and staffed with servants.

He was a successful army officer who enjoyed life to the full. He stood six feet three, and, as a long-distance runner, had a fit and muscular body, full of energy. His features were fine and his eyes sparkled with fire and humour. He was a friendly, fun-loving rascal, witty and fond of practical jokes. A natural performer and a brilliant raconteur, he had bundles of charisma and a big heart. He was unafraid of the world and what it held for him: he was always going to succeed, no matter how often he might falter along the way.

Hugh Aitchison Green was born in Hanging Shaw, Glasgow, on July 30, 1886. The second-eldest of six children, he grew up in a fine, middle-class family of business people, all working in the wholesale fish trade. His teenage fascination with the world of travelling theatre, especially vaudeville, was discouraged by his parents; in those days, most 'respectable' people frowned upon the actors' itinerant lifestyle and apparent irresponsibility.

The young Hugh only loved it more, and he was still dreaming of a career in show business when he became engaged to a beautiful Scottish lass called Minnie Stoddart – a close family friend who jilted him, literally, at the altar. The reasons for her cold feet are now lost in time, but it's possible she realised at the eleventh hour that Hugh, who jokingly referred to himself as a 'bad boy', was simply too impulsive and too unpredictable to be a suitable husband.

Hugh's parents were shattered by Minnie's sudden withdrawal; they had loved her every bit as much as they would later dislike Violet Price, their future daughter-in-law. Heartbroken and humiliated, Hugh, at twenty-one, had nothing to lose, no reason to stay in Scotland, when on May 3, 1908, he and his family boarded the ocean liner *Cassandra* and set sail from the Clyde towards a new life in western Canada.

This drastic move was organised by Hugh's father, Daniel, who feared he had tuberculosis and had been advised that the pure, prairie air would cure him. However, he was never medically diagnosed as having TB, and he did live on to a ripe old age. The location was isolated, rigorous, primitive. The family almost starved there during their first year. And prairie farming didn't agree with Hugh, who lamented, 'All the farmer needs is brawn, and I have both muscle *and* brains.' When he did use his brains, in a succession of entrepreneurial schemes, he invariably ended up going cap-in-hand to his father for financial salvation.

Returning to Glasgow before the year was out, Hugh was no more successful in his enterprises, and he tried but failed to infiltrate the regional entertainment scene. By the spring of 1910, broke and in need of a cash handout from the ever-obliging Daniel, he rejoined his parents in Prince Albert, Saskatchewan, opened a general store with his great friend Jock Cameron and entered into the community life of the small town. He spent much of his leisure time in the local social club, and soon began to perform his own comedy skits and vaudeville routines.

Sadly, his attempts to break out of Prince Albert and into the wider performing circuit, travelling as far away as Winnipeg, met with as much success as his Scottish forays and his 'surefire' business deals. As for the shop, it was barely breaking even. Hugh's parents, however, were beginning to flourish, having abandoned farming. They kept the farm itself, which they loved, but went into a successful water-bottling business.

By the time the First World War broke out, on August 4, 1914, they were despairing of their 28-year-old 'wastrel' son and wondering when he would ever grow up and settle down. They didn't know it then, but Hugh was beginning to see a route out of his rural *ennui*. It was paved with gold . . . and fish.

Hugh and his brother Dan signed up to the Canadian army, but my grandfather had no intention of actually going into combat. He envisioned fighting the war from London, where he would see to it that Canadian soldiers, dug into the trenches in France, could depend on a 'lovely piece of cod' to eat every day from home waters off the Grand Banks of Newfoundland. He packed his trunk and moved to Ottawa, determined to find a way of selling Canadian cod to Canada.

With an outrageous combination of blarney and bluff, he managed to secure a meeting with Sir Sam Hughes, the Minister of Militia. Hughes was arguably one of the most powerful men in all of Canada then, although he was heading for a fall; in 1916, the Prime Minister, Sir Robert Borden, was forced to sack him for insubordinate behaviour, accusing him of many irregularities including 'patronage' – awarding contracts and appointments to people who caught his fancy.

Sir Sam liked Hugh Aitchison Green so much that after only one conversation, he promoted him to major on the spot, granted him a lucrative contract to supply fish, and authorised him to direct its safe passage from the North Atlantic to the French battlegrounds, via England. Now, that was not a bad day's work.

Arriving in London to take up his position on Sir Sam's personal staff, Major Green had wealth, prestige and good looks

– everything it took to attract a voluptuous Violet Price.

Violet was a great beauty. Her sex appeal still smoulders out of old, faded photographs from her youth; it transcends time. She was a large woman, about five feet nine in height, with a full figure and an impressive bustline. Her hair was naturally blonde, her lips were thin, and her eyes were a dewy, greenish-blue that could suddenly freeze into an icy stare, immediately transfixing the recipient. Rubens painted women like Violet.

She met Major Green early in 1917, possibly at a regimental party. They were worlds apart, socially; Violet would normally not have been moving in the same, rarefied circles as the Major. She had never worked, and had no occupation.

She was born on January 20, 1895 in Caterham, Surrey – contrary to my father's claim in his 1965 autobiography, *Opportunity Knocked*, that she came from Warlingham, Surrey. Violet was an only child living in the Manor House, where her father, Irishman John Morrison Price, was in service as a gardener. Within seven years of her birth, John had become a dairy farmer, and the family, including John's widowed mother, Isabella Price, had moved out of the grand house into one of the estate's adjacent buildings, Manor Farm.

John would later die of bovine tuberculosis, and his will does not indicate that he had made a lot of money in life, despite my father's assertion that he was a 'prosperous Irishman'. The Price family were not impoverished, but they certainly were not 'of the manor born', or even well-off. Notably, they had no servant. Violet was probably expected to help around the farmhouse. She would have seen how hard her mother, Alice, worked to raise a child and look after her husband and an elderly Isabella single-handedly. Violet clearly wanted no such lifestyle for herself.

She was glad to see the back of her boring, country life in Caterham after her father John was diagnosed with TB, presumably contracted during his many years working with cattle. The family moved to London, no doubt for better medical attention, and settled at 251 Junction Road in the northern area of Tufnell Park. But Violet still wasn't happy. By the class-ridden standards of the early 1900s, this was a 'downmarket' address.

What she dreamed of, and saw in Major Hugh Green, was her chance to go up in the world. They enjoyed a whirlwind romance, which would result in marriage only months later.

Violet adored the Major's dashing good looks and cheery personality, his social standing, his title, his prestigious West End address, his bank account and his connections. He was going to introduce her to a fashionable, glamorous life in London, and he would make her the head of an enormous house, The Orchard, in Meopham, where the couple would spend occasional weekends.

In that spectacular home, she, Violet, would have servants and all manner of good things to eat and drink without ever having to lift a finger. She would wear the finest clothes, and she and the Major would become a 'couple of note'. Together, they would go to the races at Ascot, where they would hobnob with the gentry and, even grander, the aristocracy. Violet Price, giddy with her good fortune, saw her world expanding ever upwards on the arm of Major Green. He, in turn, was besotted with her.

It's unlikely he had told her that prior to meeting Sir Sam Hughes and securing his rank of major and his lucrative fish contract from the Canadian government, his life achievements had been expensive failures, paid for by his father Daniel Green. It's also unlikely he had warned her that his affluence might have a time limit: the Major's contract to supply the troops in France with 'a lovely piece of cod' – canned and salted – would last only as long as the war.

But she wouldn't have changed her plans, whatever he'd said. This was England in the early twentieth century, and the prevailing class divisions did not readily allow a young lady such as Violet the opportunity to meet and marry a man of Major Green's apparent stature and accomplishment.

The wedding took place on July 26, 1917 at the fashionable St James's Church, Piccadilly. Hugh Aitchison Green had just turned 31 and his new wife was 22. The witnesses were John Price – Violet's father – and Colonel Charles W MacLean, the Major's best friend. They had met in Canada, and had much in common. A Scot, like Hugh, Charles W MacLean was big, strong and athletic. A self-made man, he emerged from a humble background to excel in the army, and by marrying well he gained social acceptance at the very highest levels. He was inspirational to Major Green and later to my father, Hughie, who would be friends with the Colonel's three children.

Colonel MacLean was 32 when he married his first wife, Martha Fulford, the nineteen-year-old daughter of Senator George Fulford of Brockville, Ontario. The wedding took place on the Fulford family yacht, moored at Quebec City, and was attended by no less than Sir Wilfred Laurier, the seventh Prime Minister of Canada. Indeed, he gave away the bride, whose father had been killed a year earlier in a car crash.

Martha and her baby died in childbirth two years later and Colonel MacLean went on to inherit an enormous part of her family's fortune, built on sales of a medicine called 'Dr William's Pink Pills For Pale People'. The Colonel also acquired the late senator's plans for an extravagant mansion and experimental farm, and he subsequently built this estate in Pointe Claire, Quebec – the town where I live today, just outside Montreal.

After Martha's tragic death, Colonel MacLean found another love, and she followed him over to London in 1917. Violet was awestruck by the Colonel and by his new fiancée, heiress Doris Aldous. She was everything Violet aspired to be – a woman of means and social standing.

When the war was over, Violet would sail first-class to the New World and she would stay in the MacLeans' mansion, Mull Hall – later described by the *Illustrated London News* as 'one of the finest and most beautiful homes ever built in the Colonies'. She and Major Green would not, however, live in Canada. They would visit there when it suited, and money would never be an issue. Violet was going to be a true, society lady.

They were an odd couple, really – a classic case of opposites attracting. Major Green's eyes danced and twinkled; Violet's were stern and penetrating, and her smile was thin, sometimes simpering. Major Green always looked pleasant, relaxed and self-confident; Violet Green wore the distant look of a *grande dame*: elevated, unapproachable. She was hugely impressed by the top-drawer people she was meeting through the Major but, at the same time, she felt humble and insecure in their company, which may explain the regal bearing that she wore like a suit of armour from the earliest days of the relationship.

What she did have in common with her husband was ambition. The Greens were determined social climbers, theatrical and keenly aware of appearances. They loved posing for photographs. Today, they would be jet-setters, A-list celebrities.

At first, they lived happily and in luxury. They had money, property, servants and status. These were the 'Ascot days', Violet's dreams come true – the rewards of her marriage. She thoroughly enjoyed their glittering life in London and their visits to The Orchard, the colonial-style, Victorian country house about 27 miles away, in Meopham, Kent.

There's little of historical note in Meopham. One of the oldest cricket clubs in England is located there, which wouldn't have interested the Greens, and the windmill on the common worked up until 1927. The couple's real interests were closer to home and hearth. They revelled in keeping dogs, and they threw their doors open to hundreds of guests. It was fashionable for persons of note to have country retreats for weekend entertaining, and both the Major and Violet were eager to be written into the social calendar.

Major Green knew The Orchard would impress his friends, which in turn, would improve his chances of making good connections. It was all part of the game of life for him, and he loved it. This magnificent house was a symbol of his recent streak of luck and success. Just a few years earlier, he had been running a modest general store in Prince Albert.

The Major had had very little education, but through the sheer force of his personality, initiative and determination, he had proved to himself that it really wasn't what you knew but who you knew that truly counted. That and knowing how to make a deal. Life was all about making deals. More important than anything, though, was the Major's desire to make Violet happy. Waited on by a full complement of staff, she must have felt very queenly, very important indeed. But the idyll couldn't last: within two years, cracks were already appearing in the marriage. Major

Green's slavish devotion to Violet, and her willingness to exploit it, created an imbalance that paralleled almost exactly the state of their physical relationship. She wanted; he tried to give. Violet, figuratively, castrated her husband.

The Major's ebullient personality subsided; he became subservient to the wishes and well-being of the spouse he worshipped. And although I'm sure he did everything possible to fulfil his marital duties in the bedroom, he simply wasn't up to the demands of Violet's libido. As a result, he meekly looked the other way while she took a succession of lovers.

None of this troubled Violet greatly. What did concern her was the very real spectre of diminishing finances, and the accompanying threat of relegation from the first division of society. On top of that, something really awful happened to her: she fell pregnant.

It's most unlikely that Major Green and Violet ever sat down and talked about their future together, ever looked ahead to what their married life would be like when the Great War was over. It was an era of incredible social unrest and change. Within a few years, England would see the General Strike. Women had no right to vote or to have abortions. Many things were happening in the society around them, and I doubt that the couple ever discussed the idea of having children. Their marriage was far from healthy, but it was not a bad one in as much as they had certain goals in common and they had established an understanding. The Major doted on Violet. He could not and would not disappoint his parents with a failed marriage; they had already seen him jilted on the church steps in Scotland. Of course, divorce was out of the question in that era.

As long as the Major fulfilled her monetary needs and aided her climb up the social ladder, then Violet was happy to have her flings on the side while staying under his roof as his wife. Today it would be called an 'open marriage', accommodating the fact that Violet's sexual appetite far exceeded the Major's. But what the couple had not factored into this arrangement was a child.

Violet had never wanted children. Her mother, Alice Price, was neither Irish nor Catholic. Hailing from Wolverhampton, Staffordshire, she was a lifelong and devout Christian Scientist, and had not burdened her daughter with any sense of family duty to produce babies. Hughie, therefore, was a mistake – Violet's.

In those days, men were chauvinists. It was the responsibility of the lady to take care of birth control. Prophylactics were not widely discussed or used. They were seen as unreliable and unattractive and – worst of all – they required some cooperation or action by the male partner. It was not until after an educational campaign about contraceptives in the twenties, when condoms could be bought over the counter or from a slot machine, that they became really popular.

Family history does not record Violet's preferred method of prevention. But in 1919, when she accidentally conceived, she and Major Green were living the good life to the full, and she had no intention of allowing a screaming little bundle to disrupt her pleasure or to divert the Major's adoring attention away from her for a second.

She was known to be extremely vain. Her appearance was of paramount importance to her, right up to her very last breath. Photographs taken while she was expecting find her posing deliberately to hide the bump, and it's probable that the prospect of stretch marks added to the horror with which she viewed her pregnancy.

She could count on any number of nannies and servants to help her care for the new arrival, but Violet Green still did not want a child. She felt no maternal instincts whatsoever and made no secret of her desire to get rid of the baby. She was outrageously open, within the immediate family, about the most personal things. She would later freely tell Claire, my mother, that she had tried to abort my dear Papa. Father already knew this.

Violet would have been too scared to visit a back-street abortionist; that would have been an unimaginable ordeal, fraught with hazards, and the anti-abortion laws of the day were extremely severe. Therefore, she had to try to induce a mis-carriage, in such a way that its cause would be undetectable. She hit on the idea of a bone-shaking, high-speed car-ride, inviting one of her boyfriends to take her for a race around the quiet, country lanes near The Orchard.

Motor carriages were relatively new inventions in 1919. It wouldn't have been commonplace in those days to see such a vehicle roaring around the tiny, twisting byways of Meopham. Any unfortunate rambler, leaping into the ditch to get out of its path, would have watched, astounded, as it hurtled out of sight, wildly bouncing up and down over the bumps and jolts in the road while a woman, facing backwards in the rear, open rumble seat, clung on for dear life. Also clinging on for his dear, foetal life was her son.

Hugh Hughes Green was born on February 2, 1920 at his parents' central London flat – 8 Weymouth Court at 1 Weymouth Street. His father was 33 and his mother, 25. Hughie had two godfathers. One was Sir Sam Hughes, the Canadian minister who had given the Major his title and fish contract. Sir Sam remained close to the family until his death a year later, and his influence on the Major carried on from beyond the grave: he would regularly eulogise Sir Sam as a wonderful role model. Others who were familiar with Hughes' often arrogant and bigoted personality might have raised an eyebrow at the Major's admiration and insistence on promoting such a man so highly to his son. Godfather number two was Harry Tate, a leading variety entertainer of the day.

The Greens were now a picture-perfect family. At the time of Hughie's arrival, the Major and Violet looked like an Adonis and his goddess, cradling their beloved angel. Despite her unfaithfulness, Violet had no doubts that the child was the Major's. There wasn't ever any suggestion to the contrary, and I never saw the Major look so thrilled. Family snaps and professional shots taken later (by leading photographers, of course) show him beaming delightedly, tenderly, at his little son. Violet's first picture with Hughie is a classic studio pose: the Madonna and Child. Against a black backdrop, Violet, in profile, holds the baby in graceful hands, showing off his full face and flowing gown.

But, interestingly, no pictures exist of the radiant parents together with their new-born infant. He had come into the world

as a source of stress to their relationship, and as far as Violet was
concerned, he was an enormous pain in the ass. Having gone
through the intimate experience of childbirth, she had still failed
to make any motherly connections. On the contrary, she
immediately issued a set of terms and conditions under which the
threesome could proceed as a reasonably happy family. The
Major, infatuated and weakened by Violet, surrendered to her
orders as quickly as she barked them out.

The child would be 'parked' at The Orchard and raised by
nannies and servants. His parents would visit Meopham at
weekends – but not all weekends. Although Violet enjoyed the
countryside and the parties, she would never forget the years she
spent yearning to break out of the pastoral uneventfulness of
Caterham. London, with its lights and sparkle, was where she
wanted to be, and they would keep their London address
uncluttered with an infant.

She would have her little flings but would be discreet enough
not to bring any shame upon the Major as the cuckold he was and
would be. That would be 'their little secret'. She would travel
freely, with and without her husband as she saw fit. Baby Hughie
didn't figure in her plans here either. Violet had a taste for first-
class ocean-going and outrageous pampering, and did not want
the nuisance of a child in tow. She was not in any way prepared to
be a mother to her son.

It conjures up such lonely images, the thought of one small child
and a nanny rattling around in this very large mansion. Even the
servants lived in houses on the outer edges of the estate.

The Orchard had been built at the end of the nineteenth century
on three acres of prime Kentish land. A handsome brick structure
with square-leaded windows incorporating stained glass, a
veranda and a first-floor balcony, it's full of attractive, period
features including high ceilings, wood panelling and carvings,
and fine joinery.

It boasts a reception hall, drawing room, conservatory, dining
room, billiard room, sitting room, library/study, kitchen and
breakfast room, a utility room, domestic offices, a cloakroom,

cellars, seven bedrooms, two bathrooms – and a viewing tower at the top of the house. All of the rooms are spacious; the billiard room alone would equal the square footage of most people's homes today. There is a coach house and cottage, as well as a range of outbuildings in the grounds.

Since the days of my father's residence, there have been relatively few changes to the house and grounds. The duck pond has dried up and the tennis courts have been removed, although the 'changing house' and 'tea-room house' which once served them remain.

Hurtfully, and for reasons of his own, Father never told me anything about Meopham. He said nothing to me in his lifetime of the splendid house in which he spent his early childhood. Only later did I discover that The Orchard existed, that he revisited it more than a few times shortly before he died, and that he shared some of his memories with the presiding owners, Freddie and Kirsten Stuckey and their son, Ben. He told them how his parents would visit on weekends when they were not away travelling and, intriguingly, referred to his full-time carers impersonally as 'the staff'. There was no mention of a name or even the word 'nanny' or 'nursemaid', no clue as to who these people might have been. It was as if he had lived in the house alone.

He talked to the family about a ride in the hay cart and how thrilling it was, but he didn't say who was driving the cart – presumably one of the groundsmen. And when he recalled feeding the ducks in the pond, he did not refer to anyone being with him, passing over scraps from the bag of bread. In his recollections, he fed the ducks alone.

Similarly, Father never spoke of having any little pals. Possibly, he did play with other children, but if so, he never mentioned it to Freddie, Kirsten or Ben. I find all of this to be hauntingly bizarre; a picture of the child, Hughie, in a state of almost total isolation and friendlessness.

Major Green squeezed in as many weekend visits as he could, and Violet accompanied him when she felt like it. As much as the Major lived for the time he could spend with his adored son, there was no prospect of a permanent reunion. To all intents and purposes, the Major had become the 'glue' that stretched in two different directions to bind the family threesome together, however loosely, and he had to keep Violet happy.

She was in charge and the Major would do what he was told – an arrangement acknowledged by both parties, to the point that there was no need for argument or strife. They never raised their voices to each other. The Major would reflexively go along with whatever Violet decreed. In public, they presented a reversal of their real roles. Violet would not openly embarrass him – which would have detracted from her regal status – and most people, in passing, saw her as a dignified and attentive wife.

Hughie's view of his parents, even as an infant, was more insightful and instinctive. He saw them come and, inevitably, he saw them go. He never felt part of a united family, since they weren't one, and he didn't have the chance to live through their daily interactions. Had he shared their home, he might well have grown up accepting Violet's domination of the Major as a normal, domestic circumstance. As it was, his mother's cool and self-serving disregard for his father – and him – hit home in a series of shockwaves. He began to dislike her intensely. And his devotion to Major Green became tainted with primitive feelings of disappointment and then contempt that would harden as the years went by.

The Major came from a large and loving family. He knew what the needs of the child were; he had been able all his life to rely upon a nurturing, supportive network of relatives. He loved his kith and kin. Yet he could not be the role model that he knew he should provide for his innocent son.

Young Hughie was immensely proud of his father, a man with commanding features and a deep, loud voice that demanded respect – that is, when they played together in the park, or kicked a football around. But in the presence of Violet, the Major would wilt, retreat. He would tread on eggshells. He was quite unable to offer strength, protection or any of those positive qualities that a child seeks in the male parent. Your dad is meant to be the strongest man in the world. This was an incredibly sexist time, and men were meant to be visibly dominant. Hughie loved Major Green, as I did myself, but neither of us were able to respect him. My father came to despise very early in life those he perceived to be 'weak' men, and as an adult, he could not abide their company. The root cause of this was, undoubtedly, his father.

Major Green was horribly weak. I saw that and my father before me had seen that and been deeply hurt as a result. The Major could have taken a stand for Hughie, his son. He could have taken a stand for me, his grandson, in the face of Violet's ongoing cruelties. I was regularly interrogated by her. She would say, 'Come here, Christopher, and tell me . . . do your mother and father fight?' The Major would see me squirm in confused unhappiness at being asked such a question, but he never would intervene on my behalf. He would merely look sad and embarrassed and then glance away or, more often, just silently leave the room.

The Major loved Hughie, and he loved me too, but for all of his great charm and confidence in public, he was a coward in the face of his beloved Violet. And that would eventually kill him.

By the time Hughie came along, the First World War had ended, and so had the Major's profitable fishing contract. The Greens were staring at the possibility of financial catastrophe which for Violet, in particular, was terrifying.

The Major was desperate for money to keep his marriage together – he couldn't live without Violet – and was rushing wildly from one entrepreneurial scheme to the next. As it turned out, he had all the right ideas at the wrong time. He made deals to promote leisure activities such as miniature golf, a Lilliputian village and holiday camps (with no less a person than Billy Butlin). He also went into business with an outfit called the Goudey Gum Company, producers of 'Oh Boy' chewing gum. It tasted awful, but rather than change the recipe, he paid a team of young men to dress up as sticks of gum and dance along the streets, persuading kiddies that their parents simply must buy them a packet. The kiddies were smarter than the young men in their costumes, who received a pittance for their efforts.

Without exception, these ventures flopped disastrously. But the Major had one project in the making which would eventually hit paydirt, and that project was called Hughie Green.

Before that, however, the Major and Violet were forced to eat humble pie. By the turn of 1926, money had become so tight that they'd had to sell The Orchard, and Hughie's life in loveless splendour had come to an end. The six-year-old Hughie was returned to London. His parents were living in a terraced house at 7 Park Road, Marylebone, opposite Regent's Park, but his own whereabouts for that year are unrecorded. It's possible, although very unlikely, that he spent short periods of time at his parents' address. What *is* known is that the Major and Violet travelled extensively in America in this period. Given their financial constraints and their tendency to put their own pleasures before their son's, they were unlikely to have paid a maid, a housekeeper or a nanny to look after Hughie during the months they were away.

In all probability, he was boarded out to live with his maternal grandmother, Alice Price, who lived about three miles north of the Greens at 95a Golders Green Road. This would shortly afterwards become Hughie's permanent address and a place where Alice provided a whole new experience for her grandson: a home filled with happiness.

According to everyone who knew her, Grandmother Price was a lovely human being. Hughie adored her, and she loved him unreservedly. She was one of the few truly significant people in his life. He often reminisced fondly about his trips to the local cinema with Alice. However, she was not a mum or a dad. She was a surrogate for both of them, and Father must have instinctively realised this, as children do.

In 1927, Hughie had his first-ever holiday when Major Green took him to Canada to visit the town of Prince Albert. Violet did not accompany them. On their return, Hughie moved in with Alice. She sometimes accompanied the family on subsequent trips to the coast, but despite her presence, there's nothing especially joyful in the face of the tiny, good-looking Hughie, captured in black-and-white photographs playing cricket on Bournemouth beach in 1928.

By now, Hughie had become a pupil in the preparatory department of the Francis Holland Church of England school at Clarence Gate close to London's Regent's Park. It was his first recorded school, and a mere minute's walk away from his parents' home, but still Hughie remained with his grandmother, Alice.

By the end of the summer term, 1928, the Major had removed him from the school. Possibly, this had to do with the concluding remark on the child's annual report: 'Hughie is *intelligent* and *will do well* [underlined] *when* [double underlined] he has *learned* [double underlined] to *think* [heavily underlined four times].'

I can well imagine that the Major took offence at the remark and its hostile underlining. You didn't talk about *his* son in that manner or tone! The Major had no time for schools anyway. He had hated his own as a youngster, had once led a student rebellion, and had been threatened with expulsion many times. He hung on by the skin of his teeth through his father Daniel's personal appeals to the headmaster.

Leaving Francis Holland, Hughie was enrolled at Egerton House School in Dorset Square, Marylebone, for one term only. Although this was, again, very close to his parents' home, Hughie stayed on with Alice Price and commuted from Golders Green.

Alice, sadly, was becoming unwell and by the turn of 1929 was unable to look after Hughie full-time. She sent him to St Margaret's, a boarding school in Bromley High Street, Kent, primarily because it was near the home of her sister, Emma. Dr David Jenkins, later Bishop of Durham, was a pupil of St Margaret's, along with his younger brother Graham, but neither attended at the same time as Hughie. Dr Jenkins later declared that Miss Symons, who ran the institution with another matronly lady, was 'somewhat crusty and no-nonsense of demeanour'. The school later moved to a new location around the corner from the High Street, where it would take a direct hit from the Luftwaffe during a raid in the Second World War. It never reopened.

It was from St Margaret's that Hughie, aged nine, sent a telling letter to 'Dear Mummy and Daddy', who were abroad. Hughie wanted his parents to know that the May weather was very wet, and the apple tree in the garden was in blossom. He rather mournfully related that he had had a cold and spent two days in bed. After touching on a couple of routine family matters, he signed off with words and a drawing that revealed his growing hurt. In large, bold letters, he wrote, 'Love, Hugh, *this for daddy*,' and indicated with an arrow the large and numerous X-kisses he was sending to the Major. To the right of this outpouring of affection, he sketched a sour, unsmiling face, tersely labelled 'mummy'. He received no kisses as a child from his mother, Violet. In turn, he was sending her only a raspberry from St Margaret's.

The Greens were not doing well financially, but they continued to travel internationally throughout 1929, either for pleasure or business. Major Green, as ever, was chasing the big deals that he hoped would shore up his flagging fortunes. Hughie addressed his letter to the couple in Boston, Massachusetts, where they were visiting the Major's brother Jack, a fish wholesaler. The Major also took the chance to meet with the Goudey Gum Company Of Boston, securing his rights for UK distribution and sales.

It was during this trip that Violet met her in-laws in Canada and America for the first time. Journeying on from Boston to Prince Albert, Hughie's parents returned to the UK via Montreal. There, they met with Major Green's great friend, Colonel Charles MacLean, who was living in his fabulous, Pointe Claire mansion, and borrowed money from him for their son's education.

At the start of the next school year – September 1929 – Hughie moved back to his grandmother Alice's house in London and became a pupil of the elite and expensive Arnold House School, which still exists in Loudoun Road, St John's Wood. The Major was keenly aware of the prestige such private schools bestowed not only upon the pupils but their parents. The Wall Street Crash would send a financial shudder around the world on October 24, the Depression years were starting, and Major Green wanted to remain in the company of the well-to-do. He had spent the money from his fish contract, he had sold The Orchard, and his Mayfair days as an esteemed major with the Canadian forces were a distant memory. But appearances had to be maintained: Hughie could not be seen in a grammar school with the 'lesser classes'.

Father remained at Arnold House for four years, apart from a twelve-month gap when, aged eleven to twelve, he apparently received no formal teaching. He was nevertheless a bright and promising student when he was taken out of the education system completely in December 1933. The following February brought his fourteenth birthday – which was the then minimum, legal school-leaving age.

Grandpa Green had had no interest whatsoever in his son going to school. His only wish was for Hughie to be on the stage; he relentlessly pushed him into the theatrical spotlight at every opportunity. Of all his money-making schemes, this was the most ambitious, but also the one that would finally pay big dividends.

Little more than a year after leaving Arnold House, Hughie would become the highest-paid child entertainer in the UK, and a movie star to boot. The Major would be able to live out his own fantasies and lost dreams through his boy. Violet would have access to the piles of cash he generated, and would maintain her status in society.

Together, they were about to destroy any chance that Hughie Green would ever have of being a 'normal person'.

3

The Leader of the Gang

Major Green worked tirelessly with Hughie from the earliest age to teach him vaudeville songs, impersonations and comedy skits. This escalated when Hughie was six. Until then, the Major had had to cram the training sessions into snatched weekends at Meopham. With Hughie in London, his father grabbed every chance to see him at Grandmother Alice's house, or to have the youngster visit 7 Park Road. The Major adored him, and he saw in him a star – the star he had always wanted to be himself. He taught him literally hundreds of tricks and tips.

Shortly after Hughie's move to London, the Major took him to see his godfather, the popular variety star Harry Tate, performing at the London Coliseum. Harry had a small aeroplane as a prop for one of his sketches, and after the show, Hughie told Harry that the propeller hadn't been turning fast enough. He was promptly invited to come back the next night, get inside the plane and turn the prop at the correct speed. It was Hughie's first stage performance – hidden in a model aircraft at the Coliseum.

A little later, in 1927, when Major Green took Hughie on his first trip to Canada, the Major insisted that his son take part in the ship's concert, reciting 'The Old Lady In The Market Street Car'.

By the time Hughie was ten, he was entertaining cinema audiences. Having spent many an afternoon at the pictures with his Grandmother Alice, Hughie had come to love the movies and was enthralled by their stars. He made up scrapbooks, listened to what was then called the wireless and, like many other children of

36

his age, dreamed innocently of one day taking centre stage himself. Unlike other children of his age, he did something about it.

In those days, there were usually one or two live performances between reels. As Father told it, he simply decided one day to approach the manager of his local cinema in Golders Green and offer him five shillings – 25 pence – to be allowed to perform. (Personally, I doubt that there was any schoolboyish spontaneity about this; it smacked of Major Green, orchestrating the initiative from behind the scenes.)

The cinema manager was impressed enough with the lad's talents to ask him back the next Friday to present a short routine. And when the big day came, Major Green, Violet and Alice sat nervously in the auditorium while Hughie acquitted himself with great aplomb and revelled in the warmth, the *acceptance*, of the applause. Within a year, Hughie was treading the boards of a more exciting venue – London's prestigious Garrick Theatre, where he performed a 'trial audition' in front of a live audience. This was really the beginning of the Major's campaign proper. From then on, he would be indefatigable in his efforts to make connections and to promote his boy.

At this point, the Major's own parents began to express alarm. His mother Margaret – known affectionately as Maggie – told him that she would rather see Hughie being raised as 'a shepherd in the Highlands'. As far as his immediate family were concerned, Major Green lived his life through his son to a degree that was unhealthy for both, and he was pushy and manipulative with it.

Maggie and her husband Daniel had travelled from Canada to Scotland and England in June 1931 to celebrate their golden wedding anniversary, and they could see at first hand what was happening. Their worries were crystallised by the young Hughie's absence from school. Aged just eleven, he had been taken out of full-time education for a year so that Major Green could get on with the 'more important' business of building a child star.

To satisfy legal rulings, he hired a governess, the improbably named but adorable Pussy White. She cared for Hughie deeply, and she came to dislike the Major and despise Violet for their treatment of the child. Despite being a true professional, Pussy rarely got to open a book or to teach her pupil anything. She was seldom allowed any time with Hughie at all. Her role, simply, was to be around in case the authorities should start checking up on why the boy was so frequently missing from the classroom.

The Major was quite single-minded in his ambitions for Hughie who, at age twelve, on May 12, 1932, took his next step up the show-business ladder. This was the occasion of a 'Grand Children's Concert' in aid of the Royal Northern Hospital in Golders Green, which had launched a fund-raising campaign. Allegedly organised by Hughie and a 'school chum' called Ralph Goldman, the show took place at the local All Souls' Church in Hoop Lane. Contributing to the seventeen 'turns', Hughie sang 'The Trousers My Father Used To Wear' and delivered a monologue entitled 'Coffee Cups Derby'.

'God Save The King!' cried the programme, which cost all of two old pennies. 'God save young Hughie and Ralph!' cried the hospital, which received the princely sum of four pounds and three shillings. 'God save Major Green!' cried anyone who knew that the Major had put up the five-shilling deposit to book the hall and had been the organiser and recruiting agent for the unusually talented mix of children on the bill.

My father always claimed, romantically, that he and Ralph 'just thought it would be a great idea to round up some kids and put on a charity show'. Ralph, allegedly, sorted out the ticket sales, and Hughie took care of everything else – an unfeasibly tall order for a couple of twelve-year-olds. In all the newspaper coverage of the day, no one thought to ask how two small boys, without consider-able help, could have promoted, scripted and directed such a big production, and how, seemingly out of nowhere, had managed to discover so many fabulous, young performers. Interestingly, Ralph's sister Hesta, one of the kids who 'just happened' to be around, was already operating professionally under the name of Baby Sunshine.

Major Green's fingerprints were all over the production, its organisation and its business aspects, and Hughie and Ralph simply took the credit. But this was all part of the masterplan, the

Major's promotion of Hughie as a child genius who was destined for great things in show business through the sheer force of his brilliance and desire for the theatre. It would not do for the Major to be seen to be behind the wheel. Indeed, he went to great lengths to present Hughie as a Boy Wonder following an irresistible calling *despite* the parents who were naturally concerned for his education and well-being. He should've been so lucky . . .

The Boy Wonder duly announced a second benefit for the hospital, this time in conjunction with a genuine schoolmate, Lauri Lane, who would later emerge as a key character in Hughie's career. Lauri and his actor father, Lupino, were undoubtedly cultivated by the Major, who was always on the lookout for useful contacts. On this occasion, however, Lauri dropped out of the project at an early stage because of school commitments, and Hughie received all the credit for production and direction of the concert, held on December 15, 1932 at St Alban's Hall, Golders Green. Hughie once again recited 'Coffee Cups Derby', the cast included a wider element of experienced child performers and the hospital was handed an even more impressive six pounds and twelve shillings.

At the time of the first show, Hughie explained that he had wanted to do something for the hospital because his grandmother Alice had been a patient there. Alice did indeed have a history of chest complaints, and Hughie would have been dismayed that she had fallen ill. He may well have visited her in one of the wards – but there is no evidence to support this. And her name was not linked to the second concert.

At this point, Hughie was making nothing financially from his show-business ventures. This was all about charity work, and in those days most people saw only the generosity of such selfless activities as Hughie's. But few realised better than Major Green the power of doing 'good works' and what advantages could arise from them later. Decades on, via international charity spectaculars such as Live Aid, those advantages would become more widely understood.

The hospital concerts generated an enormous amount of goodwill and publicity for Hughie, but more importantly, they sowed the seeds of what would become Hughie Green's Gang Show – a famous, touring revue performed entirely by children.

Hughie was twelve years old, and the Major had already tried and failed to get him into Hollywood. He secured an important part for his son in a movie called *Cavalcade*, which was being made by the Fox Film Corporation, with a package deal including a contract for a breathtaking £10,000 a year. Back in 1932, that was real money.

But the Major ran up against one big problem in the shape of British law. According to the Children (Employment Abroad) Act of 1913, no child under fourteen was permitted to leave the UK for the purpose of singing, playing, performing or 'being exhibited' for profit. The penalty for the parent or guardian infringing this law could be as heavy as two years' hard labour.

The Major was incandescent with rage. He vowed to fight the Government and its stupid, bloody laws about child exploitation. He railed loudly at the Home Office, accusing them of ruining his son's chances in life and trumpeting that Hughie's mother would – *if necessary* – accompany him to Hollywood and supervise him there. But what mother would not *insist* upon going with her pre-teen son if he were travelling 7,000 miles across an ocean and a continent? There was certainly no indication that Violet wanted to go to America with Hughie. At the time, she believed that this was just another of the Major's numerous crackpot schemes, and one which robbed her of his attention. Despite all the Major's huffing and puffing about his boy being an English superstar in the making, the Home Office would not budge: no exception would be made for Hughie, even in the 'safe custody' of his mother.

The whole sorry saga was reported in the *Daily Express* dated September 15, 1932. 'Boy Denied A Film Star's Career' boomed the headline to a story which stated, 'Hugh is broken-hearted. His father is bewildered and not a little indignant.'

It's probably safe to say that Major Green was more broken-hearted than his son, and that he was more than 'a little indignant'. The Home Office did not react too kindly to the hostilities he fired off in the press. They were not about to be bullied by the Major, and the authorities began to take an interest in Hughie's welfare. The Greens were officially informed that they were under suspicion of child exploitation, and were cautioned. Realising that he would have to tread more carefully in future, Major Green returned Hughie to Arnold House in 1932 to sit out his last two years in the classroom, with Pussy White on standby to cover any ensuing absences.

Hughie spent most of this time being intensively coached for stardom by the Major, although he somehow found time for other interests. He won prizes for his drawing. He was fascinated by trains, ocean liners and aircraft, and he would read anything and everything about them, remembering every detail. He took an interest in politics. And he was an accomplished student.

Many years later, Hughie, with his mother, Violet, present, would tell an interviewer, 'It was inevitable that I drifted into the theatre . . . I was a dreadful scholar and hopeless at maths. The ominous warning, "This boy will never succeed," kept appearing on my term reports.'

This was absolutely false. Both he and Violet knew it was a lie. The comments on Hughie's report for his last school term range from 'quite good' and 'very keen' to 'very good' and 'excellent'. His maths performance was summed up as 'Good. Has worked hard and done well.' There was nothing 'inevitable' about Hughie going into the theatre, nor did he 'drift' into it – he was firmly steered by parents who were quite unmoved by the academic achievements and potential of their son.

Arnold House, a boys' prep school, prepares its pupils to transfer to St Paul's School for Boys by age fourteen, and from there to Oxford or Cambridge University and the hallowed professions and classical, literary pursuits of gentlemen. The Major was having none of that nonsense, but he was aware that very few boys from 'good backgrounds' opted out at fourteen. He wanted Hughie at least to have on his record that he finished school at this fine and challenging institution.

The Major hadn't needed education himself, striding out to meet the world head-on with a shrewd and streetwise business acumen and the gift of the gab. He determined that the same would be true for Hughie. Sending him into the adult workplace at the earliest possible moment, neither Major Green nor Violet even considered that they were depriving or exploiting their boy. Violet didn't give a damn about him one way or the other, just as long as he didn't inconvenience her. She may have been resentful that the Major lavished so much time on Hughie, but she was really only concerned about her husband making enough money to return her to a life of finery. She was also preoccupied with her continuing bedroom liaisons, away from the eyes of the family.

The Major, with typical tunnel vision, was convinced that he was giving Hughie a wonderful start in life because it was what he would have wanted for himself. Hughie Green, for his part, spent the rest of his life bitterly upset that he had not received a full, formal education and would lash out at anyone who made him feel intellectually inferior. But back in his early teens, Hughie raised no opposition to the plans that were being made for him, fearing that if he did not go along with the Major, he would lose his love and interest. He received no warmth or attention from his mother. What would happen if he went against his father's wishes for him to be a star? Would both parents then be lost to him?

Hughie was too young to understand that real love cannot be gained from anyone if they do not have it to give, like Violet, or if they give it in the wrong way and for the wrong reasons, as the Major did. None of which is to suggest that young Hughie had no aptitude or enthusiasm for performance. On the contrary, he was brilliant, a natural. It wasn't as if he hated show business and had to be forced, kicking and screaming, onto the stage. Simply, he had no choice in the matter. His career had been chosen for him.

*   *   *   *   *

In January 1934, while his former schoolmates were trooping back to their desks in Arnold House after the Christmas holiday, Hughie was already on the verge of a massive breakthrough – courtesy of Lupino Lane. Lupino was the father of Lauri Lane, Hughie's school pal and his initial collaborator for the second

Royal Northern Hospital benefit. An acclaimed stage and film actor and director of twenty years' standing, Lupino would later have the distinction of performing the Lambeth Walk for King George VI and Queen Elizabeth, the late Queen Mother. He knew some very influential people, not least the top brass at the BBC, and it was through these friendships that a leading BBC executive called Bryan Michie joined the audience at a London production featuring Hughie and Lauri.

The show, *Come! Come!*, staged at the Rudolph Steiner Hall in Baker Street on January 11, was the third benefit for the hospital, and it was a bigger and more elaborate affair than anything Hughie had so far attempted. It also raised more money – a whopping £25. Introducing the *Gang Show* for the first time, it had Hughie producing, Lauri directing, and both boys acting, with Father in the leading role.

'Revue Is A Serious Business!' raved the *Daily Express* with an enthusiasm equalled by Bryan Michie, who immediately offered auditions – at Broadcasting House – to both Hughie and Lauri. Michie had been attracted to the hall that night by Lupino's name and connections, but the teenagers' performances had been thoroughly deserving of the opportunities now on offer.

Hughie passed his audition for the top BBC radio programme *In Town Tonight*, and he wrote and recorded a fifteen-minute spot that included his soon-to-be signature song, 'The Wearing O' The Green'. This led to his starring role as Emil, supported by Lauri Lane, in a serious radio play titled *Emil And The Detectives*, which in turn triggered a flood of work offers for *Hughie Green's Gang Show*, with the Gang all hand-picked, rehearsed and ready to roll. Major Green had struck gold.

Writing about these events in his book, *Opportunity Knocked*, Father was at great pains to cast himself as the boy next door who had happened to get a break. 'Although we were happily nibbling away at the big time,' he contended, 'our lives were perfectly normal – too normal if you counted school and homework!'

Hughie had already left school.

He added, with even greater imagination, 'Being normal kids, in fact, almost lost Lauri and me the chance of doing our first straight play, *Emil and the Detectives*. We arrived late because we had been playing football. The beautifully dressed, prettily turned-out, highly scented young gentlemen from a dramatic school, who were also at the audition, stared at our satchels, muddy knees and faces in amazement and disdain.'

It's most unlikely that either the Major or Lupino Lane would have missed out on going to Broadcasting House with their boys, and the idea of the Major allowing his protégé to be muddied up with dirt on such an important occasion is even more fantastic. A cute story, but then Father never did let the truth get in the way of a good anecdote.

Equally fanciful is Hughie's account of his next big accomplishment – a two-night engagement at the Fortune Theatre in London's Drury Lane. The way he told it, he just turned up at the theatre and asked a cleaner to take him to the boss.

'He showed me to the office of Mr Frank Lloyd, who not unreasonably hedged at the prospect of doing business with a fourteen-year-old. A couple of letters from my father, however, convinced him that any show I produced would not lack financial backing.'

With so much at stake, there is no way that Major Green would have just let Hughie jump on a bus to go and negotiate for two nights in a prominent theatre. The Major's involvement would certainly have amounted to more than sending 'a couple of letters'. He wanted West End exposure for his boy, and as Hughie said, he provided 'financial backing' – to the tune of hiring the venue. Significantly, this was the first time that Hughie had acknowledged any help at all. It would also be the last time the Major tried to pretend that Hughie was a one-man operator.

The Fortune Theatre show, held on April 30 and May 1, 1934, was again called *Come Come*, but without the exclamation marks of its predecessor. It was an expanded version of the earlier production, with more young performers and a broader variety of acts. Some of the children were already established in the business and all were now under the umbrella of Hughie's Gang. The Major had evidently been very busy securing new talent.

Featuring in the show for the first time were two sketches. The Major was keen to show off Hughie's acting skills, because he was looking to the movies – and, still, to Hollywood. In another significant change, the production had no charitable purpose. It was all to make money for the Greens, and even the price of a programme had risen, to sixpence.

Lauri Lane had dropped out of the picture completely. This was a Hughie Green venture, with the rising star acting as compere, director, producer and principal performer. As for the Major, he was fast becoming known as the man behind the hottest talent in town – Hughie.

*   *   *   *   *

Harry Tate had been responsible for his godson's first taste of the stage, even if the boy had been hidden from the audience in a model plane. Now, Harry came back into the picture to bestow another favour upon Hughie: he invited him to appear for a week in Eastbourne, beginning on May 14, 1934, for a fee of £5. Hughie was hired as Harry's young sidekick, a part often played by Harry's own son.

Barely pausing for breath, Hughie then dashed out on a UK tour with the *Gang Show*, which found them feted as celebrities wherever they went. Crowds of fans, held back by police, lined their exit route from every stage door, exuding a friendly and supportive adoration rather than the wild hysteria that would unnerve later generations of pop stars.

Essentially, the *Gang Show* continued in the tradition of the gypsy circuses which once travelled the country with an assortment of fat ladies, bearded women, two-headed children, giants, dwarves and mutants. Child performers were very much a novelty and not a legitimate, mainstream proposition. They attracted suspicion, mockery, dismissal. They were *weird*. But the capabilities of the children in Hughie's entourage, promoted with great skill by the Major, changed that forever. Hughie and his Gang blew away the stigma; they made the genre of child entertainment widely acceptable in the UK for the first time.

The tour ended on an unforgettable high for Hughie when, on
August 27, 1934, he and the Gang started a week-long residency
at Sir Oswald Stoll's revered old vaudeville theatre, the Alhambra
in Leicester Square. Father was overwhelmed as he gazed up at
his name in lights for the first time. He was equally awestruck to
be ushered into the Number One dressing room, which he
described as 'a holy of holies rustling with memories of the great
artistes who had used it' – people of such legendary stature as
Sarah Bernhardt.

'Top of the bill after only six weeks in the business!' he would
later quip, more casually, for sure, than he felt at the time. But for
once, the excitement of the occasion was not completely shared
by the audience. For all of its glamour and prestige, the Alhambra
held a warning for Hughie and the Major – that children, no matter
how talented, were more attractive to warm, family audiences
than to the stylish habitués of London's theatreland.

Despite this, the event raised considerable interest, and the
Major was quick to act upon it. Within 22 days, the Gang were
back on the road, and Hughie's fame – and misfortune – were
sealed. For the next five years, up until the outbreak of the
Second World War, he would rarely sleep in the same bed two
nights running. He spent his days in any number of anonymous,
provincial dressing rooms and his nights in equally interchange-
able hotels as he criss-crossed the length and breadth of
England, Ireland, Scotland and Wales. The Major worked him
like there was no tomorrow. And according to fellow Gang-
member Ella Wilson, he was often out there on his own, without
either parent.

Violet obviously wasn't interested in the endless slog of
touring and Major Green had appointed a personal manager,
Archie McCulloch, to keep the machine running smoothly on the
road and to report back to him at the London headquarters he had
set up for Hughie's promotion. Eventually, he would open a swish
new office on Percy Street, off Tottenham Court Road, launched
with a lavish oyster party.

Hughie was also accompanied on his travels by singing and
dancing instructors, a secretary and a chauffeur. Intriguingly, he

claimed that a male tutor was on the payroll. This tutor was never named, and Father insisted that if he ever approached him with a book, he would tell him, with typical charm, to 'fuck off and get me a beer'. In fact, the only recorded 'tutor' that Hughie ever had was Pussy White, and the person who fetched the beers for the touring fourteen-year-old star was Archie McCulloch. Major Green was anxious to convey that Hughie was travelling with a teacher. It made things look better in the eyes of the authorities and that element of society which would snobbishly question the value of a youngster who had left school at fourteen.

* * * * *

Hughie Green's Gang Show was entirely structured around its star, who was visible to the audience at all times. He was the master of ceremonies, introducing the acts, and he conducted the band. He danced with the chorus. He was the headline artist, singing songs, telling jokes, rattling off well-polished patter, enacting comedy skits, and turning out immaculate impersonations of figures including Maurice Chevalier.

Behind the scenes, Hughie was tireless in organising and training the other children. Their excellence was vitally important. It meant that Hughie's name quickly became a guarantee of quality, and this later enabled the Major to have two or three *Hughie Green Gang Show*s out on the road simultaneously – without Hughie. The crowds would turn out anyway, because they trusted the name.

But back in the early, founding days of the troupe, people came along primarily out of curiosity. They had heard Hughie and the Gang on the wireless, they had put imaginary faces to the voices, and they were intrigued to see their heroes in the flesh. Before long, though, curiosity turned to true fandom.

There were usually two shows a day, each lasting for about two hours with a twenty-minute interval, during which mums and dads could buy choc-ices and sweeties for their children – encouraged by a jovial Hughie, who was adroitly on a percentage of the takings.

As his celebrity grew, he became 'Chum Chief' of the 'Chum Club', a children's feature in the *Glasgow Daily Record*. It was another brilliant scheme of the Major's, creating both publicity and money as he set up links with other children's clubs around the world and with 'honorary chums' including the Hollywood kiddie sensation Shirley Temple, the only slightly older British actress Nova Pilbeam, the up-and-coming screen star Margaret Lockwood and the beautiful Gracie Fields.

Yet, for all of the pally atmosphere of the *Gang Show* and the 'Chum Club', Hughie was extremely lonely in the crowd. He had been brought up in an isolation that was both physical and emotional. Dispatched to Meopham as a baby to be looked after by 'the staff', he had been denied the precious gifts that should be the birthright of any infant – his mother's arms, the holding, the scolding, the nurturing and the loving that most parents give unreservedly. Major Green offered Hughie an aberrant love and attention in exchange for the chance to live his own thwarted ambitions through the hapless child. His parents, for cruel and selfish reasons, then took my father from one world of illusion – The Orchard – to another, which was the theatre. And this ensured that he would miss life's second, critical stage of development, the one in which children identify with a peer group and freely interact within it.

Hughie never had any time at school to make friends, to enjoy the fun and to take the hard knocks in the playground that teach interpersonal skills and tolerance for others. In every spare moment, he was being instructed in the art of entertainment by the Major. By the time my papa was fourteen, he was no longer what one would call a child. He had been forced to grow up, to take charge, and many of the basic human emotions he should have come to understand through normal childhood growth had been cut off forever.

The Major had forcefully instructed Hughie that the Gang must look up to him at all times as their boss. A gang, by definition, must have a leader, and Hughie was it. He had to maintain a distance from the other boys and girls, otherwise he would lose control over them and, therefore, the show. He had to be able to discipline them if they should in any manner jeopardise the professionalism of the act. Show business was serious work. It was not meant to be fun. Hughie must be constantly beyond any suspicion of immaturity.

Indeed, the Major was furious on the one occasion that his son did indulge in a bit of adolescent tomfoolery with three other members of the Gang. They had gone together to Lake Alvaston in Derby for a photo session involving a wind-up submarine that my father had bought. This was yet another scam, intended to portray Hughie as a 'normal' boy out playing with his chums, but it all got a bit *too* playful when Hughie fell into the water. It was a trivial, funny incident, but unfortunately for my father it found its way into the *Nottingham Guardian*. Other children fell into ponds, raged the Major. But Hughie Green The Star did not. No such juvenile antics should undermine his authority. He was special. He was not like other children. He was an *artiste*. That is what he was told all his life, even if the public were told something different.

One of the boys at the lake with Hughie that day was Toney Entwistle. He later changed his name to Anthony Beauchamp, married Winston Churchill's daughter Sarah, made a fine reputation as a society photographer, and committed suicide on August 18, 1957 with barbiturate tablets. He had gulped down a succession of small doses which, cumulatively, were fatal. Before he died, he tried three times to call Hughie, who had continued to see him over the years for drinking sessions. My father had instructed his private telephone switchboard not to disturb him before 9 a.m., since he had had a late night. However, the operator became worried by Toney's progressively faltering speech. She phoned to wake my father, who immediately returned the call, but it was too late; Toney was already dead.

Ironically, he was the only Gang kid with whom Hughie ever established any kind of relationship. At the height of Gangmania, Hughie had around two hundred children on his payroll and his relations with them were absolutely not those of a child with his peer group. According to Ella Wilson, he could be sharp, disdainful and imperious. At an age when most teenagers are learning how to take orders, he was giving them. He was uptight and very serious about everything. Newspaper articles from the era relate that Hughie was authoritarian, and would not put up with any nonsense in rehearsals, once reducing a little girl to tears by telling her that she was no good and to 'go home if you cannot take your work seriously'.

Journalist Ruth Maschwitz, reporting from run-throughs of the Fortune Theatre *Come Come* production, said he 'stands over his little troupe like a dragon and does not spare their feelings'. She had overheard Hughie telling another small girl, 'You are rotten and must pull yourself together.'

He later confided to Ruth, 'It's no good being nice to the kids. They don't understand. Children are very difficult to handle. At the slightest sign of kindness, they fool about and giggle.' He said this at the age of fourteen.

In training, Father would personally rehearse any member of the cast who needed improving. By the time the Gang went out on tour, they were all expected to be at top performance level – but if someone wasn't cutting the mustard, they were dismissed. Hughie was too smart to allow such a firing to be based on personal dislike; what counted was how each performer was being received by the audiences.

He was no less critical of the venues themselves. If, on arriving, he found something wrong, and he usually did, he would issue instructions to have changes made, be it to the lighting, the sound, the emergency exits and procedures, or even the set-up of the dressing room.

When the curtain went up, Hughie was always prepared. He made it all look so very easy. Any nerves disappeared instantly. He was in his element because he would hear that glorious sound – the applause – and no one enjoyed it more than my father. As John Heyman, his manager in adulthood, later told me, 'Your father needed applause and attention more than anyone else I have ever managed; only Richard Harris came close to Hughie in that regard.'

Momentarily, he had some appreciation of what being loved actually felt like.

*   *   *   *   *

One day when I was about ten and living in Baker Street, I went with a friend across Regent's Park, and we crept through a hole in the fence into London Zoo. It was a cold, rainy, autumn day, and the zoo was pretty much empty. We went to the parrot house. I knew many of the keepers, and one of them showed me a new bird which had arrived. It was beautiful, about two feet long, but I was upset by the size of the cage it was in. There was no room for him to move around with ease, and he certainly could not fly. The keeper explained to me that the parrot had been in this cage since he was born. They were going to try to introduce him to larger cages until one day, hopefully, he would be happy in a big aviary with other birds of his size.

Realising that I was still upset, he added, 'You know, Chris, this parrot is quite happy in his cage. It's all he has ever known. He is fed and watered and has not been physically hurt by anyone. We're the ones who are hurt because we know that he should really have been allowed to flap his wings and fly.'

This little incident impressed me greatly. I still wonder if that parrot ever did make it to the large aviary. And every time I think about those few minutes at the zoo, I think about my father. Out on the road with the *Gang Show*, he was too young to know about adult worlds or children's worlds, or what age his friends should be. All he knew was the 'cage' of his immediate environment. It was too tight and too restricting for him ever, later, to be able to 'flap his wings and fly'.

Hughie had no real friends, with the exception of Toney Entwistle, who was really just a colleague he quite liked. Both on and off the road, my father was surrounded by adults at all times. To some extent, this was a by-product of show business and his position as the leader of the Gang. But at the same time, Hughie had no pals of his own age outside show business. His parents actively discouraged it; they did not want him wasting his time with 'normal kids'. Violet couldn't stand children, and the Major decreed that Hughie should be concentrating full-time on his career.

As their son became more successful, they wanted to maintain total control over their property, their cash-cow, and it suited them that he was alone. When Hughie had a problem or a worry,

without any confidantes or any ability to communicate personal
things to others, he could only turn to his parents. And that is just
what they wanted. By comparison, the other Gang children
seemed perfectly happy and well-adjusted. They were treated
well on tour. Their food, accommodation, transport and general
well-being were given the highest priority, and they had lives and
friends outside the theatre.

Some of the Gang children had been discovered by chance. The
Major spotted Ella Wilson, innocently performing as a child in
Scotland. On another occasion, some of the troupe heard a little
boy whistling as he sold sweets on a station platform. A few days
later, he was in the *Gang Show*, whistling his way around the
country as Willy Mars. The Major had chosen this stage name and
had then secured a profitable advertising contract for Hughie to
promote Mars Bars – 'Stars Eat Mars'. Magazines and newspapers throughout Britain were subsequently treated to images of
young Hughie hanging out of a first-class carriage window in a
station, holding up his Mars Bar.

Hughie was, of course, a 'lifer' in the Gang, and while a few
others, like Joey Hopkinson, a promising comedian (who was also
at the lake the day that Hughie tumbled in), went on to successful
performing careers, most of these wonderful kids simply grew up
and dropped out to have a normal life when their voices broke, or
they returned to education. Then other children would be found to
take their places.

Everything was above board with the parents of the Gang.
Indeed, it was often Hughie who dealt directly with this vital
group of adults, answering their queries and soothing any worries
that might arise. They were 'pains in the ass', he later told me.
'They drove me fucking nuts.' But they were given proper
contracts for their young ones, they were consulted at all times,
and they were always made to feel involved and respected.

This was not the age of ambitious mummies and daddies
shoving their offspring onto the stage. There were no big
children's talent contests – that would all come years later with
the introduction of television, particularly in America. Indeed,
such parental behaviour, if witnessed, was considered suspect by

the Home Office and the British legal system. Major Green and Violet were not your average guardians.

The parents of the Gang members cared greatly for their children and wouldn't have dreamed of abusing them in the way that the Major and Violet were exploiting Hughie. Not even his fellow-performers cottoned onto the realities of Hughie's life, on tour or at home. They viewed the Major as sometimes intimidating but, generally speaking, a very nice and kindly man. Violet remained in the background.

But the truth was that of all the things the Greens did or did not do for Hughie, the most satanic was the degree to which they isolated him. They denied him the ability to make and keep friends, to communicate within his age group, to feel or give affection or love. His 'chums' worked for him, and he worked for his parents. Eventually, he would rebel. But not before the fateful night when he walked in on his mother, Violet, having sex with a total stranger. It would be a shattering moment, and one in which his feelings about his parents, and the world, changed instantly and forever. Hughie's ruin would be complete.

4

Gold Dust and Chicken Sandwiches

By the age of fifteen, Hughie Green had become the hardest-working, highest-earning child star in the UK. He was chalking up an incredible 700 live performances a year. He was touring relentlessly with the *Gang Show*, playing matinees as well as two concerts a night. He was making live and pre-recorded appearances on the radio, he was starring in pantomime, he was making records, he was an orchestra leader and he was also turning out regularly for benefits and charity events.

His annual net income would have been somewhere between £15,000 and £20,000, which was a fortune at a time when a small bungalow cost an average of £250 and a male factory worker earned roughly £1 a day.

Yet, it was impossible for my father to fully appreciate what he had, because he had no experience of normal life. Stardom to Hughie had been like passing an exam to anybody else. He was expected to succeed, and he did. He was then showered with accolades and told he was a genius. Show business was his destiny. Had he been 'discovered' at, say, twenty, then his achievement might have meant a great deal more to him.

Most children have toy cars; Hughie had a real, deluxe car complete with chauffeurs. He would never feel the excitement of Christmas. But none of this interested Major Green and Violet.

Hughie had become a famous and fabulously well-paid little person, and he was their greatest asset.

When Father was onstage, the Major lip-synched along with every word of the patter and songs and jokes he had taught his boy to deliver. Nothing thrilled him like the roar of the crowd. The youngster's success also vindicated Major Green in the eyes of his beloved Violet. His project had taken off! Hughie had become his greatest accomplishment, and the Major was awash with the cash – Hughie's – that he knew would keep his marriage together.

He enjoyed the good life too, but it was less important than his perceived duty to Violet and his blind ambition for Hughie's career. Seemingly, he was unable to recognise his own cruelty towards his son. He thought he was giving him everything – and that was the Major's sickness. His love had become deviant; it wasn't pure, from the gut. It was forcefully motivated by all of the hopes that he channelled through the innocent child.

If Hughie had not turned out to be such a brilliant vehicle for the Major's own broken dreams, then I'm sure he would have loved his son as devotedly as he had in his babyhood and would have done his best to care and provide for him. He would have gone on to some other entrepreneurial venture, albeit with disappointment, while Hughie would have continued his schooling and probably found a happier future in which he would have been at peace with himself, excelling in law or business or maybe even politics. And Violet would have stayed with the Major until he could no longer support her at an acceptable level.

Violet, however, had found in Hughie her ticket back to the champagne and celebrity lifestyle she feared she had lost forever when the fish money started to dwindle. He became important to her for the first time in his life. She luxuriated in the opportunities he created. This is not to say that she suddenly developed any maternal warmth towards him. She didn't. She would only ever bother to show up for his concerts if they happened to be in London, attended by the rich and famous. She had no inclination simply to support him. Never in her life did she come to love him as a son, although he became more tolerable for her. But she certainly wanted to know what Hughie was doing, and with whom. She was determined to supervise the Major's control over 'their property' and his cash.

There was no love, in its real sense, among the Greens. But when Hughie started making incredible sums of money and the future shone with limitless possibility, the three became bound together, bizarrely and obsessively, like a triad. Violet needed her husband and her son for as long as the goose kept laying the golden eggs. The Major had everything to lose. He truly wanted and needed both his wife and Hughie, and to have both, it was imperative for him to keep the boy in line, working unquestion-ingly. If the money ran out, then so would Violet. His unconditional love for Hughie had become conditional – and the strings effectively strangled the child's emotional future. He would have no understanding of decent, giving relationships, inside or outside the home, and he would never know what it is to be loved and to love in return. Eventually, the Major's terror of losing his wealthy protégé would lead to his own death.

And as for Hughie, he was trapped.

His parents spent his money freely and without guilt, never even dreaming of investing anything for him. They fully believed that his cash was their entitlement. Hughie was in their debt – forever. After all, Major Green had dedicated his life to his son, transforming the snotty-nosed little schoolboy into a star in record time. Here was Hughie, coasting through the Depression with his own luxury cars, drivers, valets and secretaries, and his parents had made it all possible. They never allowed him to forget that most young men were lucky to have a bicycle and a lowly job in some trade or factory. He had to be eternally grateful and, of course, obedient. He could never even think of leaving his parents' 'generous' directorship.

They approved of nothing they could not control, and their most successful means of ensuring Hughie's compliance, apart from establishing his indebtedness, was the vague threat of parental withdrawal. Their form of 'love', no matter how superficial, twisted and malnourishing, was all he knew, and he dreaded losing it. If he were to alienate his dad, who could he turn to then? Not Violet; she was locked in with the Major. What would happen to the

Gang? Who would promote him? Who would 'care' for him? Hughie had already lost his respect for his father. Now, his surviving, instinctive love was turning to fear. And that fear would swell and fester until the day that Hughie initiated an incident that would kill Major Green.

Publicly, the Greens treated Hughie as though the sun rose and set on his bottom. He was their magnificent gift to the world, and they basked in his reflected light. Violet travelled in a Rolls-Royce coupé, and she swept around high-profile parties and dinners swathed in mink, dancing to the orchestra, sipping champagne and nodding, small talking and exchanging her thin-lipped smile with any number of famous and important guests as she set about acquiring a minor fame-by-association of her very own.

She had made a thrilling entrance into society as the wife of a leading, uniformed army officer, but it had all been based on canned Canadian cod, and she'd had to grin and bear her husband's less-than-glamorous nickname of 'The Fishmonger General'. She much preferred her new role as the grand and beautiful mother of Hughie Green, entertainment's most sensational child prodigy. After all, the fish business didn't get you the whole dining room in London's exclusive Maison Prunier restaurant.

That's where the Greens held Hughie's fifteenth birthday party, an extraordinary event which found the young star surrounded by two dozen adults including actress Hermione Gingold, publicly smoking a cigar, and a delegation of top BBC executives – the gods who could make or break an entertainer's career. No other children were present.

As usual, Hughie's parents had failed to consider his enjoyment or his needs, even on his birthday. Having denied him a formal education and the opportunity – and therefore the ability – to make and keep friends of his own age, they were now, unapologetically, wringing everything they could from their son.

*   *   *   *   *

They were fucked up, totally, and it took me years to realise the extent of it. Of the two, Major Green was the more dangerous: he

was lovable. I myself would have a youthful but fleeting devotion
to him. People often noted that he was vulgar and unpolished but
they still warmed to his naturally charming manner. He was a
brilliant conman and a coward. If he hadn't been so weak, he
would have shown Violet the door. If he hadn't been so screwed
up, he would have encouraged Hughie to follow his own dreams,
whether they included show business or not.

When they were out together, Violet respectfully walked
behind the Major, but most people got her number as a shallow,
self-centred tyrant who had emasculated her besotted husband,
and this worked to the Major's advantage. They disliked her so
much they didn't look at his warts and wrinkles as closely as they
might otherwise have done.

The couple had finally agreed to share their home with Hughie
when he was fourteen. They had moved to a new apartment at
36 Clarewood Court, Seymour Place, in London W1, and in
October 1934 Hughie insisted on moving in too, accompanied by
his beloved Grandmother Alice. Father had learned that Alice
was terminally ill with lung cancer and was distraught at the
thought of losing her. He couldn't bear to imagine her passing in
some impersonal hospital bed. Thanks to his resolve – and his
undertaking to pay his parents' rent and other household
expenses – Alice was able to remain with her family. She would
die at Clarewood Court in July the following year in the bedroom
next to Hughie's.

Father, however, would rarely enjoy the novelty of actually
living with his parents: he was out in the provinces, touring to
support them, while the Major ran a fantastic propaganda
campaign to convince the public that Hughie was a normal, happy
little boy who was never tired and who just wanted to work
because it was all such good fun. In fact, Hughie knew full well
that he was not 'normal', he was afraid that he had been turned
into a freak, he knew he wasn't loved in any meaningful way, and
he was upset and angry that he had been made the family
breadwinner. Seemingly, he never complained. The concept of
respecting one's elders carried more weight with children in the
thirties than perhaps it does today.

But all of his childhood demons and fears would resurface time and again throughout his life. He never came to terms with the roots of his hurt. He would explode into a familiar, violent rant in moments of rage, 'What do you think I am? A fucking freak? A fucking pathetic, peep-show freak on the pier? All I am worth to anyone are the pennies falling out of my pockets. Apart from the fucking pennies, no one gives a fuck about me.' Then, trembling, tearful and hysterical, he would scream in a hellish, childish cry for love, 'Well, I'm going out and I probably won't come back. And no one will care if I get hurt. No one will fucking care if I die in the bloody gutter.'

I last witnessed this performance only two years before he died, and it all went back to his five years on the road with the *Gang Show*, working all hours of the day and night for the benefit of his parents. There were tremendous pressures on him to be an 'adult'. It was the only way to make the Gang work. He had to be seen to be in control, manipulating and cajoling other children of his own age to keep the show running smoothly. He could never show any hint of weakness or, heaven forbid, shed a tear, or give in to a yawn.

He carried the responsibility for the whole show on his young teenage shoulders, and that anxiety would also reverberate down the years as he bellowed drunkenly, on more than one ghastly occasion, 'If the fucking show is no bloody good, no one ever thinks to blame the bastard that fucked up the lighting, or the sound, or the piss-arse idiot who couldn't write a funny joke for me. . . Oh, no, they'll just say, "Hughie Green stank." I get all the shit thrown at me, and that is why people will fucking well do what I tell them to do. I'm the fucking star!'

Father's tirades, especially when he was in full flight and loaded with booze and Benzedrine, could be spectacular. Grown men cowered.

From the earliest age, he was burdened with the knowledge that there is only one way to go when you are at the top, and that is down. People liked winners and not losers. They only cared for you when you were number one. He had had it drummed into him by Major Green, that 'second place' was not good enough. As an adult and father, he often repeated the Major's credo to me,

'Chris, just finish first. Cheat, lie, do what you have to do to win and no one will question how you got there. That might not sound nice, but it's just the way it is. No one likes a failure.'

He was taught that the only thing worse than coming second was making excuses for it. That was weak. Only weak men made excuses; strong men never did. Thankfully, most of us are taught that we should take pride in a race well run, even if we don't finish first. We are allowed to be 'weak' from time to time, to make mistakes and excuses for ourselves and to learn tolerance for others who may not always finish first either. My father never received any moral instruction. Everything was black and white, never grey, to the Major who, notably, failed to see his own craven weakness where Violet was concerned.

It was from this emphasis on strength and leadership that my father's intolerance for 'weak men' and homosexuals arose. Hughie's era was incredibly homophobic, and the stigma attached to a gay man was considerable. When he wrote about the 'beautifully dressed, prettily turned-out, highly scented young gentlemen' who had attended the audition for *Emil and the Detectives*, it was with a deliberately and typically insulting sneer, although in private, he would use much more abusive words.

Hughie would grow up identifying with the macho, male stereotype, but in adulthood he liked few people. He was uncomfortable with children, and he insisted that most women were 'stupid cows' who had to know their place – although he was always respectful and caring of elderly ladies. He had little patience with people he perceived to be fools, but he did like unusual characters, and was very impressed with intelligence and demonstrable accomplishment. Even his inveterate homophobia could be set aside if that person was interesting enough, brilliantly gifted or a top name in show business.

Scared of losing his grip on success and scared of disappointing the Major, Hughie was hard on himself and on other people as the *Gang Show* toured the country. The anxieties that plagued him were things unknown by most other teenagers, and he would later resent his parents for instilling in him such a fear of failure. This would remain with him for the rest of his career. So too would his tight-fistedness and mistrust of other people, which stemmed from his bitterness at having had to bankroll his parents. Never financially generous towards others, he was an embarrassingly poor tipper in restaurants. If I dined with him, I would always insist on paying the bill because I knew how much he suspected people of taking advantage of him. Conversely, he was deeply appreciative of anyone buying him lunch, or footing his hotel bill.

Father's stressful and abnormal lifestyle took its toll when he began to complain of a tight chest. The young Hughie must have heard a lot about chest conditions. Major Green's father, Daniel, had uprooted his family from Scotland and transplanted them in the middle of nowhere in Canada after convincing himself he had contracted TB. Violet's father, John Price, had died from bovine pulmonary tuberculosis when Hughie was two, and her mother, Alice Price, had suffered from chest ailments for years before her death from lung cancer. Both Violet and the Major were worried by the scourge of TB. London was still burning bituminous coal for heat, and the fogs and dampness concerned them. Any health issue, especially involving the chest, was reason for alarm. And so when Hughie complained of breathing difficulties at the age of fourteen, he was rushed to a doctor immediately.

Dr Laszlo Banszky wasn't just any old doctor. He was a brilliant and charismatic Hungarian in his early thirties who practised at 12 Devonshire Street, near London's famous Harley Street. His approach was truly progressive, mixing traditional with alternative remedies in his efforts to treat both body and mind, and his reputation impressed Major Green, who firmly believed in alternative medicine.

Dr Banszky agreed that Father had a weak chest – Hughie later diagnosed himself as an asthmatic – and the doctor then decided on two courses of action. One was to inject Hughie with gold dust. This, perhaps, is not the sort of help we'd expect today from the local doctor, but gold dust, very finely ground-down, has been used in medicine since ancient times. It is seldom allergenic and can be mixed with any number of solutions either to be injected or painted onto a body surface, such as the throat – a treatment I later received myself from Dr Banszky.

The exact formula of the mixture used is usually exclusive to the prescribing doctor. Gold is inert; it does not react chemically with anything else, it doesn't rust or deteriorate, and that, of course, accounts for its age-old allure and value. I doubt that Father had any idea about the chemical properties of gold, but it was just the thing to treat *his* medical problems. Other little boys might be given an aspirin, but he was a 'Star' and would be cured by gold dust.

The doctor's second prescription for Hughie was Benzedrine, an amphetamine better known today as speed. In the thirties, it was commonly prescribed for a wide range of ailments, including asthma because it dilates the bronchial passages. Hughie took it via an inhaler. Banszky gave it to Hughie primarily as a decongestant. He realised that Hughie's tight chest was a product of his lifestyle, a manifestation of the severe pressures he was constantly experiencing. He was almost certainly suffering from anxiety attacks, not asthma, and while the doctor may have commented on Hughie's 'weak chest', he was really trying to treat the pain of this young boy's mind. For Father, that *was* the good doctor's golden touch.

Dr Banszky immediately became his surrogate father. He could see that my father was in urgent need of kindness and attention, and he was genuinely caring of his patient. In return, Hughie worshipped the man he affectionately called Latzy, and was shattered when he died in 1965.

He would often tell me, dramatically, about their first meeting, 'Yes, Chris, it was Latzy who told me the sad news that I would always have a weak chest. Without Latzy and his miraculous gold-dust treatments, I doubt that I would have survived. He saw I was an asthmatic when no one else could figure out what was wrong with me.'

In reality, my father enjoyed excellent health as a young person. Only in the last decade of his life did he experience real chest infections, and these were largely related to lung damage sustained in a near-fatal car crash. But after that first consultation, he ran to see his beloved Latzy almost every time he coughed. Part hypochondriac, part attention-seeker, he was an impressionable boy weighed down by expectation and desperation to be noticed.

His parents' main concern was to keep Hughie on the stage, making money. He had to be dependable or risk ruining his reputation and career. Indeed, my father never missed a curtain going up. But if he even hinted he might have to bow out of a show due to illness, that unerringly attracted the interest of Major Green and Violet. Anxious to keep him happy, they would indulge him with any number of visits to Latzy. It was no financial sacrifice for them because Hughie was paying for everything anyway. And Hughie revelled in the undivided attention of his father-figure and doctor.

When Latzy died many years later, his successor, Dr Hare, inherited his formula for the gold-dust mixture. But Father became disenchanted. The treatments weren't working. Why couldn't Dr Hare work Latzy's magic? His frustration became so profound that he wanted me, as a medical student, to dedicate my life to rediscovering Banszky's secret and to open up a clinic specialising in gold-dust treatments. In truth, it had done nothing for him physiologically. The magic was Banszky himself, a man my father had looked to with love and admiration.

If the gold dust was a harmless panacea, then the Benzedrine was quite the opposite. It had only entered clinical medicine in the late twenties, and the potential for its abuse as a slimming aid, for example, or as an unnatural source of energy, was not appreciated at the time of my father's initiation. Many have looked back at this era, at such tragic stars as Judy Garland, and named Benzedrine as the precipitating factor in their descent into drug addiction.

Benzedrine is a stimulant of the central nervous system. Its effects include elation, wakefulness, alertness, enhanced self-confidence, aggression, talkativeness, loss of appetite, increased initiative and restlessness – most of which would have benefited a young boy working to the very limits of his endurance. But the withdrawal effects may include severe craving for the drug, depression, fatigue, inertia, paranoia and psychosis.

Father never went anywhere without his inhaler – and by also indulging in alcohol, he set out on a treacherous path. Alcohol may appear to give a boost, but it's a depressant, a downer. By mixing it with Benzedrine, an upper, he triggered a chemical see-saw reaction in his brain. Physically, he careered from super-human activity to utter exhaustion and collapse, and the terrifying temper tantrums, nastiness and impaired judgements that characterised his behaviour were clearly fuelled by this volatile combination of drugs.

Major Green and Violet didn't give a damn that Hughie was drinking alcohol at fourteen. As long as he was on the road fulfilling his responsibilities to their bizarre triad, as long as the Major could march around the sumptuous, London offices in Percy Street and Violet was welcomed at fashionable restaurants and exclusive stores, Hughie could do what he liked when he was out on tour.

When my father found the Benzedrine made him too twitchy to sleep, he would demand a calming shot of booze from his manager, Archie McCulloch, who went on to accommodate his growing taste for liquor. Archie, Hughie told me, was 'a good shit', and he was perhaps the best friend he had during this period. Archie had no wilful desire to hurt him and, viewing him not as a teenager like the rest of the Gang but as a young adult, would cater to his every whim on the understanding that things should never get out of hand to the point that Major Green would have to be informed.

My father never considered himself to be a drug abuser, which he clearly was. His prescriptions 'legitimised' him, and he wanted nothing less than death by hanging for anyone in the illicit drug trade. His lifelong drug abuse – and total denial of the same – was yet another consequence of his monstrous upbringing and a contributing factor to his catastrophic life as a real adult.

*　　*　　*　　*　　*

The Greens were aware that as a rising showbiz family they needed to create an endearing image for themselves, and to this end the Major organised a string of newspaper articles which would paint the same cosy portrait. Everything was wholesome and jolly and good, clean fun. That was the scenario that put the bread and butter on the table, and it was endlessly reinforced in interviews, which often took place in the room next door to where Grandmother Alice lay dying.

Hughie, said the propaganda, lived a regular, contented home life, when in fact, he knew only dressing rooms and hotels. He was the 'boy next door', a happy camper who loved his pets and his model trains as much as he adored his work. That was also bullshit. His life was bleak and joyless. He didn't have the pets described or pictured in the press, and there was no train set. They existed only as props. Hughie's dog, Mickey, was actually the Major's, and my father rarely saw the animal since he was always out on tour. His pet monkey was brought in for a photo shoot and just as quickly dispatched, and the goldfish that 'travelled with him' didn't.

Ironically, these were all things that the teenage Hughie dearly wanted. He received outrageously expensive presents, he had his own car long before he was old enough to drive one, but he hankered after the possessions that normal boys prized and later, as an adult, he would secure them. Clearly trying to compensate for what he never had as a child, he would keep pets and a train set, which he installed in my bedroom. As he added to it, the table was extended, and extended again, while my single bed was, accordingly, moved ever closer to the wall. Mama would say, 'Hughie, have some conscience, soon you will have Christopher sleeping under Clapham Junction,' but expansion continued. Hughie needed his train set.

The press, in the thirties, was kinder, more trusting and less intrusive than it is today, and none of the reporters ever dreamed of investigating the Greens and their fresh-faced young protégé. Had they scratched the surface of the charming domestic story they were proffered, they would have found a clear case of psychological child abuse. The authorities, too, had lost interest in Hughie's doings.

Years later, his daughter Paula Yates would also be allowed to slip through the social services' safety net with tragic consequences – despite the media's relentless scrutiny and exposure.

The triad, though, was in the clear back then. No one knew that the Greens' glossy, family happiness was a sham and that Hughie was being obliged to collude with his parents in a gross deception. Many of his later-life colleagues and acquaintances have described him to me as a 'pathological liar', and that can only be attributable to the training of his parents.

Major Green liked to brag that Hughie had won a scholarship to St Paul's School for Boys, and, subsequently, Father would repeat this. However, there is no record of any scholarship. Hughie, the Major insisted, was a gifted baby, with a miraculous ability to listen to gramophone records and learn them off by heart – at the age of one. Only a little later, he just happened to pick up the famous vaudeville songs, patter and routines, all by himself.

If the Major was full of hot air, Violet was just as bad. It was a 'mystery to everyone', herself included, where Hughie found his talented Gang members – clearly, she'd forgotten about the Major combing the country to look for them. She talked about Hughie, at eight, forecasting his own appearance at the Alhambra Theatre, and how she and the Major would have stamped on such an ambition if they'd thought he was serious. Then there was the story of Hughie training dogs and performing impersonations at the age of three. Most outrageous of all was her contention, 'I'm real proud of my Hughie. . . sometimes even I feel like asking for his autograph.' The Greens were deliberately surrounding their son with smoke and mirrors which would disguise his true condition of being overworked, thus ensuring the smooth progress of his career and earnings.

Hughie heard and repeated these same stories many times. He had probably convinced himself that they were true, just as he seemed certain he had watched the great fire at Madame Tussaud's in 1925 and had witnessed scenes from the General Strike in 1926. He must have had telescopic eyesight: Hughie wasn't living in London then.

The stories became more outlandish as time went on. The great French entertainer Maurice Chevalier had been present at Hughie's birth! Grandmother Alice had duetted so beautifully with film idol Walter Pidgeon at The Orchard that three-year-old Hughie burst into tears of emotion! The grand house was packed with famous actors and actresses every weekend!

Neither Chevalier nor Pidgeon were even in England in the years of these remarkable events, and I have no knowledge of my father ever meeting Chevalier, although he did impersonate him brilliantly. There's a small possibility that he may have been introduced to Pidgeon in Hollywood, but there was no big friendship. And while the Major and Violet did eventually meet many of the showbusiness celebrities claimed to have been at their weekend parties, this was only through Hughie's fame and long after The Orchard had been sold.

The most fascinating interview of all appeared in 1973. It was given jointly by Hughie and Violet, who lied in a fantasy harmony as they worked over all the old ground and, again, dropped the names of Chevalier and Walter Pidgeon. Violet glamorised her origins and her past, and lied for the sake of expediency and self-interest. She consciously knew she was not telling the truth.

But I don't believe that my father was a liar *per se*. He was a complex being, on the one hand deceptive, delusive and secretive and, on the other, excruciatingly honest, logical and forthcoming, which got him into a ton of trouble later in his career. He could not express the shades of grey between these two extremes of his character.

He knowingly perpetuated a lot of bullshit, just to fall in with his parents' propaganda. Other stories he remembered from childhood, or heard repeatedly, and internalising them as his own, wove them faithfully into his legend. But I'm convinced there were times when he desperately wanted a lie to be a reality. Hughie knew that Maurice Chevalier was not there to welcome him into the world, but he clung to the myth because it was comforting: it meant that his birth was happy and wanted. Similarly, he embraced the delightful childhood tales that the

Major and Violet spun so persuasively to the media because he needed to reinvent his past as something innocent and happy. In my view, he would lie to make everything all right, and then try to believe it.

*   *   *   *   *

Hughie began work on his major film debut in the summer of 1935. Veteran of one small bit-part, he took the leading role alongside Margaret Lockwood and his godfather Harry Tate in a movie called *Midshipman Easy* – director Carol Reed's first film, and an adaptation of Captain Frederick Marryat's popular novel. A seafaring drama filmed on a limited budget as a 'quota quickie' – made to satisfy the Government's ruling that a certain percentage of films shown in British cinemas must be home-grown – it was a minor success financially and critically, but never a classic.

The British film industry was very much the poor relation of Hollywood, and it was the Major's ultimate goal for Hughie to be successful there. He had not stopped seething over the lost *Cavalcade* deal, and to his further infuriation, another British child star, Freddie Bartholemew, was launching a successful acting career in Hollywood – aged ten! It appeared that his aunt and guardian, Cissy, had taken him there for a holiday and simply never brought him back.

The Major was kicking himself; he felt he'd been outsmarted. To add insult to injury, Hughie had failed an audition in England for the title part in MGM's *David Copperfield*, which was now shooting in California – with Freddie in the starring role. Even more annoyingly, it was later nominated for an Academy Award. The movie that did win 'Best Picture' was *Mutiny on the Bounty* – a sailing epic which had dominated London's West End while *Midshipman Easy* worked its way modestly around the provincial cinema circuit.

It was time for the Major to strike back! Having passed fourteen, Hughie could now legitimately work in America with a magistrate's permit and a deposit of £100. But rather than pursue any further negotiations with the authorities, the Major decided to circumvent the law and set up a solo tour of Canada and the States with Hughie performing only for charity. Since he would make no money, he was, therefore, not 'working'. The US and Canadian charities, all well-known and respected, were so grateful to have the 'Boy Wonder' raising funds that they offered to cover all of the travel and accommodation expenses incurred by the Major, Violet and Hughie.

Hughie's charity work would attract attention, help him build a reputation for generosity as well as talent, and put him in the right places to make influential contacts. It was the Major's intention that Hughie should achieve the highest level of recognition in the States, paving the way for his triumphant entry into Hollywood as the successor to such legendary British imports as Cary Grant and, later on, David Niven.

And so, in the autumn of 1935, the Greens set sail. Violet left a few days ahead of her husband and son to 'visit friends', and apparently she was not alone on that ocean passage; she was enjoying another of her flings, with an unknown gentleman. Hughie, meanwhile, was saying goodbye for the time being to his first-ever girlfriend, the *Gang Show*'s Kitty Machree – a pretty, dark-haired teenager with a sparkling smile. The Major had undoubtedly warned his son not to get too closely involved with members of his Gang, since any such liaison would compromise his authority, and an unintended pregnancy – heaven forbid – would create massive problems. However, Hughie's relationship with Kitty was tolerated since it seemed primarily romantic, even naïve. None of his relationships with women would be so innocent again.

Violet rejoined the Major and Hughie in New York City's famous Algonquin hotel at the end of the tour. From there, they travelled by train to Toronto, where they checked into the magnificent Royal York Hotel.

Hughie was to be uniquely honoured the next day. The Lord Mayor of Toronto had invited him to a luncheon sponsored by the Ford motor company. There, he was to be feted for his marvellous charity work, along with Fred Waring and his orchestra – the most

popular big band of the day. And the fifteen-year-old Hughie
would have the privilege of conducting Waring's band! With such
an exciting day ahead, he decided on an early night.

The Greens had taken a suite with bedrooms on either side of a
uniting lounge. Hughie ordered chicken sandwiches from room
service, ate them and went to sleep. Waking around midnight, he
realised to his dismay and fright that he'd been sick all over
himself and the bed. It was dark, he was in an unfamiliar place,
and he did what any young boy would do – he ran across the
lounge to his parents' room and opened the door.

The lights were on, and Hughie found himself blinking in
horror at the sight of his mother, Violet, having sex with a man
he had never seen before. Panic-stricken, he ran out of the
suite and into the corridor outside. There, he was confronted
with a vision that filled him with even more confusion and
disgust: sitting on a small sofa, head cupped in his hands, was
the Major, weeping.

I was never told what happened next. Parents and child must
have reached some uneasy agreement, because Hughie sailed
through the luncheon the next day with his usual aplomb. But he
later confided the nightmare experience to my mother and she, in
turn, told me as much as she knew. Father was too badly damaged
by what he saw to have been able to go into any detail, even with
his wife.

Truly, it was the moment he came of age. He was, until then, an
innocent in many ways, and nothing could have prepared him for
such a traumatic discovery. For the first time, he became cruelly
aware of his mother's infidelity, and he realised that there was
nothing 'normal' about his parents. (He also refused to eat
chicken – or any type of poultry – ever again. The mere sight of a
Christmas turkey would enrage him to the point of violence.)

His already shaky relationship with Violet was, at one stroke in
Toronto, rendered irredeemable. He despised her from then on,
and was affectionate towards her only when necessary for his
public image. Unconcerned, she continued her flirtations and
affairs, with Hughie often painfully aware of them. As for the
Major – in that single, hopeless instant, he had broken his son's

heart. Hughie had already lost his respect for his father, but now his impulsive love and fear were transformed into revulsion.

Major Green was not impotent, nor was his heterosexuality in any doubt, but he was not a ladies' man. Tall and handsome and blusteringly larger-than-life, he was a diminished sort of fellow in the privacy of his bedroom, unable to keep up with a beautiful, sensuous wife whose passions were insatiable. Watching the Major weeping beneath the chandelier of the hotel hallway, Hughie immediately recognised the real helplessness of a father who had preached only strength. He saw the dominance of his cold and distant mother, and he vowed that no woman would do that to him.

And no woman did. Hughie gifted his wife, my mother Claire, with a life of torment. He treated his mistresses terribly; one of them, looking for his help at a moment of desperate need, only to be spurned, resorted to killing herself. He had any number of one-night stands, and would think nothing of having sex with a woman in his dressing room while her husband was somewhere nearby in the theatre. His sexual behaviour would become increasingly deviant. But in his determination not to become a victim like his father, and with a disturbed and disturbing logic, he would copy what his mother did when she exposed him as a child to her loveless and lustful betrayal.

He was quite indifferent when he learnt that he had impregnated a teenage theatre usherette in Birmingham only two years later. Vera May Hands could expect no sympathy or support from the father of their son, Barry, the first of Hughie's illegitimate children.

5

Hughie: His War and His Women

Girls flocked around the stage door every night to catch a glimpse of Hughie Green, leader of the *Gang Show*. They were mesmerised by this tall, thin, energetic young man with his natural blond hair, his cornflower-blue eyes and his ready smile.

Father never had any trouble attracting women. At seventeen, he could and did seek pleasure with any number of starstruck, female fans. He never liked using a condom; he said it was 'like shaking hands with a glove on'. Even though they were easily available over the counter by the time he was capriciously sowing his teenage oats, he was quick to take risks, and his irresponsibility would soon catch up with him.

By the time he met Vera May Hands, he no longer had his manager Archie McCulloch around all the time saying, 'Careful, old boy . . . got a rubber with you?' Hughie was on his own. Since spring 1937, Archie had been travelling the UK and the Channel Islands setting up tours for the Major. These would be billed as *Hughie Green Gang Show* events but would not feature Hughie himself. By now, he was a brand name and was to be marketed aggressively.

Vera May Hands was working part-time as an usherette at the Aston Hippodrome in Birmingham when Father appeared there for the week beginning Monday, May 31, 1937. During that time, they had what Hughie later described as a one-off sexual encounter, and conceived a baby.

72

Vera May was desperate to communicate with Hughie about her plight, and not knowing how to contact him personally, wrote to Archie McCulloch. He held a crisis meeting with Hughie to discuss the constant stream of letters she was now sending. It was agreed that she could become a big problem, and the Major had to be informed. He wasn't interested in whether or not Hughie had impregnated Vera May, only that the allegations stayed out of the press: such exposure could ruin his career. There was no concern for the young lady, no thought for the child, and no consideration for Hughie's feelings. This problem was not an emotional one for the Greens. It was a business matter.

Violet, totally lacking in any maternal feelings herself, felt no compassion whatever for the unfortunate mother-to-be. It never crossed her mind that Hughie should perhaps think about helping Vera May or, indeed, any other little madam trying to get her claws into the family meal ticket. Violet pinned 'the scarlet letter' onto Vera May, while secretly enjoying the disclosure of Hughie's active sexuality.

The Major was furious about the potential damage Hughie had caused, but he realised that it was an occupational hazard. He advised him to be more careful the next time, while reassuring himself and Violet that the child probably wasn't Hughie's anyway. Without knowing the circumstances, they chose to damn Vera May out of hand.

As a damage limitation exercise, the Greens instructed Father that he was not to reply to any of Vera May's letters, and he was not to confide in anyone. As long as there were no proven links between Hughie and Vera May, then all would be well. If the prospective mother did come forward publicly with her claims, it would be up to her to prove Hughie's paternity. And that would have been impossible, since blood tests at the time could only establish that someone was *not* responsible.

Vera May Hands was the only child of strict, Protestant, working-class parents who opposed her pregnancy. They ordered her to give the child up for adoption, but she steadfastly refused. She was seventeen when baby Barry was born at the Dudley Road Hospital on March 17, 1938. His father's name was left off the birth certificate, and his mother's occupation was described as 'brassfounder's viewer' – presumably meaning a quality controller of brass products.

Vera May wanted to be with her son's father, but her letters went unanswered and she could follow Hughie only through the newspapers. While her mother clipped out his press stories and stored them in a tin box, Vera May kept writing to him, in vain. Father, for his part, felt nothing for his abandoned lover or for the son he would never meet. I believe that he was conditioned to blank out anything which hurt, or which threatened the commercial safety of the triad – even though, intellectually, he knew he was a shit.

Still, Vera May Hands would not go away. She persisted for years in her efforts to have Hughie acknowledge his son. Decades later, only days after meeting Paula Yates, I would come face to face with Barry and would hugely enjoy meeting the half-brother who had been born in Birmingham almost sixty years earlier. His mother had fantasised about spending the rest of her life with Hughie Green, despite the brevity of their encounter – and she would go on to devote herself entirely to her son. Her mother, meanwhile, scanning the papers for news of his activities in the summer of 1938, would have learnt that he was in the States and Canada. And Vera May would surely have been heartbroken to know that Hughie, there, met his first great love.

The Second World War was on the horizon. Conscription was already starting, the Government was drawing up arrangements for mass evacuations, and the Major was making plans to get Hughie and the family well out of harm's way. Father's trip to the States, the press reported, was for a tour. Other articles said it was a spur-of-the-moment holiday. It was neither. Major Green was frantically trying to peddle his boy in Hollywood, to line up film work so that if war did break out, he could whisk the family out of England – while continuing with his dreams to make Hughie a hero of the silver screen.

It was in Hollywood that Hughie met a young woman called Nancy, and it was love at first sight – although the burgeoning relationship was a red rag to the bullish Violet and Major Green.

Alarmed at the strength of Hughie's passions and certain that Nancy was a threat to their investment in him, they crushed the romance at the first mention of the word 'engagement'.

Hughie never forgot Nancy. He would often speak about her over the years, although not in detail. I never heard her surname or her occupation or any reference to her appearance, but she was the only girlfriend that he would recall with 'love' – except for my mother, Claire, and in his deathbed will, a later girlfriend, Yvonne. He told me more than once, 'Perhaps I should have married Nancy, but my mother and father didn't approve,' always hastily adding, 'But, of course, that was before your Mama.' Mother, for her part, would often sigh, dramatically, 'Oh, Nancy, wherever you are today, you had a lucky escape! Why didn't you marry him and save me?' In view of everything she had to endure from Hughie, I sometimes think she was only half-joking.

Stopping off in Montreal on the way home, Hughie signed up a French-Canadian lumberjack, Big Joe Beauchamp, to sing with the *Gang Show*. Back on English soil, Father told journalists that he had found Hollywood 'very artificial' and was glad to be home. But he wouldn't be home for long. On September 3, 1939, Hughie was entertaining in Glasgow when war was declared on Nazi Germany. The Gang was little more than a skeleton by the time of their last performance a month later. Most of the members had joined the war effort.

By now, some 38 million gas masks had been stockpiled for use by the British public, along with a million and a quarter cardboard coffins. Food rationing was introduced in January 1940, and Hitler launched invasions of Denmark, Norway, the Netherlands, Belgium and France in April. The Blitz began in September, and London was slammed for 53 terrifying nights in succession.

Hughie, meanwhile, was eating steak on the other side of the Atlantic Ocean. He told me this appalled him. He was bitterly ashamed of being made to abandon the UK for the safer shores of the States and Canada. At the beginning of the war, the USA was neutral. And the Dominion had rejected conscription as it was practised in Britain, whereby any soldier who was called up had to go where he was told; he could be sent to the frontline in any participating country. In Canada, when a soldier was drafted, he would only be expected to fight within Canada for the defence of Canada. He would not be ordered to fight overseas unless he had volunteered to do so. The Major figured that if Hughie were called up in Canada, he would be given a rifle and told to guard a bridge or something, thousands of miles from any combat or danger.

Back in Britain, the Government was worried that Hitler would isolate the islands and starve the inhabitants, and a 'Dig For Victory' drive was in full force. Every garden, no matter how large or small, saw rhododendrons replaced with radishes. A piggery was built in Hyde Park, and in Kensington Gardens cabbages were growing where the flowers used to be. House-holders began keeping chickens and other farmyard animals.

Hughie knew all this. He knew that his former audiences in the provincial towns and cities – those same places which had for so long suffered unemployment and poverty – were now in dire straits while he was eating steak in Montreal, Boston, New York and Hollywood. The guilt never left him. For all of his disdain for others, his respect for 'the little people' who made him a star knew no bounds. He had been truly humbled by his exposure to others less fortunate than himself and he never failed to stick up for the wholeheartedness and generosity of the very people who had the least, materially, to give. He knew how they lived, what songs they liked and what jokes made them laugh, and he knew their joys and fears. His famous 'populist touch' came naturally. He saw no division between himself and the man in the street, only a difference in luck or opportunity.

And so in October 1939, when the Major rushed the family away from the bombs and bullets of the Second World War, he undermined his son's sense of fair play and injured his self-respect. Hughie was hurt and angry that he would not be able to stand alongside his fans, his Gang and the millions of other patriots defending the country, and he hated leaving the two people who truly cared about him: his doctor, Laszlo Banszky, and his godfather, Harry Tate, who later died after a heart attack in wartime England.

The Greens travelled first to Montreal, where they lived in a rented apartment in downtown's Summerhill Avenue. The Major was busy establishing a business headquarters when Hughie and Violet drove together to California. There, Father filmed his first Hollywood movie, *Tom Brown's Schooldays* – an adaptation of Thomas Hughes' classic 1857 novel about life in a Victorian boarding school. Hughie had a minor role as a class bully; Tom Brown was played by his old nemesis, Freddie Bartholemew. Released in May 1940, the film did well at the box office, and to this day it routinely appears on TV.

Father followed on with a summer season at the Hollywood Playhouse, in an improvised comedy show called *Meet The People*, and a seven-week residency at the prestigious Coconut Grove nightclub, located in LA's swish Ambassador Hotel.

The Major eventually joined his family in LA, where they lived in a rented house just off Wilshire Boulevard, only a couple of miles southeast of Beverly Hills. During this period, Hughie – and his parents – rubbed shoulders with a host of famous Hollywood stars, many of whom Violet would later claim to have entertained at The Orchard.

With his stage show highly acclaimed and full of hilarious impersonations, it really did look as if Hughie Green was about to become an international star. Over eighteen and able to work legally in America, he was performing for as much money as the Major could negotiate. But Hughie's conscience continued to trouble him. He felt guilty that he was contributing nothing to the war effort, especially when friends of his in Canada were volunteering for service rather than waiting to be called up, and were heading off to Europe. In his own words, 'I felt like the serpent in the Garden of Eden.'

In tandem with this dissatisfaction, Hughie's past returned to haul him over the coals. On the eve of his coming-of-age in February 1941, he sat down in the Montreal apartment with the Major's typewriter and wrote an essay titled *Twenty-One Tomorrow*. Surveying the pros and cons of adulthood, he ventured, 'You can get married without anyone being able to say "yea" or "nay", and if you care to do this or that you can, with no let or hindrance from a family who have possibly guided you with great skill and care during the precarious years of childhood and youthful madness up to this point.

'The other side of this picture is the one where you count up the misfortunes of the situation; when you realise gone are the easy, comfortable days of school and college where the "old man" was a cinch to send you pocket money, pay your fees and generally push the unsociable and hard side of the world away from you. Gone are the days of running up tailor's bills, club bills and suchlike, without any other security than a good and rather tireless father to pay them for you.'

There may have been a reference to Nancy in his stinging sentence about the right to marry without permission. For the most part, though, Hughie was writing not about himself but, bitterly, about the person he wished he had been. He would have liked to know those 'easy, comfortable days of school and college' when your father paid the bills, provided the pocket money and sheltered you from the 'unsociable and hard side of the world' – all the things that the Major did not do. Hughie would have loved to have gone to college. By now, he had been paying his parents' way for quite some time, and there was every indication he would have to carry on doing so. Clearly, there was a lot of bad blood between him and his parents, and a growing discontent within Father himself.

It was in this frame of mind that he did something quite extraordinary. He celebrated his twenty-first birthday not at some star-studded party, but by volunteering to fight overseas in the Royal Canadian Air Force – without telling his parents. He had summoned the courage and will to stand up to the Major and Violet. He knew full well that they would both be absolutely furious. And they were. They were horrified by his insubordination, by the wartime dangers facing their star and by his treacherous bid for freedom. This was the greatest calamity that had yet befallen the Major in his masterplans for maintaining the triad that was the Green family. Losing control over Hughie or losing him in wartime action amounted to the same thing: the Major's dreams would be shattered.

Hughie's resolve had not in fact come suddenly. Back in England in 1938, against the Major's orders, he had taken flying lessons in Bournemouth, and had secured his 'A' pilot's licence the next year after two months' training at Doncaster Aerodrome. He would have been ready and willing to join the RAF had he stayed in England to be called up. As a child, Father had been fascinated by travel and transport. Now, flying solo in an airplane, he had found his greatest high, a complete escape from his parents, his pressures and everything that was wrong with his life on the ground.

Before this, Hughie would never have contemplated any act of disobedience. Where would he go if he left his parents? They had isolated him to the extent that he had no friends or support network outside showbusiness, and only employees inside it. And after years of being pampered by an army of attendants, he was quite unprepared for a life on his own.

Hughie was also painfully aware that his parents were growing older, and depending on him for their income. He was unable to shake off the eternal 'gratitude' that they demanded from him, even though he, increasingly, could not stand being with them, and their impropriety was beginning to embarrass him. Something happened, though, when Hughie came to Montreal in those early years of the Second World War, something which ignited the spark of defiance into a flaming rebellion. He had taken up with Claire Wilson – his future wife and my mother.

Claire, her family and her friends opened up a whole new world to Hughie. They were not members of his Gang and they were not Hollywood celebrities. They didn't give a damn that he was a 'star'. In any case, 'stars' in the Montreal of that day were more likely to be hockey players. These new friends were intrigued by Hughie the person and not by his career and status, which was something he had never experienced. Their very independence made him feel like a coward, but they also gave him the encouragement to take charge of his own destiny. He had found peer group support for the first time in his life. These people were unimpressed by the Major and Violet. Indeed, they individually grew to dislike them, although their influence over Hughie was by example and not by preaching or criticising his parents.

Father's redemption should have been at hand. But he still wasn't ready or able to cut the strings that bound him inescapably to his mother and father.

Major Green went into a frenzy of activity to have Hughie removed from active service in the Royal Canadian Air Force. He couldn't get Father's volunteer application withdrawn, since Hughie was able-bodied and of legal age. But he tried to have his military function transferred from action to entertainment. The Major contacted a London producer chum, Lee Ephraim, who by chance was in New York City. Unbeknown to Hughie, the Major explained that his son was keen to play a patriotic part in the war by appearing in a show that would cheer on England's campaigns. Ephraim's friend Guy Bolton – a playwright who had co-written popular musicals including *Oh, Boy!* and *Anything Goes* – was putting together just such a production. *Golden Wings* was an RAF tale, filled with pro-England propaganda, and Hughie reluctantly travelled to New York to meet Bolton.

To his horror, he was offered the part, although it would depend on financial backing being found for the show. Sitting it out in Summerhill Avenue, Montreal, he took a telephone call one day which informed him that he was being called up for duty in the air force. It was wonderful news for him and a disaster for his parents.

The train that carried R.104851 A.C.2. Green h, for two days and two nights to Regina, Saskatchewan, left Montreal's Windsor Station on May 22, 1941. Hughie, heading towards his new career as a Link training instructor, struck up a conversation on the train with an American called Art Teulon. Desperate to fly but barred by the US military because of a childhood leg injury, Art had volunteered for the Royal Canadian Air Force, whose entry requirements were less strict.

He was quiet, almost taciturn, and quite unlike the chattering classes of show business. He had no interest in Hughie's wealth or fame. Rather, they bonded over a shared passion for flight and speedboats, wine, women and song. To Father, Art was the embodiment of all that was American and good, and the two men that day established a lifetime friendship.

Arriving in Regina, Hughie was afforded no special treatment and the living conditions were primitive, but he liked it that way. Perhaps for the first time in his life, he felt he was doing something important. But things weren't perfect yet: all through that hot, prairie summer, he dreamed only of flying, and he was overjoyed to be promoted to sergeant in the autumn and sent to a flight-training school in Windsor Mills, Quebec.

Happy and confident, with his parents 2,000 miles away in Montreal, he had no idea what strings the Major was pulling behind the scenes – but he found out when he was informed that his father had secured his leave from service to appear in *Golden Wings*, which was going into production straight away. Full of shame and resentment, Hughie swapped his air force uniform for a costume and appeared alongside actresses Fay Wray and Signe Hasso in a show that travelled through Wilmington, Delaware, Washington, DC, and New York before coming to an abrupt and dramatic halt.

Golden Wings arrived at the off-Broadway Cort Theatre, one of the oldest and most beautiful venues in the area, on December 8, 1941 – the day after Japan's shock bombing of the Americans at Pearl Harbor. The USA, previously neutral, had now entered into the Second World War, and its people were no longer seeking entertainment from a play about England's military exploits. *Golden Wings* was grounded on December 12.

Most fellows would have thrown in the towel, but not Major Green. He immediately tried to use his influence to get Hughie stationed in Ottawa, where he would lead a military band. With that idea rejected, he followed on with another suggestion. He wrote an article in November 1942 for the *Montreal Daily Star*, proposing, to no avail, that Hughie should be employed to organise an air force show.

Father was humiliated by his father's interventions on his behalf. He felt manipulated. The other lads in the RCAF were aspiring to wear real aviator's wings and fight for the good cause. Hughie didn't want 'play wings', nor did he believe that his theatrical displays were of any significance in the middle of a war. Of course it had been a privilege to work with the fabulous actors appearing in *Golden Wings*, and it had been thrilling to perform on Broadway, but the timing was wrong. The applause that Hughie wanted was from Claire and his new-found friends back in Montreal and in the air force. He was eager to prove himself. Above all, he wanted to fly.

The *Montreal Daily Star* article was published primarily to announce that my Papa had finally earned the most precious thing in his life: his wings. But only days before the RCAF ceremony in Brantford, Ontario, on November 19, a big secret slipped out. Hughie had rebelled, again, behind the backs of his parents: he had married Claire.

Hughie was fifteen and Claire was two years younger when they met for the first time aboard the *Empress of Britain* in Cherbourg harbour, France, in September 1935. The liner had stopped to pick up other first-class passengers en route to Canada. The ship was the last word in elegance, luxury and service. Owned by Canadian Pacific Railways (CPR), it was the flagship of their North Atlantic fleet.

Claire's great-grandfather, Duncan McIntyre, was a founder and first executive Vice-President of the CPR. The empire also owned the splendid Royal York Hotel in Toronto, a 'city within a city' and a place of great architectural splendour where Hughie nevertheless spent one of the worst nights of his life, having witnessed at first hand his mother's marital unfaithfulness. Hughie was sailing to Canada for the opening of the charity tour that would end in this harrowing discovery. But as he strolled along the decks with Claire, his thoughts were not of the future but the past. He was still mourning his dear Grandmother Alice, who had died only eleven weeks earlier, and he confided his unhappiness to Claire. Endlessly sympathetic, she in turn told him about the lady *she* adored, her Grandmother McIntyre. The youngsters spent the rest of the journey together.

When Hughie returned to America in the summer of 1938 on his pre-war, fact-finding mission, he had travelled to Montreal to recruit the mighty lumberjack Big Joe Beauchamp. At the same time he took the opportunity to look up Claire.

Finally arriving for an extended stay in Montreal after the war broke out, Hughie again contacted Claire, and they became inseparable. The dark-haired Claire was charming, beautiful, graceful and almost ethereal in her appearance. She carried an understated elegance, a great femininity. She was, at the same time, remarkably modest, witty and intelligent. She belonged to the cream of Montreal society, and the Greens were thrilled, seeing opportunities in Claire's fabulously wealthy and well-connected family – although it never occurred to them that the relationship would become serious. That would be no good for business at all . . .

Claire and her sister Pam lived in a mansion on Peel Street, right at the top of the hill in the centre of Montreal's fabled 'Golden Mile'. Half the wealth of Canada lived within a couple of streets' radius. Claire had come to hate the suffocating privilege of her upbringing. She was rather a 'naughty' little girl, who was straining at the gates of home, aching to explore the world beyond. She never liked the house on Peel Street, complaining that the windows were too small; there was never enough light.

Her Grandmother McIntyre, who owned and ruled the mansion, was a person somewhat to the right of Queen Victoria in ethics and outlook. Known affectionately as Makin, she took on most of the parenting, since Claire's father, Bradley Wilson – the youngest son of Major General Wilson – was a drunk.

Bradley – my grandfather – was also shell-shocked, continually suffering flashbacks to his worst experiences as a Gunnery Officer in the First World War. There was the day he came across some magnificent horses stuck fast in the mud and bloody mire of Flanders, and had to shoot them as an act of mercy. And then there were the 'Huns' who startled Grandpa when they jumped down from the hayloft brandishing rifles. Reflexively, he discharged his Smith and Wesson pistol. He would later lament, 'Oh God, Chris, the look in their dying eyes! The horror of it all!' A drink would take away the visions of the mud, the horses and the Huns – until the next time.

Bradley regularly disappeared to the family's country house at Ivry in the Laurentian mountains and he took Claire's mother with him. The former Helen McIntyre, my beloved Grandmother Wilson, entrusted her children to the care of her own mother, Makin, reasoning that my Grandpa was unlikely to cause serious social embarrassment when he was hidden away in the family retreat. Like Hughie, Claire had grown up hating 'weak' men. This was how she saw her father, Bradley. He didn't work, he didn't own the house they lived in, and she deplored his drinking and the strain it put upon her mother, Helen.

Although they came from different worlds, Hughie and Claire shared common hurts, and they were in perfect harmony sexually. Mother once, unabashedly, told me: 'No one compares to your father in that department,' and he returned the compliment.

Claire – born on February 20, 1922 – was twenty years old when she eloped with Hughie. She had no reason to run away. She wasn't pregnant. Her parents wouldn't have opposed the union and neither would Makin, her devoted grandmother. Makin was tremendously fond of Hughie. She admired his wit and intelligence, although she recognised that he was a flirt and she harboured doubts about his ability to be responsible. She was also appalled by the Major and Violet, disgusted by their manipulation and fleecing of Hughie and worried about the prospect of their interference in any future marriage. Yet Makin was prepared to give the union her blessing, and she was deeply hurt that her darling Claire could not have shared the secret with her and had run away in such a clandestine manner.

Claire's parents, Helen and Bradley, were none too thrilled when they learned of the marriage, but they bore the news stoically. Helen and Hughie disliked each other, and my father despised Bradley. Helen was extremely well educated, spoke three languages and held opera and ballet in the highest esteem. This annoyed Hughie, whose world was vaudeville, and he would storm out of the Peel Street drawing room on Sunday afternoons at the sound of the first aria, usually returning for dinner with liquor on his breath.

Hughie insisted that the elopement was necessary because Helen Wilson would not have approved and would have tried to block the marriage. In truth, it was for Hughie's benefit entirely.

He was soon to get his wings, and he wanted to cement his defiance of his parents by getting married too. But he didn't want them to know about it; they would be livid. They would see Claire as a threat to their power over him and his money, and they could easily get the marriage annulled, since Claire was still five months short of twenty-one.

In September 1942, Hughie and Claire were pronounced man and wife in front of Hughie's co-pilot, close friend and best man Art Tuelon and a lawyer who had set up some private deal whereby the underage bride could be married. After the ceremony in Montreal's unfashionable East End, the newlyweds repaired to the Windsor Hotel, where they bribed the hall porter with $5 to keep their secret.

The new Mrs Green went straight to their room while Hughie popped out to buy tobacco and immediately bumped into his father, enjoying an evening stroll. Major Green was astonished to see him. Hughie explained that he'd been at someone's wedding and was soon to catch the train back to camp. The Major insisted on Hughie walking him home. Hughie recalled, 'I don't think he had ever walked home so quickly in his life. I left him on the doorstep, yelled a goodbye over my shoulder and ran like hell all the way back to the hotel. If Claire had left me there and then I wouldn't have been surprised.'

Hughie and his new wife managed to keep their secret for six or seven weeks until Claire, overcome with guilt, blurted it out to her former nanny, who encouraged her to tell Makin. Hughie then had to make the bombshell confession to his parents.

Only days later, Father received his wings at Brantford, and Claire was there to see them pinned on. Also present were the Major and Violet, still burning with rage that their son had married 'the Wilson girl'. She was now the enemy, and they would have to do something about her.

* * * * *

The Golden Mile was characterised by the most incredible homes with arches and turrets and acres of garden, and the Peel Street mansion was one of the grandest. This was where Hughie and Claire started their married life, and Father loved it as much as Claire loathed it. The matriarchal Makin ran a gracious and happy house. Staff were loving, loyal and treated as an extended family. A favourite personality was the nanny, Maria McKinnon Low, who was known endearingly as 'Nannie' and had remained in the household even after Claire and Pam were old enough to look after themselves. It was a true taste of homely, family life that Hughie relished but never understood.

Art Teulon soon followed him into matrimony, and his wife Nancy became Claire's best friend. She saw Mother's righteous hurt as the Major and Violet vented their dislike for her, and provided support and reassurance.

The Greens blamed Claire for the dramatic downturn in their fortunes. She was depriving them of their star and his income. In retaliation, Claire began referring mockingly to her haughty, self-important mother-in-law as 'The Violet' – a name which has stuck through the generations. In one letter to Nancy Teulon, dated March 28, 1945, Claire wrote, 'The old Violet is going to New York next week. A big break for everybody, and I hope and pray that she will be away all the time Hughie is back.'

Other close friends of Hughie and Claire included Morna and Ian MacLean, the children of Colonel Charles MacLean – the Major's close pal, who had built the incredible Mull Hall estate outside Montreal. Doris, the second Mrs MacLean and mother of Morna and Ian, was the lady who had so impressed Violet during her courting days in London. With the two families now living as neighbours, 'Aunt Doris' had been keeping a concerned eye on Hughie's predicament with the Royal Canadian Air Force, and the Major's shadowy manoeuvres.

Kindly interceding, she secured for Hughie a wartime stationing in Ferry Command in Montreal. Hughie would serve with honour by flying from a home base of Dorval, and the Greens would still have their boy close by – not quite out of harm's way, but at least not piloting Spitfires over England, or bombers over Germany.

Ian MacLean was among the friends who had volunteered for service, and that was one of the factors which had spurred a conscience-stricken Hughie into his decision to sign up. Indeed, Ian went overseas where he was made a prisoner-of-war.

Now, at last, Father too could be proud of his contribution to the conflict, and he was a brave and distinguished aviator.

On the home front, things took a new turn in 1944 when Claire gave birth to the first of her two children. My sister Linda came into the world in a private maternity room in the Royal Victoria Hospital. Hughie lurched in much the worse for wear and snapped, witheringly, 'A girl, born on April 20, Adolf Hitler's birthday. Just another little bastard . . .' Mama's private nurse steered him out of the room while Claire rolled over in the bed and vomited. Still, the birth had been uncomplicated, Linda was a beautiful baby and Claire was surrounded by delighted friends and relatives.

Hughie's outburst was a pointer to the problems in the marriage, even in these early stages. Over the next couple of years, they worsened. Father had promised Claire that he would put her first and his parents in a respectful, but removed, second place. But he couldn't do it. The Major and Violet were ever-present, and they made it clear that Claire was in their way.

Father was regularly away flying missions, and Claire raised no objections there, but when he returned, he would spend a disproportionate amount of time with the Greens. The situation deteriorated when the Major launched another of his entrepreneurial ventures. He built a recreational 'Dude Ranch' in Chamcook, New Brunswick, complete with horses and all manner of family holiday attractions including an elephant that painted pictures with its trunk. Claire was allergic to horses, and had to stay behind at Peel Street while her husband dutifully visited his parents in Chamcook.

Claire realised that her husband was always going to spend most of his time away from home. When he did return, his shadow would fall across his parents' doorstep first, and that doorstep was never far from hers. She also recognised that Hughie had no idea what a home was. He adored the Peel Street mansion, but he treated it more like a grand hotel than a place for personal relaxation. He was always on edge. He could never grasp the spirit of Christmas. And children, those most precious people who turn a house into a home, held no appeal for him.

He was drinking too much and too often, and Claire abhorred it; she disliked her own father for that very reason. Hughie was also still on Benzedrine – a popular drug among long-haul aviators – which made him unpredictable, bad-tempered and sometimes frightening. Claire had good reason to fret about what lay ahead, and she would later pine for the warmth of the house she never appreciated on Peel Street.

As for Hughie, he knew that the Major and Violet were ruining his marriage. He didn't want to lose Claire, or Makin for that matter, but despite repeated promises and genuine efforts, he was unable to sideline his parents for any length of time. Hughie, in truth, was as cowardly as any of the 'weak men' he so vigorously condemned. Claire was preparing to cut him loose, to return him to his rightful place in the triad, having confronted the saddest truth of all, that he was incapable of giving love.

Father later declared that he had been under crushing pressure to keep Claire in the style to which she had become accustomed, but it was an unforgivable lie. Mama neither expected nor wanted a life of luxury. She'd had that since she was born, and it hadn't made her happy. Tragically, all that she wanted was for Hughie to love her.

*   *   *   *   *

Germany surrendered on May 7, 1945; the conflict in the Pacific ended on September 2. Hughie intended to stay in Canada, as did Major Green and Violet. The Dude Ranch had been a fiasco, and they had lost their investors' money. Hughie was one, and it would be his last big hand-out to his parents. To the dismay of Claire and her family, the Major had also solicited cash from some of their closest and most affluent friends.

The Greens turned to their friend Billy Butlin, who set them up as part-owners and managers of a proposed holiday camp: Butlins Canada. It was a brilliant idea, and it looked as if they would pull it off until the former naval base Cornwallis – the site they were buying from the Government – was suddenly reclaimed by the Navy.

The Major had been dabbling again in canned fish, and yet another scheme – to sell a collection of religious artworks he had hastily assembled before the war – similarly failed to rescue the Greens' situation in Canada. Hughie loved the country from one end to the other, but he saw little excitement in service after the madness of the war years. The boys were no longer flying into uncharted skies at a moment's notice to do heroic things. They were regimented, disciplined, inactive.

Art Teulon was pursuing a career in civil aviation, and while Hughie saw a fascinating potential there, he realised that there would be no immediate entry into the cockpit. There would be a lot of hanging around, and Father was never one to wait. He turned in his RCAF uniform and embarked on a campaign to become a radio and theatre star in Canada. Makin financed his abortive efforts, and continued to provide a home for the threesome, free of charge. Claire became suspicious of Father's interest in her family wealth – the classic fear of the rich heiress – and in the early autumn of 1946, she told her grandmother that she could no longer see a future with Hughie Green. Makin was heartbroken, but not surprised. Things were clearly hopeless. Hughie and his parents were inseparable, and there really was no prospect of a tolerable family life for Claire and little Linda.

Claire and Makin devised a plan. Divorce was out of the question, so Hughie, they decided, should be persuaded to return to England while Claire and Linda stayed on at Peel Street. They doubted that Father would object too loudly, and they knew that the Major and 'The Violet' would be overjoyed. Time would pass and time would surely heal. But something happened quite suddenly that would wreck this perfect outcome. Claire discovered that she was pregnant again. I was on the way.

6

Fear and Loathing in Montreal and London

They were praying for another daughter. According to the 'Victorian logic' of high society, a boy child was significantly different from a girl and should always be accompanied by his father. Makin and Claire were aware that Hughie had little interest in his first child, Linda, but were equally sure that he would be pressured to act conventionally if the baby were a boy. He wouldn't leave his son behind in Peel Street, and the rescue plan for Claire, Linda and the unborn child therefore depended on that arrival being a girl.

I was born on July 24, 1947. It was the hottest, most humid summer then known in Montreal. I was overdue by almost a month, and everyone had tired of waiting for me. Even Makin had gone on her annual holiday. Claire's parents, Helen and Bradley, had wilted in the oppressive heat and had retreated to their country home at Ivry, where cooling breezes rippled off Lake Manitou. Family and friends alike had all left town.

Mama did not like the doddering, family doctor who was attending her. He was not prepared for the dangers accompanying my arrival. Weighing in at more than ten pounds, I was a breach delivery, and the umbilical cord that scarred my face almost killed me. My mother's heart stopped beating, and she, too, nearly died.

Hughie was in the UK, having been contracted to deliver an airplane from the States. Commissions to sell and ferry aircraft, usually old crates, had become a much-loved sideline for him; they paid him to keep flying. He received a telegram which informed him that Claire had presented him with a son. It was followed that day by another telegram offering him a small part in a children's film about the popular sheepdog Lassie. In the States, it was called *Hills of Home*, and in the UK, *Master of Lassie*. It boasted an all-star cast including Janet Leigh. Father responded to the second telegram. Rather than return to Canada to meet his heir apparent, he travelled to Scotland to negotiate his next contract. However, he made sure he had a say in my name – Christopher Hugh Whitney Green.

I was lumbered with 'Hugh' to please the Major. And Whitney arose from the fact that Father had been trying to curry favour with the wealthy Whitney dynasty in the States. He had hoped to bag me an impressive godfather by naming me in their honour, but he was unsuccessful – just as he had been unsuccessful in securing Gracie Fields as Linda's godmother. At least he didn't saddle Linda with the singer's name.

My birth was a lonely and traumatic experience for my mother. I doubt that she missed her husband's presence, given his behaviour when Linda was born, but she suffered a severe, post-natal depression that coloured her feelings about me for all time. Like my father before me, I wasn't wanted by my mother. I wasn't wanted by Hughie either. Had termination been the routine option that it is today, I'm convinced I would have been aborted.

Returning home from hospital, Claire, in a long, silk housecoat, descended the fabulous staircase in Peel Street with her newborn son in her arms to formally present him to the staff. The assembled staff were enchanted, excited. Nannie, beaming radiantly, stood a few steps in front of the receiving line. Claire walked into the grand hallway and straight to Nannie, who had reflexively extended her arms. Ignoring the smiles of everyone around her, Mama ordered tersely: 'Nannie, take it!' Nannie did take me. Without another word, Mama turned and went up the stairs alone, to a stunned and embarrassed silence.

*　　*　　*　　*　　*

It would be some time before I met my English grandmother, Violet Green. She had left the Major in the spring and returned to London, taking a flat on the mezzanine floor in Chiltern Court, just where Baker Street crosses Marylebone Road. Violet had been talking about leaving the Major since 1939. He'd been rushing around England spending a lot of Hughie's money on religious artworks he knew nothing about so that he could sell them in Canada. She didn't want to be poor again, and she knew from fiascos like 'Oh Boy' chewing gum that the Major didn't always hit the bull's-eye. Hughie had no long-term guarantees of showbiz work in Canada or the States, and Violet saw that if the war carried on for a long time, then the family would be spending money but not necessarily making it.

Like Hughie, but for reasons that had nothing to do with conscience, she was miserable about leaving London when the war broke out. She never imagined there would be a bombing campaign in England – it was widely believed that Hitler wouldn't dare. The experts were wrong again when they predicted a short conflict. If Violet had guessed that she would be stranded in Canada for nearly eight years, she would undoubtedly have demanded a financial settlement from the Major so that, bombs or not, she could have waited out the war in England.

Violet wasn't keen on Canada, but the Major managed to win her over by the promise of travel in America. He had lined up contacts and possible work for Hughie in Hollywood, and that certainly did put the sparkle back in Violet's eyes. She'd never been to the West Coast. Indeed, she fell in love with sunny California. She lived a glamorous lifestyle in LA, met celebrities galore, and was happy to stay for an extended visit. The Major, however, wanted to settle there, and he worked hard to make it happen. The couple were sick with disappointment when the bombing of Pearl Harbor, and Hughie's entry into the Royal Canadian Air Force, put paid to their ambitions.

Violet hated Montreal. She needed wider spaces for her various dalliances, which she conducted anyway, to her family's humiliation and everyone else's raised eyebrows. Violet was a city girl, and compared to London, Montreal was boring and claustrophobic, a one-horse town where gossip spread quickly through the society grapevine. One infamous affair was with the manager of an elite hotel resort in the Laurentian mountains. Claire would regularly commiserate with Hughie over his mother's wanton antics.

In Montreal, Violet also felt out-classed and out of her depth. The Greens lived well but not magnificently in a rented apartment in Summerhill Avenue. She was jealous of the wealth and status of Claire's family and the MacLeans, who had always overawed her. The Greens had infiltrated the highest social circles, not least through Hughie's relationship with Claire, but Violet found them intimidating and also tedious compared to the glittering company she had kept in London and LA. Hughie had ruined everything by marrying Claire, his Hollywood career had not materialised, the family fortune was gradually diminishing, and Violet saw no further reason to stay in Canada.

Major Green's relatives out in Prince Albert were scandalised and openly critical. A wife should not leave her husband – especially a wife who was almost certainly returning to a lover in London. The Major was shattered, frantic to make another fortune and get Violet back. For this he needed Hughie, and he decided again to become his manager. Father was less than delighted; he wasn't a child any more, and his outlook on life had changed since the war. But he was missing the adulation and applause of his earlier fame. In July 1945, he secured a summer contract with the Canadian Broadcasting Corporation, airing coast-to-coast with *The Hughie Green Comedy Show*, which was produced by ex-Air Force pilot Jackie Rae. Unfortunately, it wasn't that funny, and while Father complained about the standard of the scriptwriters, it was his own fault that the contract wasn't extended. Backed by Makin's money, he then organised a touring production featuring ex-servicemen, which also flopped.

The Major had been disappointed by the recent failures of his own ventures, especially Butlins Canada. He had anticipated an expansion, with holiday camps dotted all over the country, and he had of course intended for Hughie to front them as the star entertainer. Never one to give in, the Major was pulling every string he had to get Hughie back into the frontline of show business in both Canada and Hollywood.

Actor Ben Lyon, who had helped Hughie to his role in *Master of Lassie*, now turned up trumps again by engineering a small part for Father in another MGM movie, *If Winter Comes*. A remake of the classic tear-jerker, it featured star performances from Walter Pidgeon, Violet's favourite actor, and Deborah Kerr. The two movies kept Hughie filming on location in Scotland and LA, while also flying old planes from one destination to another, for all of 1947.

Hughie imagined himself at the beginning of a rapid rise in Hollywood, but it didn't happen – and for this, he blamed Sir Stafford Cripps, Britain's Chancellor of the Exchequer. Sir Stafford introduced a crippling tax on movies imported from America, with the resulting cash invested in the British film industry. Hughie claimed that this made Hollywood films so expensive to import that UK sales dropped, and the Americans were then less inclined to make movies with British appeal. Therefore, he contended, there was little need in Hollywood for young, British actors such as himself.

In reality, while the industry in both countries hated Cripps' tax, UK distributors carried on bringing in Hollywood films and the Americans continued to hire British actors including Cary Grant, David Niven, Rex Harrison and James Mason. In holding Cripps responsible for the sudden demise of his Hollywood movie career, Father was simply looking for someone to blame. His childhood stardom in the UK had been stellar, and his inability to repeat it in the States and Canada was difficult for him to accept.

Closeted away in Peel Street, we saw little of him during that couple of years. He liked to explain, with the air of a martyr, that he was always out earning the money to pamper us. Really, he was just doing the usual: whatever he wanted. Hughie made his last theatrical appearance in New York, but not on Broadway, in December 1948. The production of George Bernard Shaw's

Captain Brassbound's Conversation at the City Center Theatre was critically acclaimed, but it brought him no further offers of work.

*   *   *   *   *

His name was Mr Pepper, and he was the man who changed Hughie's fortunes in the new year of 1949. Our safe and sheltered existence in the splendour of Peel Street was about to end. Mr Pepper, a BBC representative, invited Hughie to return to England to cover for radio presenter Carroll Levis, who was on extended sick leave. Levis, a Canadian by birth, had introduced the talent show to the British airwaves, but had suffered a nervous breakdown. His brother Cyril, replacing him, did not have the magic to keep the audiences tuning in, and Mr Pepper looked to Hughie for a solution. He asked him to devise another 'discoveries' show to replace Carroll's.

Father was thrilled to be invited, finally, into the bosom of a station that had sternly overlooked him as a child star. Remembering a programme he'd heard on a rural radio station in western Canada, he created his own talent show called *Opportunity Knocks* – and it restored the lost listeners, in growing numbers, as it ran from February through to autumn 1949.

The series was just finishing when Hughie summoned Claire to bring Linda, Nannie and me to England to live with him. It had been arranged that we would be moving into 169 Chiltern Court, the block where Violet lived. While we waited for it to become available, we took a flat in Berkeley Court, across the road, as a five-month sub-let.

We travelled by boat from Canada and then by train from Southampton to London. At the end of that long journey, the welcome we received from Hughie was a dark pointer to what lay ahead. Opening the front door, he snarled, 'I'm busy, why did you have to arrive now?' He then instructed Mama to take us into another room until he had finished his work. This cold and disdainful greeting was witnessed by Father's personal assistant, Betty Raymond, who never forgot Claire's evident hurt and her own disgust at Hughie.

Hughie had had an affair with Betty during the war. He was often in London, delivering warplanes from Canada to the British forces, and he courted her during these stopovers – without mentioning his wife and daughter. When Betty found out, she ended the liaison. After the war – and the affair – were over and Hughie was back in England, he recruited Betty to his staff. A former worker for the British intelligence service, she was a no-nonsense lady who would grow to loathe Hughie Green. She told Mama about her innocent part in the infidelity, and they became lifelong friends. Betty worried about our future; she knew that Hughie was not the marrying kind.

Even more worries surrounded us when Father was unex-pectedly informed that his contract for *Opportunity Knocks* would not be renewed. He was indignant, disappointed, confused and angry, since he had attracted millions of listeners – and the BBC was virtually the only outlet for professional entertainers in the UK. A 'Carroll Levis' show called *Spot the Winner* then abruptly appeared on the air, although Levis was still ill and did not himself appear in it. Father, meanwhile, was told that he was 'too American' for British audiences. His career had suddenly ground to a halt on both sides of the Atlantic.

He then received two fateful telephone calls, both unsolicited, from disgruntled managers in the Carroll Levis organisation. They told Hughie that top BBC officials had accepted bribes to shunt his show off the air and reinstate Carroll Levis Organisation programming. Hughie immediately set in motion an internal BBC inquiry and a full Scotland Yard investigation. Acting on this information and supported by Viscount Hailsham QC, who agreed to be his counsel in the High Court, Hughie filed papers to sue the BBC. The action would drag on for five long years, and then it would financially ruin us.

*   *   *   *   *

Violet had been keeping her options open. She had not been playing the archetypal, devoted wife, keeping the home fires burning in London for her family. After the collapse of the

Major's Butlins Canada project, she had prayed for Hughie to succeed in Hollywood. That would have enabled her to enjoy her freedom in London while the Major paid the rent, visited occasionally and lived the rest of his life with Hughie, thousands of miles away.

The reality was a dreadful disappointment. Hughie's potential as a source of income had faded, and he had dared to marry and have children. But there was hope, she felt, in *Opportunity Knocks*. Hughie might still be able to resurrect his career in the UK. She could then upgrade her living accommodation and enjoy, once again, the good life she had previously taken for granted. Hughie certainly seemed a better bet than the Major, who was keen to come back and put Wall's ice cream out of business with a 'more colourful', competing brand.

Violet had kept her figure, looks and libido, but at the time of her husband's projected return, had received no better offers from any of her men friends. Practical as ever, but with resignation, she liaised with the Major to prepare for the arrival of Hughie, later his family and, finally, her husband himself.

Father by no stretch of the imagination wanted us with him in London, but it was a social and professional necessity. The war was over and he was earning decent money again in England. He could not be seen as anything but a jolly nice family man doing a jolly nice family show for his audiences. Makin, at the same time, was insistent that Hughie accept his family duties, in view of the fact that I had been born a Christopher, not a Christine.

Claire felt equally trapped by the arrangement, while Violet, reasoning that knowledge is power, wanted only to keep her son and hated daughter-in-law close at hand. The Major was thrilled to be reunited with his Violet, and he made all the arrangements, as always. Finally, we were all together in Chiltern Court. Mama, Papa, Nannie, Linda and myself lived five floors above my grandparents Green, who immediately embarked on a campaign to isolate and intimidate my mother Claire and, hopefully, effect her estrangement from Hughie.

Their physical proximity was a major weapon. They knew that their son would always call in on his way up to the fifth floor and that they would be important confidants, now that his best friend, Art Teulon, was living an ocean away. However, the Major and Violet could not be totally sure that their son would tell them everything, so they tried to enlist a spy. Victor Hallums was one of the two men who had told my father about the BBC bribery plot, and he went on to become his show manager. Vic is outraged to this day by a brush with Violet in the Chiltern Court foyer. After asking for 'a moment aside', she offered him cash induce-ments to spill information about Hughie and Claire. Insulted and incensed, my 'Uncle Vic' went up to flat 169 and reported the conversation to Hughie, who simply replied, 'Yes, Vic, I'll take care of it.' Whether he did or not, no one knows.

Violet went on to try to make spies of Linda and me when we were older, quizzing us about the relationship between our parents. Her icy, penetrating gaze and intense monotone were more exquisitely terrifying to us than anything Disney could have invented.

My grandparents wanted information to use as a wedge between Papa and Mama. They must have been overjoyed in 1951 when Claire packed our bags and rushed us back to Montreal after finding out that Hughie had taken a mistress. He had met Pat Hughes – an aspiring actress – when she worked in some capacity on *Opportunity Knocks*.

Another woman in the *Opportunity Knocks* entourage enlightened Claire, who had already made many allowances for Papa. She had accepted the existence of his illegitimate son, Barry Hands – which he'd confessed before they married. She had forgiven his wartime encounters with Betty Raymond, since he'd been miles from home and comfort, flying perilous missions, and had not humiliated Mother in her own circles. But in the full flush of youth and beauty, enjoying a satisfying, marital sex life, she was cut to the core to learn that her husband was flaunting a lover.

In Peel Street, Montreal, the ever-loving but conventional Makin told Claire that we were welcome to stay as visitors but not as long-term refugees. Her granddaughter would have to return to Hughie. However, Father didn't know this. With Claire gone, his mistress seemed less interesting. He needed Claire, too, to uphold his reputation as an upstanding family man in his ongoing legal battle with the BBC.

Hughie finished the affair, which he later described as 'a meaningless chapter of incidents'. He came cap-in-hand to Montreal requesting another chance, and Claire wearily agreed. We were going back to Chiltern Court.

Hughie couldn't stand the sight of Linda and me. He had no idea what it was to be a child, because he'd never been one. He didn't know who or what we were. He'd tell us, scornfully, 'When I was your age I was a star. . . and just look at you.'

Linda has publicly denounced him as a 'monster'. He wasn't a monster, but he wasn't a very nice man, and his temper tantrums were explosive and unpredictable. I never knew him as 'Daddy'. It was 'Yes, Father,' or 'No, sir.' The man terrified me. There was nothing about me that he appeared to care about, and he never lost an opportunity to belittle me. He was very tall, loud and forceful. I was a small child.

On Sundays, usually after a drinking session, he would call me into the living room and test me on topics that were way beyond the reach of a boy my age. If I could not say the seventeen times table, he would scream for Mama and bellow, 'Claire, this boy is a cretin. Art Teulon's son is brilliant, a genius. Why did you produce a fool like this for me?' Mama would then plead the case for both of us, beginning with an anguished, 'Oh, Hughie. . .'

Of course, I came to believe that I *was* stupid, Father was angry at Claire because of it, and in turn, that was why Mama really wasn't very fond of me – along with my noisiness and all the other things that upset Hughie and, therefore, my mother. I knew she was not a happy person. In private conversations, she instilled a terrible guilt in me by talking about the sacrifices she had made, and how she had stayed on with Papa only for my future benefit.

She would be in bed beside Hughie when he insisted upon a hurtful, Saturday-morning game. He would call me into the bedroom as I was on my way out to the children's show at the Classic cinema in Baker Street. He would be sitting up with a breakfast tray and would make me play 'double or nothing' for my pocket money. 'Nothing' meant no movie. During these sessions, he would usually produce a small, pink, plastic doll from a drawer. He would place it in the breast pocket of my shirt and sneer to Mama, 'Look at your son. He has a dolly in his pocket. Claire, you gave me a little queer.' And my mother would again have to defend, plaintively, my very being.

I was all too often the 'ham' in my parents' rotten sandwich. I was too short, too thin, too dumb, too baggy-eyed. I really wasn't much of a kid. When the letter came to say that I had passed the dreaded Eleven Plus exam, my father called the headmaster of Herewood House, my private school in Swiss Cottage, demanding, 'Are you sure there hasn't been a mistake?' Turning to Claire, he barked, 'Your son must have had a horse-shoe up his arse,' and then, without any hesitation, asked me directly: 'Did you cheat?'

My worst-ever experience of Hughie in early childhood occurred one Christmas Day. Lurching into the apartment, drunk and belligerent, he found Mama, Linda, Nannie and me wearing party hats, trying to create some sort of festive atmosphere. Flashing back to the chicken sandwiches and the vision of Violet with her lover in that Toronto hotel room, he picked up the turkey, occupying pride of place at the centre of the table, and hurled it out of the window.

There were few tender moments between father and son back then, although one spring day when I was about ten, he truly amazed me. I had taken a tiny duckling, which had followed me through Regent's Park, back to the lake, only to see a female duck kill it. Hughie listened sympathetically to my heartbroken story and talked to me gently, kindly, and reassured me that there was nothing we could do when Mother Nature decided to take her course. He acted towards me as I always hoped he would one day – with loving attention.

Claire was a distant mother, but nevertheless I adored her. Even as a little boy, I felt it was somehow my duty to protect her and, by extension, Linda, from 'The Growler', who was Hughie. Yet, I never felt secure, and I would spend the first 48 years of my life trying to win her love and respect.

Occasionally, she read to her children, and that was so special. I vividly recall her reading a story about Tin Lizzie from the *Beano* comic, and on another occasion, passages from one of Richmal Crompton's *Just William* books – and later still, chapters from Tolkien's *The Hobbit*. I was enchanted as much by her as the stories themselves.

My mother much preferred Linda to me, but I never held that against my sister. She was beautiful and talented, and I looked up to her with awe. She, too, was cold towards me, I felt, no doubt following Mama's example.

Linda only ever took me out twice that I can remember, and she had been told to do so. For the first jolly outing, she walked me, and my short legs, around the many churches in our neighbourhood. She was going through a religious phase then; her room was a shrine, festooned with images of the Virgin Mary, postcards of the Lord's suffering and candles galore. I was exhausted and utterly miserable.

The second excursion was even more of a disaster. Linda and her best pal took me to the children's animal enclosure of London Zoo, bought me petting food to give the goats and chickens, and then disappeared when a thunderstorm broke overhead, leaving me panicked, surrounded by a pack of jostling, smelly llamas, drenched through, and facing the journey home on my own. Linda seemed to have forgotten about me. We have since had a few laughs about this incident, but at the time, it seemd to me that Linda took no pleasure in having a younger brother, or worried about my safety. As children, we never went out together again.

We only ever came close in moments of fear, huddled under the bedclothes during a Fatherstorm, when he crashed home drunk and raving. Sadly, that became a lifelong pattern; there had to be a family crisis to unite us. In times of contentment, Linda's phone call never came.

At 169 Chiltern Court, we knew four different types of family life. The 'first life', when Hughie was away, was relatively normal. Both Mama and Nannie relaxed enormously. Linda and I would have friends in to play, we would roam around the flat rather than be confined, quietly, to our rooms, and we would

throw balls, wrestle, do gymnastics and all the other things that
were forbidden when Papa was at home.

The 'second life' was the tense period before he returned. For
me, these were the worst times. I developed a nervous tic at five
or six years old, causing me to blink my eyes rapidly. When I
felt a 'blinking attack' coming on, I would count the 60, white,
fluffy balls that hung from the pelmet covers, one by one, and by
the time I'd done that, I would have recovered. I constantly
listened for the front door opening, a sound that could reduce
Linda and me to cowering, shaking wrecks if Father was
obviously entering in a rage.

On one memorable night, Papa opened the door loudly and
aggressively, signalling that he was drunk and spoiling for
trouble. I heard terrifying sounds in the hallway, which faded as
they progressed into my parents' bedroom. I strained my ears to
hear; I knew something dreadful was going on. Suddenly, I heard
the reassuring voice of 'Uncle' Vic Hallums, who had just
arrived. I heard him say, 'All right, Claire, I'm here now. I'll take
care of him.'

Mama later told me that she came within seconds of killing
Hughie that night. He had passed out on the bed after being sick,
and rolled over into his own vomit. Mother, holding a damp towel
to clean him up, instead found herself pushing his head downwards into the suffocating mess. By his timely arrival, Vic saved
Hughie's life and Claire's liberty.

Strangely enough, the 'third life', when Hughie was in
residence, was one of the easiest times for me. The anxiety of
awaiting his arrival was gone, The Growler was at the other end
of the hall, my friends wisely stayed away, and I quietly withdrew
to stay out of trouble as much as possible.

Sometimes, Father would 'park' people on us, like Florrie
Leadington, his elderly showbiz friend. I would be ordered to keep
her company while she watched TV – a relatively new and exciting
invention. I remember vividly the day of the Queen's coronation –
June 2, 1953. Florrie sat in the big, stuffed chair in front of that tiny
screen, and she must have been the only one of the unprecedented
television audience to fall asleep, snoring distinctively, as the

spectacle unfolded, with a commentary by my hero, Richard Dimbleby. Waking, Florrie waved a small Union flag around wildly, cooed 'God bless her' innumerable times, and farted with abandonment – much to the amusement of both my sister and me.

Whenever Papa left for yet another trip, the tension of his 'visit' lingered throughout the rooms, and this was our 'fourth life'. Mama would wring her hands at whatever havoc had unfolded and Nannie would tut disapprovingly. My mother would always tell me that she felt responsible, she was sorry and she would make it up to me one day. I would come to realise how fortunate I really was, she said, and one day, when all I could see was her 'empty chair', then I would be sorry. Papa's tirades were straightforward, if illogical, but my mother's created dread, bewilderment and even more guilt.

As the lady of the house, Claire could never cope, a fact she was endlessly ribbed about by Betty Raymond and another close friend, her upstairs neighbour, Wendy. My mother had spent her life being looked after by servants, and she had never been exposed to the working end of the kitchen. That much was evident when Nannie would take her annual three-week holiday. A favourite family story was the day that Mama cleaned the oven wearing long, white, silk evening gloves.

The real linchpin of the family was Nannie. It was Nannie who ran the household and raised us. It was Nannie who cooked, cleaned, washed, scolded, bathed us, wiped our bottoms and took us for walks. She was 'Nannie with the cuddly arms', and it was her bed I'd run to when I was scared of bogeymen in the dark.

She looked after me for many years with a kindness and abundant love I would never know from either of my parents. Without my Nannie, I would have been totally lost. I can never dwell for long upon my love for her: my tears just trip me up.

*   *   *   *   *

Chiltern Court is a monolithic structure; very big, very heavy, with long corridors and countless doors running the length of its nine floors and two basement levels. Deep underneath runs the

London Underground, a hot and dusty world that seemed excitingly cosmopolitan. I lived moments of true, Gothic horror at 169 and on the mezzanine floor where my grandparents lived – moments that still loom large in my nightmares. But at the same time, it was a glorious place that held many wonders and delights for a little boy growing up.

A wartime German doodlebug rocket had burnt out the back of Chiltern Court. My friends and I claimed it as our playground. The flat, dangerous, concrete slab that was the 'roof garden' was, to us, a place of mystery and adventure. High up there, we fed the pigeons, collected their dead for ceremonial burial, and looked across all of London from the 'birthday-cake' parapet.

The Chiltern Court restaurant was situated on the ground floor, with the windows of its bar sections opening onto the back. We'd wait there to see what tidbits the jolly old folk at the tables would pass out to us. Smith's crisps were a favourite, and if we got really lucky, the packet would be half-full and still containing its little blue twist-bag of salt. Out on the main street, below Chiltern Court, were the shops, and none held greater wonder for me than Smith's Book Store where the manager, a Mr Channel, allowed me to sit for hours, poring over the captivating children's books.

Inside the back of Chiltern Court, where the doodlebug had wrought its fiery havoc, the flats were structurally sound but mostly empty, dirty and forlorn. We saw them as magical, new territories to be explored away from the gaze of adults who would have disapproved of our experiments with a five-pack of Woodbine cigarettes, or our furtive scanning of our friend Harrison Mark's nude magazines.

Flat 169 was sparsely furnished, and the sofa and chairs that we did have were large, frumpy pieces which the Major and Violet had dug out of storage. The linoleum on the kitchen floor was cracked and would no longer 'take a polish'. In the other rooms, there was very little carpeting, although we had a few, threadbare, dark-brown rugs, also donated from the mezzanine floor by my grandparents.

There were no homely touches, no paintings on the walls, or a piano. The kitchen's gas appliances were antique, and the electricity system required voltage adaptor boxes because we received our electricity supply from the tube-train system. My room, which originally I shared with Linda, had a single bed, a desk, a play-box for my toys and a small night table, before Father's train set appeared. In the late fifties, when Hughie began to make some real money, he had the flat professionally painted and furnished.

But the lack of luxury never bothered me as a child. I did enjoy the arrival of the annual Christmas food parcel from Peel Street, prior to the end of rationing in 1954. But my real pleasures were simple things like travelling on the tube, taking a bus, roaming around Regent's Park with its tennis courts and zoo. I had imagination, I was seldom bored and I had no problems making and keeping friends.

My best pal Mike lived in Berkeley Court, where we had stayed for our first five months in London. Another great friend, Karin, lived in Chiltern Court with her mother – Mama's friend Wendy – and her grandma, Lady Latham. Karin and I did our best to avoid the head porter, the pompous Mr Bacon, who dressed like a Rear-Admiral, while making firm friends with the regular porters and lift operators, especially Paddy who was stationed at the northwest doorway, known as 'Paddy's entrance'. However, we liked the dark, dingy staircases more than the lifts, since they gave us a clear view through the downward spirals and a perfect location for spitting competitions.

* * * * *

Father's battle with the BBC rumbled on for five years. The stress turned his hair white before he finally lost the case on May 27, 1955, after twenty, nerve-racking days in the High Court. He had accused the Corporation – and eight individuals connected with it – of allegedly conspiring to prevent him from being employed or re-engaged or otherwise making any contracts with the BBC as the producer of *Opportunity Knocks* or any similar variety entertainment. Hughie had also sought damages against the defendants: the BBC, two of its executives, one representative of the Official Solicitors office, two management agency staff and Carroll Levis, his wife and brother.

The BBC, Buckingham Palace and the Houses of Parliament were the three British institutions that were in those days inviolate and beyond reproach. Yet Papa, with typical bravado and fearlessness in the face of the establishment, was not prepared to be swindled by anybody, least of all the BBC. He had grown up believing that institutions – the schools, the Home Office – served only to block his stardom, and he had taken on board the Major's defiance of such obstacles.

Hughie's single BBC radio series of *Opportunity Knocks* had been a solid success, attracting thirteen million listeners and more as the weeks went by. This was only marginally less than the figures for Levis, a tremendously popular broadcaster. Hughie fully expected to have his contract renewed, since Levis was still unwell. To tell Father that he was not to the public taste was therefore an insult to his intelligence and a confirmation of corruption in the corridors of power.

He stuck his middle finger up at the BBC in his own defence and in the name of his audiences, the 'little people' that he adored and respected. He was not going to have some bunch of 'sanctimonious bastards' deciding what they did and didn't like when the ratings and the fanmail spoke for themselves. And he went to court in the knowledge that if he lost the case, he would also sacrifice his career as an entertainer in the UK.

Vic Hallums testified that *Opportunity Knocks* caused concern within the Carroll Levis Organisation because it was so successful. The Levis team did not want to be eclipsed and forced out by Hughie's programme, especially in view of the money that could be made from touring a show around the country if that same show was also on BBC radio.

My father took a lot of abuse as the hearing progressed. He was said to be an arrogant, egotistical, irritating, insincere, gushing, money-grabbing, jealous and delusory pseudo-American who had a chip on his shoulder and could not admit to his own failure. Although many of these descriptions could well have applied to Hughie in other aspects of his life, he was, in my opinion, acting and speaking honourably in his reasons for bringing the action and in the way he conducted it. He had a sound case and he should have won, but he came unstuck for various reasons.

To prove to the jury that all eight accused people, in tandem with the BBC, committed a conspiracy against him was too complicated to pull off. It was also difficult to verify that the various monies and gifts referred to were bribes paid within a conspiracy, rather than simply loans or personal presents. Father's two key witnesses were Levis managers. Vic Hallums, who claimed he was aware of the corruption and had taken part in it to a small extent under orders, and David Delmonte, who also admitted involvement, were less educated than their opponents in the court room, and less expensively dressed. They were sitting ducks for the legal snipers.

It was widely believed that Father had been shafted, but he couldn't prove it in court, and the experience changed his worldview: it was the beginning of a lifelong paranoia that people were out to get him, and he would become fiercely litigious. His court costs were fixed at £30,000 – no small amount in those days – and we were immediately bankrupt. Father stood tall, tense and grim in the High Court to receive the verdict, but couldn't resist a word in the ear of Carroll Levis on his way out. Levis had put on a brilliantly flamboyant performance in the courtroom, which Hughie, as a professional, could only admire. After hearing Father's words, Carroll looked at the surrounding crowd and said, 'What Hughie Green said to me just then is my private business. But . . . it was one of the nicest things said to me for a long time.'

Years later, I asked Father what nice things he could possibly have said to Carroll after five years of bitter acrimony and a losing verdict. Hughie replied, whispering theatrically, 'Carroll, you are a prick. But you are a *big* prick!' Levis was quoted the next day as saying, 'Hughie is a great little guy!'

If there was anything to be gained from the whole, unfortunate mess, it was Father's new and lasting show-business association and friendship with Vic Hallums, a fine, loyal and honest gentleman. And if there was a last laugh to be had, it was a huge one. Only four months later, Papa starred alongside Billy Cotton,

Harry Secombe and the glittering cast of a gala show marking the opening night of independent television – the new Channel Nine.

Hughie Green was about to become one of Britain's most popular TV entertainers.

7

Paula: A Child is Born

We were bankrupt, and the bailiffs came to strip our flat. Papa had to give up his wristwatch, but there was little else of value for them to seize. Mama said, 'Oh, good riddance, most of it was hand-me-down rubbish anyway,' although we all felt violated. My own worst moment came when I saw them looking around my room and feeling the curtains. I shook with fear when I thought they were about to take my beloved toy-box, but, luckily, they didn't want it.

The stigma of being bankrupt in 1955 was akin to having leprosy. Some of our 'friends' crossed to the other side of Baker Street rather than pass us by on the pavement. The nannies from 'nice' families would not let their charges play with Linda and me. And Mama was snubbed by neighbours in the local shops.

The mud flung at Hughie in the High Court and reported as front-page news had stuck. He was treated with the contempt that befitted an embittered opportunist who'd had the temerity to take on the mighty BBC. Had the jury's verdict been different, he might instead have been lauded as some sort of contemporary Don Quixote, tilting at the windmill of injustice and foul play within a sacrosanct organization – which he was.

However, Hughie did have his supporters. Among them was Billy Butlin, who phoned immediately after the High Court ruling to offer him work at his holiday camp in Skegness. He was back, at last, among 'the people'. At the end of every night, there were autographs, as usual, at the stage door. Father always made time for his fans, especially elderly people and disabled or sick children, for whom he had genuine compassion and performed numerous benefits. 'It's their pennies that make me pounds,' he would always say, and he would fly into a fury if he heard anyone insult the ordinary, working families who made up his audiences. He was indebted to them.

My sister Linda was on the receiving end of his rage on what was a rare, family outing to Brighton. It was a hot summer's day shortly after the High Court verdict, and I was hugely excited at the prospect of being taken out on the pier. First, we had lunch. Hughie and Claire ordered drinks at a pub, while Linda and I ate packed sandwiches. But there was tension in the air. Father was in a bad mood, and it soon became clear that the closest I would get to the pier and all its marvels was looking at it.

Hughie wanted to drive back to London immediately after lunch, but Claire – trying to rescue the day – persuaded him to sit on the beach with us. It was packed. A baby was crying just next to our few square feet on the pebbles, and a young lad started misbehaving, for which he received a good clip on the ear from his dad. This startled and upset Linda. She remarked, 'We shouldn't be on a beach with all these common people,' and Father went ballistic. He snarled at Claire that she was raising us to be 'bigoted snobs', pointed at the pier to our left and thundered, 'It was good enough for *me!*' He immediately drove us back to London in tense and stony silence.

Hughie would not have sat on the beach in Brighton by choice. His sort of beaches were in Bermuda, or Florida. But it was his hard work at places just like Brighton Pier that had paid for his exotic holidays, and the dad who clipped his son's ear was exactly the sort of fellow who would take the family to see a Hughie Green show. To call him 'common' insulted Father greatly. By implication, his show was 'common' also.

The BBC didn't want *Opportunity Knocks*, but Hughie wasn't about to sit around licking his wounds. By the end of 1950, he had taken the show to Radio Luxembourg, where it enjoyed a success-ful 95-week run. Tape-recording had arrived by now, and the show was taped at Star Sound studios in Baker Street, just a couple of minutes' walk from Chiltern Court. Sometimes Father allowed me to tag along, and I found it all tremendously exciting.

The series' first big star discovery was a singer called David Whitfield, who collaborated with Father on and off over the next few years and who was extremely conceited. One day, just after Hughie's bankruptcy in 1955, he arrived at the flat in Chiltern Court, boasting about having 42 suits. Pointedly, he asked, 'How many do *you* have, Hughie?' Hughie wouldn't be vulnerable to such jibes for very long.

Major Green offered to put up the money to get his son freed from bankruptcy, on condition that Father signed a management agreement with him. Hughie refused, but the Major and Violet would never give up their attempts to get their 'star' back. In 1957, Hughie applied for his release from bankruptcy with money borrowed from Makin, Claire's ever-loving grandmother in Peel Street, Montreal. He never fully repaid her. Claire, burning with shame, said that he had, but my father later confessed that he had not, even though he would soon amass a veritable fortune.

Hughie Green was coming back – and he would revolutionise light entertainment in Britain.

*   *   *   *   *

There were howls of disapproval over the introduction of independent television, which brought the BBC's monopoly to an end. Far from welcoming the new channel, luminaries led by Sir Winston Churchill were sure it would be a vulgar influence on the public. Churchill was not keen on showbiz types, including Hughie, probably because his daughter Sarah was so attracted to them. Her first husband, Vic Oliver, was a music hall artist. Her second husband, photographer Anthony Beauchamp, had committed suicide after trying and failing to contact my father. He had been one of the directors of the early TV series *Fabian of the Yard* at the time of his fatal overdose.

Hughie had a new vision for entertainment, one that would cater directly for the working public and would also involve them.

In short: the game show. As he eloquently put it, 'People do not want three hours of fucking *King Lear* in verse when they get out of a ten-hour day in the fucking coal pits, and fuck anybody who tries to tell them that they do.'

The concept of *Double Your Money* – proposed to Hughie by TV and radio man John Beard – fitted his vision perfectly, and he jumped at the offer to present it. On September 22, 1955, the London broadcasting company Associated Rediffusion launched Channel Nine with an opening ceremony held at the Guildhall in London, a toothpaste advertisement, and a glitzy variety show, in which Father made a starring appearance. Before the year was out, *Double Your Money* was beaming into viewers' homes every Monday night in the prime-time spot – and it would carry on, with Hughie at the helm, for an incredible thirteen years. It was a straightforward quiz, with contestants choosing their subject from a possible 42. Each time they answered correctly, their prize money was doubled, and successful contestants would be shown into a soundproofed booth to try for the top, 'Treasure Trail' prize of £1,000. Young footballer Bobby Charlton was one such winner, before he became a sporting legend.

Hughie was in his element, clowning around and having fun with the contestants, but he was never unkind – the jokes would always be at his own expense – and he would never upstage the participants. His genius was in putting ordinary people at ease in front of a live audience, lights and cameras and bringing out the best in them. Father knew that the success of the show depended on the people rather than the format. Key to it all were the interactions between the contestants, the hostesses and the ringmaster, Hughie.

Some contestants captured the public imagination so perfectly that they were taken on as hostesses. One was the 77-year-old former charlady Alice Earrey, and the other was chirpy, cockney teenager Monica Rose. The banter and flirtation between Hughie and Monica made them the most memorable double-act of the series. Another popular hostess was the 'Wiggle Girl', Nancy Roberts, and then there was Amanda Barrie, later to become famous as Alma Baldwin in *Coronation Street*.

Amanda signed up in 1959 but only lasted a few months, later admitting, 'I just wasn't the hostess type. They were supposed to have either immense tits or endearing Cockney personalities like little Monica Rose, who got it so right she turned it into an art form.' She described Father as 'the most professional TV presenter of his kind at the time', while commenting on the gulf between his public and private personae.

Double Your Money was certainly a big hitter in the ratings, although it was roundly attacked for promoting greed and gambling – the vulgar influence that Churchill had dreaded. In fact, *Double Your Money* was all about people and not at all, really, about winning money. While it was taking Mondays by storm, Fridays belonged to another game show. *Take Your Pick*, presented by the tall and kindly Michael Miles, had started at around the same time.

Father liked *Take Your Pick* and Michael Miles. Their rivalry was purely professional. They had been the first two people to devise quiz styles that were acceptable for British audiences, and both shows had originated at Radio Luxembourg. But they were very different in structure, presentation and appeal. *Take Your Pick* was a much more complicated proposition. Its strength was its format, which incorporated elements such as the 'yes/no interlude', quiz questions, forfeits, keys, an array of prize boxes, a mystery box, booby prizes, a star prize and a treasure chest.

Hughie quickly became one of the most popular personalities on TV. While critics savaged him for being phoney and patronising, they failed to understand the real enjoyment he had always derived from his audiences. They, in turn, adored the all-embracing, man-of-the-people joviality encapsulated in his famous catchphrase, 'And I mean that most sincerely, folks.'

In the year after his Associated Rediffusion debut, Hughie personally doubled his money after being asked to present a second weekly show. With the launch of *Opportunity Knocks* in 1956, he became a broadcasting pioneer, introducing, for the first time ever, the concept of interactive TV. *Opportunity Knocks* was founded on a simple but tremendously popular formula which would keep it – and Hughie – on the air together for the next

22 years. It was then revived, less successfully, by a series of presenters, including Bob Monkhouse.

It was Hughie's baby, the TV version of the show he had created for the BBC and Radio Luxembourg. Each week, Father presented six new talents to be judged by the public. They came in all shapes and sizes. And while little was heard again of the margarine sculptor, the sailor's hornpipe dancer or the chef who could cook a dinner in under three minutes, the show discovered lasting talents such as Little and Large, Peters and Lee, Freddie Starr, Tom O'Connor, Pam Ayres, Lena Zavaroni, Frank Carson, Mary Hopkin and Les Dawson. Actress Su Pollard – the dizzy chambermaid Peggy in the *Hi-De-Hi* sitcom – tried her luck too, but finished second to a singing dog.

At the end of the show, the audience voted for their favourites by applauding; a 'clapometer', which registered applause levels, made it possible to declare a studio winner. Viewers were then asked to send votes by post – which they did in tens of thousands every week – to decide an overall winner. It was a brilliant innovation to involve the studio and home audiences so closely.

Hughie Green went on to blaze a trail through entertainment. He presented the first variety shows on an ocean liner and a jet airliner in flight. He was the only person to present entertainment on an aircraft carrier and an atomic submarine. He scored an epic triumph by being the first to use satellite for an interactive live show, between England and Australia. He pioneered the concept of Euro talent shows, with countries competing against each other, and of Scholarship Award Contests for schoolchildren. His seventies game show, *The Sky's The Limit*, introduced the idea of travel prizes, with Father fully determined to offer winning contestants a trip to the Moon as soon as this became commercially available.

He also managed to secure the services – for free – of actor and ukelele legend George Formby in a variety film called *Atlantic Showboat*, based on a voyage to Canada on the cruise ship *Empress of Britain*. Released at the end of the fifties, it also starred Shirley Bassey, Lionel and Joyce Blair, Duke Ellington and David Whitfield – he of the 42 suits.

ABOVE *My grandparents, Major Hugh Green and Violet, on their 1917 wedding day. Their selfish love would deny their son a childhood – and much more.* BELOW *Violet holds her infant son Hughie for a formal portrait – but her true feelings were not at all maternal.*

TOP LEFT *Father and son. My Grandpa Green, the Major, totally adored my Papa but it was an aberrant love and little joy would come from it for any of us.* **TOP RIGHT** *No smiles for the camera as Hughie and the Major return from Canada, November 1935. The fateful chicken sandwiches in Toronto led Hughie to a discovery that would damage and traumatise him forever.* **BOTTOM** *The leader with his Gang; Major Green counselled Hughie to always let them know that he was the boss.*

My father told me: 'You must remember that when I was thirteen or fourteen I played all those places like Poplar, Bootle and Blackburn. I played all the toughest and poorest parts of the nation in the bad old days of the thirties and I have seen poverty. There are times when you discover who your real friends are, and who are not. The greatest loyalty I have found is really from people I don't know, and most of whom I'll never meet: the people who watch my show.' My Papa's 'populist touch' was, I have no doubt, heartfelt and sincere.

Young, beautiful and to the manor born; my Mama, Claire. Papa would say that he married well.

ABOVE *Great great grandfather, Duncan McIntyre, one of the affluent Canadian Pacific Railway founders, built this baronial mansion, named Craguie, in Montreal's Golden Mile.* **BELOW** *Our family home on Peel Street. We called it 'the gate house' to Craguie. This was the house that Claire lived in when an impressed Hughie came courting.*

TOP LEFT *Mama and Papa at our Laurentian Mountains Ivry country house in 1942. They had virtually nothing in common apart from a deep and ultimately destructive fascination for one another.* **TOP RIGHT** *Just arrived in England from Canada to live with Papa. He didn't want us and Mama didn't wish to be with him. Had the baby Christopher been 'baby Christine' this fateful family reunion would never have taken place.* **BELOW** *Father, pictured in 1961 with his tragic mistress, Gwen Claremont, whose physical resemblance to Claire was uncanny.*

ABOVE *Father on the set of 'Double Your Money' with glamorous hostesses. Jean Clarke (right) was a viewers' favourite in the early days of the show.* BELOW *The day of the 'at home' interview for the TV MIRROR during 1957 turned into a drunken drama. Papa behaved badly and Linda and I fought back tears as the camera shutter clicked on.*

Mama in May of 1975 with her husband-to-be, actor David Langton, of TV's 'Upstairs Downstairs' fame. Her smile hides certain reservations.

Small wonder, then, that when Hughie died in 1997 after a lifetime of enviable success and accomplishment, even his old adversary the BBC, and that guardian of public morality, *The Times*, hailed him as 'an icon of British light entertainment' and 'the first great star of independent television'.

But equally in death, as in life, there were enemies in the shadows, eager to consign Hughie Green to history as 'a talentless fart', 'a serial womaniser' and, in the words of his own daughter Linda, 'a monster'.

*   *   *   *   *

Hughie was a faithful husband for a while – or if he wasn't, he was at least discreet. He had broken up with Pat Hughes and settled his family in London. During the BBC lawsuit years, from 1950 to 1955, he had to be on his best behaviour. In his adversity, he came closer to Claire and she, for her part, hoped that she was becoming more important to him and that their relationship was improving.

Sadly for Claire, Hughie reverted to type. He embarked on a passionate affair with former beauty queen and Bluebell Girl Elaine Smith – and the secret of the baby she gave birth to would make more impact on the life of our family than any other single event. That baby was Paula Yates.

By 1958, Father had two major TV shows of his own riding high in the ratings: *Double Your Money* and *Opportunity Knocks*. He also fronted variety shows for Jack Hylton, the impresario and orchestra leader. Ever the workaholic, Father would be out performing live when the various series took a summer break. He installed a secretary, Pam Jagger, in the flat to take over administrative and accountancy duties from Betty Raymond. Like her predecessor, Pam would also enjoy an affair with Father – although it happened years later, after his divorce.

That year, Claire, Linda and I spent our holidays in Perran-porth, Cornwall. Hughie was miles away in Llandudno, Wales, for the summer season, presenting a stage version of *Double Your Money* at the Front Theatre. Because of the TV exposure, it was a great success. He was living on his first boat, aptly named *The Rake's Retreat*.

Hughie became a regular at the Deganwy Castle Hotel. More than 250 years old, it had spectacular views over Conwy estuary and castle and had 31 rooms. The owner of the hotel was Jess Yates, who had written show-business documentaries for the Rank Organisation and Columbia Pictures. He had also produced a series of epic, biblical films starring Victor Mature. He had been honourably discharged from the army during the war with a stress-related condition which subsequently came back, along with a bout of shingles. Deciding to take life easier, he had bought the hotel in Llandudno.

Jess was also into promoting beauty pageants. At one such event, in Blackpool, he met contestant Elaine Smith. He was one of the judges, and Elaine became Miss Blackpool. She soon afterwards left for Paris to be a Bluebell Girl at the Lido and, returning, moved to Wales to join Jess. Elaine Smith married Jess Frederick Joseph Yates at the Holy Trinity Church in Llandudno on June 30, 1958, having made all the wedding arrangements herself.

When Hughie turned up in town, only days later, the pair were working hard to establish a nightclub in the hotel, complete with go-go dancers in cages – to the agitation of townsfolk in the family seaside resort. Father knew Jess in passing through show-business connections, which is why he began visiting the hotel. The two men spent hours drinking and enjoying ribald chat.

Elaine was tall, busty, sensual and flamboyant. Hughie took one look at her and saw his 'summer lady'. Elaine – a would-be actress who was little more than a chorus-line hoofer – viewed Hughie as a man who could advance her show-business career and also give her exciting sex.

Hughie didn't hesitate to bed Elaine. He had no axe to grind with Jess, and it was nothing personal. He was frequently intimate with women when their partners were in close proximity, and his manager John Heyman later ventured that this served to heighten his experience. The identity of the husband or boyfriend was never even a consideration. Jess, by all accounts, was slightly in awe of Hughie, and envious of his fame, lifestyle and money.

There is no indication that he knew, then or indeed ever, what was going on between Father and Elaine.

Hughie was 38, six feet two inches tall and a television star who was devastatingly attractive to women. Jess was only a year older, but he was ill, none-too-handsome and, according to some reports, a near-platonic partner to Elaine.

A baby – Paula – was conceived in July. She was born on April 24, 1959 at a 'maternity house' in Colwyn Bay, Clwyd. According to her birth certificate, she had no other Christian names (although Elizabeth was later added), her mother was Elaine Yates, and her father was Jess. Paula would grow up in that belief, not knowing until the very end of her life that her natural father was in fact Hughie Green.

Elaine was not the average mother. According to Jess and Paula, she abandoned her two-week-old daughter for the first of her trips to London in pursuit of a theatrical career, leaving her husband in charge of a tiny baby. Elaine has since denied this. She went on to change her name, for professional reasons, to Heller Toren, Hélène Thornton and, following her later marriage to a French man, Hélène Thornton-Bosment. She was cast in two forgettable sixties movies, and she became an author of what Father flippantly described as 'dirty books'.

Jess, emerging from bouts of manic depression, returned to show business to pursue his dreams and fulfilled them as the creator and producer of *Stars on Sunday*, a religious TV show launched in 1969. That this originated from a man who liked to drink while watching semi-naked ladies cavorting in cages was extraordinary in itself. Hughie guested on the show in 1971, confirming that Jess had no problem with him and no inkling of his teenage daughter's real paternity.

Elaine and Hughie were absolutely certain of this. She had noted her dates carefully, and it was unlikely she'd been sleeping with Jess at all at the time of the conception, since she was urgently involved with Father. Indeed, their relationship would continue, intermittently, for the next two decades. When she told Hughie of her pregnancy, he was panicked and fearful for his future. He was regarded as one of the nation's great family men,

and his contracts included routine 'morality clauses'. If Elaine
spoke out about Paula's parentage, his glittering career would be
ruined. Elaine, too, would be given 'the scarlet letter', and Hughie
clung to that as a reason to believe she would not expose him. But,
of course, he couldn't be sure.

He couldn't confide in Claire because he did not want to lose
her. She had spent five years as his moral supporter in the BBC
court case, and her grandmother had opened her purse to bail him
out of bankruptcy. Claire would not be able to face his siring of
Paula. Still, he needed to unburden his terror, and his parents were
the only people he could conceivably tell. *They* knew 'these
things could happen'; *they* had understood when Barry Hands was
born. But Hughie had failed to realise the depth of the bitterness
they felt towards him for shunning the Major's offer to manage
him again. The Major had loved Hughie to the point that he had
invested his own personality in his boy's. In making his star, he
had made himself. That Father had refused his management tore
at the Major's very being. Hughie failed to notice the emotions
that were stewing within the old man.

Violet missed the standard of living and status that her son had
once freely provided, and she was seething that Claire stood to
gain what she felt was her entitlement. Hughie, having funded
Violet's lavish lifestyle for years, saw no reason to keep putting
fur coats on her back. His parents were not impoverished; his
obligation no longer existed.

The Greens had moved to a new flat, two doors away from the
original, on the mezzanine floor. When Hughie called in and
undoubtedly told them about the baby, he could not have
imagined that they would use his fears against him. But everything points to the fact that they did. Tiny Paula had clearly
provided the ammunition with which the gleeful Greens could
now get rid of Claire.

The mezzanine floor was a forbidding place. The light was dim
and the air was musty in the corridor leading to our grandparents'
door. Their flat was like a shrine to Hughie. Everywhere I looked,
there was a picture, a painting, an open scrapbook . . .

Two living room windows faced on to Baker Street, and on the sills were a pair of very large, blue Chinese vases with darkly etched images. I thought they were ugly, and they stopped me from sitting on the high window sills. One day Violet saw me staring at these things, mistaking my loathing for admiration. She informed me that they were priceless and matter-of-factly added, 'If you should ever break or damage one of them, I will kill you.' I nearly wet myself. I took her words literally, and began to have nightmares about the vases.

Many years later, one of them showed up in flat 169. I made a mental note that if one day I should happen to inherit that 'priceless' vase, I would gently pick it up, take it to the nearest concrete floor and smash the shit out of it.

I cannot recall any occasion on which Linda and I were treated with any kindness, love or understanding by Violet. She wasn't the sort to bake cookies for her grandchildren. She had a large bosom, and she would draw me into it briefly as a greeting and then push me back. She never gave kisses. She took no pleasure from us, and only wanted to fish for gossip about Hughie and Claire.

A lady called Mrs Addiscott also lived on the mezzanine floor. She was 'the lady with the dickey-bird', a canary that sang beautifully. I was crazy about birds, and she would invite me in to whistle to her canary and hear it sing back to me. Suddenly, she stopped asking me in. When I asked why, she replied that my grandmother, a dear friend of hers, had told her I was 'not the nice little boy' she had imagined.

There were times when one of us would unwittingly upset or offend 'The Violet'. Tears would well in her icy, green-blue eyes and she would bitterly promise, '*I will remember that . . .*' Such unwarranted and quite incomprehensible outbursts had chilled Claire to the bone back in wartime Canada. They certainly scared the hell out of Linda and me. And Hughie, no doubt, had received full measures of the same as a little boy.

But we came to expect worse from Violet. She would regularly tell me, 'I have a little bone to pick with you.' I was never quite sure what the bone was, but she would punish me by locking me in what she called 'McGee's Closet', a cupboard in the entrance hall, and turning out the light. McGee, she said, was the bogey-man. One day, realising that I could see a crack of light at the bottom of the door, she had a strip of wood attached to make my solitary stays in the cupboard pitch-black and terrifying.

When Violet was not present, I could relax with Grandpa Green as we sat at the table sketching or making up scrapbooks, just enjoying each other's company. With Violet's arrival, the atmosphere would freeze instantly. Sometimes Grandpa would take me out to Regent's Park to kick a ball around. Back at Chiltern Court, he would look at me with the saddest eyes as we parted company at the mezzanine floor. He was never able to ride on up to the fifth floor, to come in for a cup of tea and see my pet budgies, the hamster or the guinea pig. He only ever visited our flat once, and even then he hovered, uncomfortably, by the front door. Violet never visited while Mama, Linda and I were living there. Major Green did show me his love, but he did not protect me from Violet, and I consequently grew apart from him.

Father didn't give a damn if we saw his parents or not – notably, he never referred to them as 'your grandparents' – but he didn't want to annoy the Major by keeping us away. Mama knew we didn't like visiting the mezzanine floor, but she didn't wish to be blamed for our absence. She once offered me half-a-crown (two shillings and sixpence, 12½p) to make a visit.

I would have been around eight when I was invited downstairs for an afternoon party in honour of the grandson of William Friese-Greene, credited by many to be the inventor of cinematography. I was camera-mad and movie-mad, and as a further enticement, I was promised ice cream. It was served in a wooden bowl, bought by Grandpa, so he said, from a North American Indian chief. I went to sit down on the big, squashy sofa and as I did so, Grandpa put his larger and heavier bottom on the cushion beside me. The sofa rocked and I lost control of my bowl, dropping a dollop of ice cream onto the carpet. 'The Violet' stared lividly at me and then the Major, hissing, 'Discipline him.'

I saw a sharp, blue light over the mantle where Father's painting hung. My grandfather had hit me hard over the left ear. In pain and shock I dropped the bowl and its contents onto the floor. The Major was even more distraught and tearful, leading me by the hand into the entrance hall, where he apologised. I knew in my heart that it was my Grandmother Violet who had hit me, using Grandpa's kind hand as the weapon. But I lost a lot of respect for him that day. He was meant to be my protector, not the instrument of my grandmother's ill-will.

I never, ever saw Hughie with his parents, individually or together. His visits to the mezzanine floor were private. There was a bizarre and hateful divide between the two households, even though we were both living in Chiltern Court. Linda and I took it for granted that this was, somehow, 'normal life' for us. There was no joint family celebration of Christmas. There was no Easter bunny, no greeting cards or presents exchanged between the floors – with the sole exception of a golf bag once sent up for Hughie's birthday. The Major and Violet deliberately created a situation of tension and attrition in the hope that Claire would 'blink first' and leave. Then they could take full possession of their boy again.

I was nine years old when I finally realised what a malignantly dysfunctional family we were. We had taken our one and only family holiday together – a sailing trip on a hired boat, ironically called *The Good Time*. Papa drank German lager for breakfast, yelled and swore constantly, and, as always, kept referring to me as 'the cretin'. This upset Mama, who was more miserable than usual during the trip. Linda was gloomy, too. She buried her head in a magazine, only looking up to smile when Father called me names. She and Mama stuck together. I was out on a limb.

I had entered a state of childhood euphoria, sitting on the back end with my fishing line in the waters of the Thames, dreaming of catching my first pike, when Papa crashed into my consciousness, beer bottle in hand. He asked me kindly if I liked fishing. When I answered 'Yes', thrilled at the interest he was showing, he suddenly turned nasty, demanding, 'Putting big hooks in little fishes' mouths gives you pleasure, does it? Did you ever think about their pain?' Finally, Papa, pulling himself up to his full six feet two inches, glared down at me and bellowed: 'Fishing! Fucking fishing? When I was your age I was a *star*. . .'

We were one totally divided, fucked-up family going nowhere together. All around us were mums, dads, boys and girls having fun on the river. I thought of my friends' families coming together to celebrate birthdays and Bar Mitzvahs. The four of us had been physically contained on one small boat, and all the things that I had known subconsciously now came sharply and fearfully into focus. We were not like other people.

*   *   *   *   *

Major Green and Violet had not succeeded in driving Claire away from Chiltern Court, even though many a young woman would have caved in to the pressure, especially in the absence of any real support from her husband. Hughie never disavowed his parents; he couldn't. He knew that no matter where he lived, they would follow him. The Major, in particular, would never leave him.

Claire's reaction was to be passive; she saw nothing else for it. She knew that as long as the Major and Violet were alive, she would never have a sustainable life with Hughie. But London, with its vibrant culture, was her adopted home, and she had no intention of running back to Montreal. She was aware that Father was incapable of giving love, they didn't get on well and they did virtually nothing together, but she was inescapably bound to him. They were 'unfinished business' for each other until their deaths.

My mother was the only person Hughie felt able to confide in truthfully about his early life. That started when he met her on the boat to Canada, opened up about his beloved grandmother, Alice Price, and empathised with her devotion to her grandma, Makin. To everyone else, he would either bullshit or talk around an issue, only inadvertently revealing something important, perhaps through drink.

But he absolutely could not tell Claire about Paula. And within a month of her birth, Major Green and Violet had started a campaign of hate mail, sent anonymously to Mama. The letters came in blue envelopes, slightly larger than standard, and they were composed from lettering of different sizes and colours, cut out of newspapers and magazines. The Major was responsible for the wording and assembly of the letters with Violet, undoubtedly, at his side, encouraging him. I noticed the envelopes because they had been addressed with an inked, rubber stamp. Mama opened the first one quizzically and the rest with visible trepidation. Once, in the kitchen, I caught a glimpse of the scary-looking text before being ordered to go away and play, while Mama talked furtively and anxiously to Nannie. Of course, I had no idea what was going on, although I sensed that it was something 'adult'.

Claire received up to fifteen letters between May and October 1959. None came while we were on holiday in St Ives, Cornwall, in July and August, but they resumed just a few days after we arrived home. Mama told me about the letters later. They were, she said, menacing but cryptic. It became apparent that the sender had knowledge of some dark, personal secret, and knew who we all were. One warned, 'Be careful of the kiddies.' Another message read, 'What is good for the Canadian goose is good for the British gander', and yet another told her, 'Jack and Jill went up the hill to fetch a pail of water, Jack fell down and broke his crown, and Jill came tumbling after. . . and you will fall too.'

The Greens were playing a wicked head-game. Mama would feel threatened and scared, and would want to scoop us up and flee to safety. Seemingly, they wanted Hughie to assume the poison-pen mail had something to do with Paula's paternity, so he would encourage Claire to move us away, fearful of a scandal about to break. They had to be careful. Such a plan would have to scare Claire without actually telling her about Paula. If she had known that truth, she could have used it to ruin Hughie, which would have defeated the object of the exercise. They wanted him, and his money, back in the triad.

But there was another secret which the Greens had not foreseen. It was Claire's. She did not tell Hughie about the letters straight away, because she had a guilty conscience too. Fearful that the letters referred to her own doings, she suffered in silence, hoping against hope that they would stop but expecting, in dread, that they would lead to blackmail; a request for 'hush money'. When they showed no sign of tailing off, Claire, seeing no other way out, showed them to Father.

This mail panicked Mama and Papa for entirely different reasons, and neither one knew what the other was hiding and fearing. Claire was in the dark about Hughie's affair with Elaine Yates and the birth of Paula. Hughie had no idea that Claire had conducted two liaisons during their years in London. One was a genuine love affair with an unnamed partner. The other was simply for fun, sex and intrigue, and it was with Sir Alexander (Sandy) Maxwell – a friend of Hughie, a former tobacco adviser to the Board of Trade and a Permanent Secretary to the Home Office. I met him at least a dozen times as a young boy, and didn't like him. He always teased me about the first time he saw me as a baby, laughing about how I had peed in my pram. He married the beautiful Lady Angela Maxwell, and I liked him even less.

I discovered one of Mama's indiscretions when I overheard Nannie telling her in a very cross tone that she should be ashamed of herself, that it was disgusting to be going out with another man and that two wrongs did not make a right. I don't believe Mama ever forgave Nannie for that piece of straight talking.

I had long been aware of Father's tendency to wander, but was profoundly shocked by the revelation of my mother's behaviour. Mama was not promiscuous and I quickly realised that she would never have looked elsewhere had Hughie been at home to tend to her physical and emotional well-being.

Claire noticed that the threatening letters spelt her name wrongly as Clare. The Major had always done this in correspondence dating back to Montreal and she mentioned it to Hughie, but he responded with silence. He did, however, confront the problem – risking unknown consequences – by calling on a friend from Scotland Yard to investigate. It was ascertained that the sender was deranged and potentially dangerous, and since one of the letters incorporated a typewritten passage, Father was asked to submit all the typed correspondence he had received in the previous six months. The detective matched the distinctive typeface to a note Hughie had received from Major Green, accompanying the leather golf bag he had given Father as a rare birthday present. The anonymous writer had been unmasked.

Mama told me, 'Your father turned to stone and said, "Claire, I will take care of this matter,"' only adding that his parents' sickness was beyond fathoming.

I guess my father went into shock on discovering that his own blood could dream of putting him, and his wife, through such an ordeal. My mother was not surprised but she was disgusted. She realised right away that the Major's intention was to separate her from her husband.

Hughie – stunned by his parents' latest stunt – then called in a flamboyant but hugely respected show-business solicitor who would go on to represent The Beatles and was known for his discretion in 'delicate' situations. David Jacobs was very tall, and he wore make-up and perfume, much to my childish astonishment when he visited our flat for an initial meeting.

Overcoming his natural dislike for homosexuals, Father issued instructions on October 23, 1959 at around 10.30 a.m. He told the solicitor, 'Scare the living shit out of my father and secure from him, in writing, an acknowledgement of what he has done, a pledge that he is contrite and will, with a total understanding of silence about this matter, cease and desist from ever doing anything of this nature again.'

My father was playing the biggest card of his life. He could only gamble that the Major, having been rumbled, would not decide that 'we'll all go down together', and reveal Hughie's deepest secrets – Paula Yates and Barry Hands.

David Jacobs went down to the mezzanine floor from 169 and rang the doorbell. It was answered by Major Green, who was confronted with a bizarre-looking stranger.

The Major's questioning gaze was drawn immediately to the clipboard, displaying his hate mail letters, in David's hand. He realised in an instant that the game was up, and reacted spontaneously.

He took a step backwards in the doorway and then lunged forwards quickly aiming a vicious kick at the solicitor.

Jacobs, reflexively turning away, felt the full force of the Major's kick on his right wrist, which shattered. He fell back against the marble wall in agony and banged his head against the lift door. He then saw Violet appear behind her husband, who suddenly stumbled back into the flat gasping, 'God damn Claire.'

They were his last words. The Major hit the ground, dead.

8

An Unnatural Death

Life had seemed perfectly normal as I left for school that Friday. The weekend was ahead, and all was well in my world. Around 11.30 a.m. I was called out of class, reassured that everything was OK, and told that my mother wanted me to come home. No reason was given.

The Number 2 bus dropped me off outside Chiltern Court, practically on the doorstep of 'Paddy's entrance', leading in to the lift operated by our favourite attendant, Paddy. There was an ambulance outside. Approaching the building, I stood aside for two men in uniform, wheeling out a stretcher carrying what was clearly a covered, dead body. It was chilling. Paddy stepped out of his lift, saying, 'Master Green, come with me, please.' He seemed strange, ill at ease. He took me all the way up to the fifth floor and escorted me to the doorway of 169. None of this was normal. I was panic-stricken.

The front hall was full of people, and the atmosphere was intense and solemn. Father was there with John Heyman and other men, one wearing white gloves. Papa stared blankly at me and called for Claire, who quickly appeared with Nannie to whisk me off to my bedroom. Mama closed the door behind us and gazed through the window across Baker Street. Turning, she looked at Nannie and said, 'Hughie says that I have killed his father.' It was like something from *Alice In Wonderland*, and I didn't like it. I had not then connected the stretcher with Grandpa Green.

Nannie, keeping hold of my hand as we sat together on the bed, told me, 'Darling, your grandfather died this morning.' I cried no tears; I was numb. How had Mama killed him, and why? It took the rest of the day to understand that he had suffered a heart attack and died. Mama had not really killed anyone.

Claire was rigid with horror, despairing that everything had come to such an ugly climax, and she was scared for the future. Nannie was tight-lipped and withdrawn. She, too, was traumatised.

Hughie's reaction was one of extreme shock, which he had vented on Claire. In fact, it was Hughie who would live with the guilt of the Major's death for the rest of his life. As the body lay lifeless on the mezzanine floor in front of Claire, Violet had told Hughie that he had murdered his father, and it was an allegation she would never let him forget.

Mama said later that Violet had not cried or shown any emotion. She was cold and practical, and her first priority was to secure her husband's will. She stated unequivocally that whatever her husband had left her would not be enough and that Hughie would be 'looking after' her from then on. She held a hurried conference with him, because they needed each other's silence over all that had transpired. They needed to be 'on the same page' when questions were asked about the Major's sudden death – failing which they could both find themselves at the centre of a criminal investigation.

But not even in this moment of supreme family crisis did 'The Violet' draw close to Claire, or hold out any hope of a truce, a united future. She showed no remorse for her part in the hate mail which had triggered this unimagined outcome. The term 'merry widow' could have been invented for Violet Green. Indeed, she was at that time a great deal 'merrier' with one of the lift operators in Chiltern Court than she had been for many years with her husband.

Some months later, Claire realised that I was still troubled over Grandpa's death. We sat together while she gently joined the dots to make at least some of the picture.

She and Papa had been waiting in flat 169 while David Jacobs was downstairs, presenting my grandfather with the 'cease and desist' order. With the Major's dramatic collapse, Jacobs – himself injured – urged Violet to phone Hughie, who dashed into the lift with Claire. The doors opened onto the mezzanine floor and Mama was faced with the image that, for her, would always encapsulate the horror of the morning.

'It was David,' she told me. 'He was slumped on the floor of the corridor. Oh God, his wrist! He was trying to hold it with his left hand, but it was broken – it was turned around. And he was ashen and in such terrible pain. The sounds he was making . . .' Mama put her hand over her mouth as tears brimmed in her eyes. 'And all he wanted was for someone to get him out of there.'

Hughie, Violet and Paddy hauled the fragrant, made-up and horribly injured solicitor into the lift and out into Baker Street, where they flagged down a taxi and told the driver to take him to hospital. David Jacobs certainly didn't want to be known as a party to the Major's death. Summoned to an inquest, he would have had to explain his legal purpose at the Greens' apartment. He could not have admitted that he was there to 'scare the shit' out of the old man so that he would cease and desist and forever shut up. That is not the way prominent solicitors go about their business. And he would have had to explain his smashed wrist.

An inquest would have opened up an enormous can of worms. When someone has died violently or unnaturally, the local coroner has to be informed. But everyone present related that the Major had simply keeled over and died, concealing the fact that there had been a brutal confrontation. David Jacobs' presence was not mentioned. Luckily for him, Hughie, Claire and Violet, the post-mortem report, dated October 28, did not lead to the coroner's court.

Major Hugh Aitchison Green was 73 when he died after falling backwards into his flat on the mezzanine floor in Chiltern Court. He was described in the report as a 'broker (wholesale fish) retired', and the cause of death was noted as 'myocardial fibrosis, coronary thrombosis'. He had previously sustained a minor injury to his right leg and often used a walking stick. When he kicked out at David Jacobs, he seemingly dislodged a blood clot from the wall of a major leg vein. This shot to his fast-beating heart and, acting as a bullet, killed him.

Quickly removing Jacobs from the scene of death, the family then called an ambulance but not the police. Police officers arrived later, when the Major's body was at the morgue, and they accepted that his passing was an act of God – even though the Major had no history of heart problems, was in apparent good health and had died unexpectedly, without his own doctor being summoned or informed.

David Jacobs told us later that the Major, keeling over, uttered the haunting words 'God damn Claire!' Jacobs himself would also die violently, a little over nine years later, in Hove, Sussex, when he hanged himself aged 56 in the grip of a black depression. It was suggested that he may have feared exposure as a homosexual – although it's difficult to imagine what could have been exposed that he had not already made evident himself through his appearance.

The dark memories of October 23, 1959 weighed heavily on Hughie and Claire for the rest of their lives. Mama would go on to tell me everything that had happened, and would invite my comments. However, it would be another fifteen years before she discovered that the trigger for the poison pen letters had surely been the birth of baby Paula. Papa, aware that my mother had told me everything she knew, would refer to that day often but never as a topic in itself. He would sum up the whole series of events, euphemistically, as 'that silly thing my father did'.

Major Green didn't leave a penny to Hughie in his will, declaring bluntly, that 'having built him up into a star in show business, he requires nothing from me'. Committing this to paper the year before he died, the Major ensured that Hughie would finally understand the extent of his hurt and anger. He left me his home movie camera, home movies, snapshots, scrapbooks and other memorabilia, but I received none of them.

*   *   *   *   *

My parents told me they were sending me to live in Canada – and of all the things that had happened to me in my young life, this was the one that left the deepest scars. It was presented as a *fait accompli*. They had not discussed it with me or considered my feelings about this most radical change of scenery. They gave me no real reasons, only that I was going on to a better schooling. There were no reassurances that I would be all right, or would be coming back, or would even be missed.

I blurted out, 'But why?' Mama's reply did not invite any discussion: 'You will enjoy it.' Claire always knew what was good for *me*, and her knowledge was never to be challenged. She would invariably add, 'One day you will understand.'

I was only twelve years old, my life was in London and I had no friends in Canada. A flood of confusion and angst swept over me. Parents are not meant to dispense with their children in such a tyrannical manner.

It has taken me many years, well into adulthood, to rid myself of the fears this instilled in me. No matter how clearly I realised, intellectually, that I was a victim of their fucked-up personalities, the nagging feeling of being somehow unworthy and deserving of such a dismissal would linger on.

Hughie had made the big decision to send me to Canada in his blind panic over the hate mail, before the Major was revealed as the perpetrator. He was sure that a scandal was about to break over Paula. He would lose his livelihood and his reputation, and he thought it expedient to have me out of the country when it all happened. As ever, he turned for help to Makin. She would take care of me, protectively and financially.

Mama had no idea why Hughie was so eager for me to leave London, but it suited her too. She hadn't enjoyed me as a child, and she wasn't going to miss me when I was gone. She would visit me only once in four years at my new school in Lennoxville. Perhaps, like Hughie, she didn't want me to be around if her own affairs should come to light. Perhaps my absence gave her more scope to conduct them . . . Claire later said that with me in Canada, she had an escape route from Hughie. However, I never bought into this explanation; she had no plans to leave Father at the time.

Linda, to my envy, would remain at Chiltern Court. Her schooldays were virtually over, and Hughie would not have been able to make a case for uprooting her and sending her abroad to a 'better school' at such a late stage of her education. Makin would not have accepted that. Also, Linda would be with Claire and, girls together, they could soldier through any emerging scandal.

Just a few weeks before he died, Major Green wrote to his sister Kit in Prince Albert, Saskatchewan, telling her that 'for some reason' Hughie was arranging to send me to Canada to be educated – despite the fact that I could have my pick of the finest public schools in England. It was a similar story to the one he had peddled about Hughie's scholarship to St Paul's School years earlier and, again, it was a lie. The letter also shows, interestingly, that Major Green knew about my move to Canada before I did.

Everything was in place for my exile, and there was no change of plan even after the Major died. But then the unthinkable happened. Makin – Claire's dear Grandmother McIntyre – passed away only a few weeks after my grandpa, on November 28, 1959. She was 90 years old.

I will never forget that night. Mama, Papa, Nannie, Linda and I sat together in the living room at 169, crying. All the tears that had not been shed for Major Green were pouring forth for a lady who had meant so very much to all of us. Hughie reacted in much the same way he had to Major Green's death. He struck out at Claire, wanting to blame her for something, anything. Exploding, he accused her of letting Makin die before she had seen Linda and me again. It was an extraordinary allegation. Both of our parents had known that Makin was failing, but neither had anticipated that she was at death's door.

Papa, while genuinely distraught at the news of her death, had other reasons to be perturbed. He had arranged for Makin to supervise my new life at boarding school in Montreal and to see to my welfare during holiday periods. He was by no means convinced that Claire's parents would agree to take on such an onerous responsibility; Helen spent much of her time hiding away with the alcoholic Bradley in Ivry, their lakeside retreat. Hughie was also keenly aware that Helen and Bradley didn't like him and, unlike Makin, would not automatically help our family in any financial emergency.

I looked at my old toy-box and wondered if I would ever see it again. Father was not around; he must have had something more important to do than to say goodbye to me. Nannie was as miserable as I was, although there was a whisper that she might be coming out to Canada to join me later, which sustained me through an emotional day.

My partings from Michael, Karin and the others in my gang of friends were brief and hurried. Once I had accepted my fate, I wanted to get it over with. I said, 'See you later,' not 'Goodbye,' to the porters and lift operators in Chiltern Court.

It was 1960, the start of a new decade and a new life for me. Mama and Linda were delivering me to my new school across the ocean. The trees were starting to take on their autumn colours as we drove to London Airport for our Trans Canada Airlines flight to Montreal.

Linda and I loved every minute of the fifteen-hour journey. We were agog at the mystery and romance of it all, and I forgot my worries for the whole time we were in the air. My grandparents, Helen and Bradley Wilson, came to Dorval Airport to meet us with a warm welcome. They were accompanied by Bradley's sister and brother, my Great-Aunt Gladys and Great-Uncle Billy.

It was a bittersweet moment, seeing the house in Peel Street again. It looked somewhat faded, and Makin – its real heart – was no longer there. She was the last of the 'great ladies' of Peel Street to pass on. Only one of the original staff – Mary, a maid – was still living in the house. Soon, the property would be taken over by McGill University – which I would later attend.

As I went to bed that night, I was conscious that everything I knew had changed, and it was not going to change back. I was sure that London would probably never be my home again, and I was aware that when I left Peel Street to go to Bishop's College School in Lennoxville – 90 minutes' drive away – it would be for the last time, since the mansion was changing hands.

Mama and Linda would soon return to England, and if they were upset to be leaving me behind, they didn't show it, or so it seemed to me. Everything seemed transitory, uncertain. From my bedroom on the third floor, I remember listening to the great, antique, table clock on the second-floor landing. Its muted 'tick-tock' sliced through the silence of the house, and on the hour and half-hour, it would chime beautifully and with authority. Then it stopped. Claire and Linda felt the same as I did – that Peel Street was saying goodbye.

Most children are very resilient, and I was lucky to be one of them. I was blessed to have Grandma and Grandpa Wilson – and Nannie, who would come back to Montreal in 1961 to retire. I was loved. My first Christmas in Canada, alone with my grandparents Helen and Bradley, had its lonely moments, but they did everything within their power to make me feel happy and wanted. When Christmas was over, they introduced me to their Eden, and it was at once mine. Visiting the country house at Ivry with them, I experienced all of the joy that I had never known on the mezzanine floor with my grandparents Green.

I missed the British countryside and the magical, coastal beauty of St Ives in Cornwall. I missed a few of my young playmates very much. But I made new friends, *good* friends, easily. I played ice hockey, I fell in love with the distinctiveness of the seasons . . . and I began to feel like the Canadian I was by birth. I had been right: I would never live in England again.

My school, Bishop's College School (BCS), was another crucial part of my salvation. It was, and is, a world-class institution with a proud history dating back to 1836. It now boasts a mixed-sex, multicultural student population, but in 1960 it was for boys only and it was an unapologetically White Anglo Saxon Protestant (WASP) establishment.

I did rather well in the Cadet Corps. I became Captain of the rifle team and we won shooting contests. I attained the rank of Staff Sergeant and won the annual 'Best NCO' medal in my last year at the school. Nobody actually enjoyed being in the Cadets, but it was an obligatory part of school life, and it taught discipline and respect for rank and tradition. Discipline and conformity were key to the school operation, and the Cadets and the chapel were the jewels in its crown. Every minute of the day was regimented, and personal expression was frowned upon.

By today's standards, it was draconian, but I responded to the dependability of the routine. It was an escape from the turmoil and uncertainty of daily life in Chiltern Court. I was attracted to the tedium and lack of excessive emotion. It was tough, but it was fair, and all the students were in the same boat. The rules, even if they were archaic and often petty, were at least understood. BCS was the best thing that could have happened to a child of my unusual and unhappy experience.

Mama and Linda, staying on in Montreal for a couple of months before their return to England, came to see me six weeks after dropping me at the school. The four-day Thanksgiving holiday was open for parental visits, and I looked forward to this unreservedly. They took a room in a fashionable motel, complete with a television, where we saw *The Flintstones* for the first time. Linda lost no time in pronouncing Lennoxville a 'dump'. After lunch in a nearby restaurant, my mother and sister told me that it was time for them to go. They had been there for a mere few hours. Unlike the hundreds of other parents who had descended on the town for the full four days, my Mama was already taking Linda back to Montreal. She never crossed the school threshold again. Nannie, however, travelled by bus in all weathers to visit me with candies and love.

Papa would later come to see me at BCS. He then decided to visit again, at which point I was threatened with expulsion. Visitations from my parents were not happy events.

* * * * *

Back in London in 1960, Hughie had taken another lover. Divorcee Gwen Claremont was not like her predecessors. She was the mistress of all the mistresses, of supreme importance to Hughie, although her feelings for him eventually turned into an obsession so disturbing that he would end his days in terror of meeting her in the afterlife. It was a real, fatal attraction.

Yet again, Father started his affair in Wales, at the end of the 1959 summer season – only a year after his productive liaison in that beautiful country with Elaine Yates. Why Gwen was there, I have no idea. It was fate. By the following year, theirs had become a serious relationship, and Gwen began to appear in public, formally, with Father.

Gwendoline Helen Hughes was born on April 8, 1916 in Acton, west London. After a brief, wartime marriage to Lieutenant Stanley Stopford-Claremont, she had lived in Kensington High Street, a more favoured residential area, with her mother Gladys, following the death of her father, James.

Gwen was the older sister of one of Hughie's previous girl-friends, the would-be actress Pat Hughes, although this appears to have been an extraordinary coincidence. There is nothing to indicate that Father knew Gwen well while he was seeing Pat, although he did later become involved to an unusual extent with the whole family, particularly Gwen's younger brother Kenneth. I'm sure that's why Gwen imagined that she could separate Hughie from my mother and have him for herself.

The physical similarity between Claire and Gwen was almost frightening. John Heyman, Father's manager, ventured: 'Claire was beautiful, willowy, graceful and feminine; Gwen was a bigger-boned, bigger-breasted, almost butch lookalike of her.' Later, when I saw a photo of Father and Gwen together, taken in 1961, I thought I was looking at my mama until her necklace caught my eye. It was too heavy, too 'butch' for Claire.

Gwen held a compelling sexual allure for Hughie. 'Uncle' Vic Hallums and John Heyman have both told me that he tried to end the relationship after only a year, but simply couldn't do it. And the lady wasn't for letting go.

The romance was going strong while I was in my last months at 169, although I knew nothing about it. Hughie would come home late and drunk on many occasions, and this was all part of Gwen's masterplan. She would sit with him, wherever they were, and encourage him to stay on for another drink, and another, knowing that Papa needed little persuasion, and she would make sure that he was blitzed before dropping him off at Chiltern Court. That was the one thing Claire would really hold against Gwen; that she sent him home so hatefully drunk and aggressive when a wife and two sleeping children would have to suffer the consequences afterwards. Hughie was on Benzedrine as well, of course, which added to his volatility.

He never hit Mama in my experience, although Betty Raymond, his personal assistant, is certain that he did. He certainly never struck Linda or me – he abused us by bullying and intimidation – but we were saved on a few occasions, apparently, by the intervention of 'Uncle' Vic, pinning Father's arms behind his back to stop him doing anything stupid. Hughie was beginning to spin out of control, but instead of obtaining psychiatric help – 'I would've driven any poor fucking shrink nuts!' – he immersed himself in ever-increasing quantities of speed, gold dust and alcohol, encouraged by Gwen, who matched him drink for drink.

One night after I had gone to Canada, Gwen was as drunk as Hughie when they parted company. A short while later, she dialled our number, and Claire answered. Father arrived home to find his wife listening to Gwen's unstoppable babble down the telephone line. What she was saying, nobody knows. But Mama instantly got the picture, she realised she was talking to Gwen, the sister of Pat Hughes, and she confronted Hughie. He was cornered. Weakly, he confessed, 'I don't understand what it is, but I just can't keep my hands off her.' Famously, Mama told him, 'Well, I'm not waiting around until you discover irresistible charms in the mother too.'

And with that, she decided to leave him.

It was coming up to Christmas 1960 in Montreal, and I was out shopping with my Great-Aunt Gladys when she suddenly blurted out the news that Father had been caught with another woman, Gwen Claremont, and that my parents were separating. It was a bombshell, exploding all around me in a department store full of tinsel and twinkling fairy lights.

Gladys had promised Claire that she would say nothing to me about it, but the secret was too big for her to bear alone. Father had been insistent that he should be the one to break the news to me next time we met. That was not until the following summer, when I returned to London during my school holiday. Claire prompted Hughie to have his little chat with me immediately. He could see in my eyes that I knew what was happening, and he said, 'Chris, I love your Mama but she won't stay with me. One day you will understand.'

That was the extent of his explanation. He never said the word 'sorry', or spoke about his feelings for me and Linda, or even tried to be reassuring about the future. As usual, the implication was that it wasn't his fault, and that we should have sympathy for him as the injured party. After all, it was Claire who was leaving *him*.

It was during that miserable summer that I also heard the truth about my mother's indiscretions. Part of the legal separation was that Claire had to disclose, via her solicitor, anything she may have done that could rear its head to embarrass Hughie and his career. One damp and overcast day, I sat with Mama beside the Regent's Park tennis courts while she filled out the papers. She was weepy, edgy and short-tempered. She looked at me, heard my unspoken question and confessed that she had 'been seen' with Sir 'Sandy' Maxwell, Father's good friend and the man who had tormented me for peeing in my pram, and another gentleman she never identified. Like Hughie in his brief 'man-to-man' chat, she hoped that one day I would understand her reasons.

Later, she would remark upon the cruelty of timing in such a short thing as a human life, and speak about fate and, for her, a love lost. But in my favourite park that day, I was a naïve thirteen-year-old, wounded and confused. Parents are not supposed to behave like this. It was bad enough to know that Papa had a mistress, but the idea of my mother with another man was just incomprehensible, so very wrong. Later, my feelings changed and I was happy that Mama had found some appreciation from her lovers, but I ached for her that she had had to look outside her marriage. She had a pulse, she had needs, and she was not by nature a promiscuous person.

Many years later, my views were echoed by Betty Raymond, who told me, 'Your father should have been knighted years ago. He was a brilliant performer, a fearless wartime pilot, an innovator in British television, and a dynamic human being who was never afraid to work, fought for what he believed in, and created and supported important charity work.

'But he was a bastard all the same. He abused your mother mentally, and he hit her during a number of his drunken rages. Your mother was not an angel either. She was a naughty girl – never wicked like your father, but naughty – and I loved her for it. She was magnificent-looking, full of charm and wit and life, and she exuded sex appeal. All the men looked at your mother. She was far too good for your father. Had he not abused her so badly and so often, and left her on her own in Baker Street, she would never have looked twice at her admirers.'

By the end of the year, Claire – humiliated by her husband's philandering in front of everyone she knew, and heartbroken by this repayment of her loyalty during the lean years and the BBC lawsuit – had escaped to Canada with Linda. She had long known that Hughie was incapable of giving love, and she repeated this sorrowfully, never bitterly, over the next few years.

She had agreed not to sue Father for divorce, since, as he pointed out, this could adversely affect his career and earnings and, in turn, her meagre, monthly alimony payment. Hughie had never intended to lose his wife and closest confidante. He was sad but resigned to the separation, although not enough to be generous in his financial provision for the family. He was delighted, though, that there was no looming divorce, since he could bat off any 'funny ideas' from girlfriends, particularly Gwen, who was hell-bent on becoming the next Mrs Hughie Green. To his great relief, he was still a married man and was therefore in no position to pledge commitment.

Violet was back in the picture in a big way, using the Major's death against Father to force his financial support. She was thrilled that Claire had thrown in the towel at last, and she decided on a different strategy for Gwen. She would keep her enemy close, but she would do it with smiles, thin-lipped as they were. Gwen accepted the hand of friendship, never realising that it was being offered manipulatively, through fear and ill-will. She did not understand the power that Violet exerted over her son.

At the same time, Violet had started to refer to herself as 'Mrs Hughie Green', relating herself entirely to her celebrity

son rather than to her late husband who was of course Major
Hugh Green.

Over in Montreal, Helen and Bradley had seen the mansion
sold to McGill University and had relocated to an apartment in
Cedar Avenue. In my school-term breaks, I stayed with them in
the luxury, high-rise Cedar Plaza, complete with air-conditioning,
a pool, an indoor heated garage and a breathtaking view over the
city and the St Lawrence River. Mary, the loyal maid, moved with
us to her own one-bedroom flat in the same building. My
grandparents Wilson had also retained their chauffeur, by
building him a garage house at the country property at Ivry.

Mama took a flat in a modern block in Drummond Street, only
two streets west of Peel Street and a minute's walk away from her
favourite Ritz Hotel. She and Linda had wanted the vacant, two-
bedroom flat, because its balcony was perfect for sunbathing.
Grandmother Wilson was incensed, incredulous that my mother,
far from wanting to welcome me back into the family fold, would
even consider taking accommodation with no room for her son.
Mama retorted that I was away at boarding school for more than
nine months each year, but her protests fell on deaf ears. She
finally accepted a three-bedroom flat in the same building and I
was back with Claire and Linda, on Drummond Street.

My mother was not delighted to have returned to her home-
town. Our family was well-known in Montreal's leading social
circles, but we had broken the unspoken rules by emigrating to
England. And now that she was back, Claire was treated
prejudicially for being a single parent. She was also bored by most
of her old friends.

It was a family joke that she could never be comfortable more
than a few blocks away from the Ritz. She wasn't interested in
skiing, tennis or card-playing, and called herself a 'porch-sport':
'I used to sit, posing, on the porch, dressed in all my fashionable
clothes, and watch the others playing.'

Mama was a cosmopolitan, city girl. Montreal wasn't big
enough, it wasn't in Europe, and it certainly wasn't London. She
could not relate to my feelings of 'becoming Canadian', and it
increased the distance between us. She loathed Ivry as much as I

loved it, and while she was pleased that I was receiving a fine education 'with our own kind', she had no affinity for those same people who, she felt, were pompous snobs.

A couple of times, over Sunday lunch, Mama would recall the circumstances of my birth, and she was very candid. She told me that she had desperately wanted a Christine, not a Christopher, and my dear grandmother, Helen Wilson, sensing my hurt, would chip in immediately, 'Oh, now, I don't think we should talk about things like that,' before giving me a warm and reassuring smile.

Nannie was present when Mama first declared that my birth was not a joyful event. She was shocked, tearful, and quickly reminded me, 'But *I* took you. You were *my* boy.'

My mother's unhappiness over my innocent arrival was something I tried desperately to 'correct' over the years. I constantly tried to earn the respect and love that she didn't have for me, and I would never refuse her anything. She knew it, too, and she would often take advantage of my 'weakness'. Linda later told me, 'The one big mistake was that you never told her "No!"' And I guess that was it.

I wish I'd told my father 'No!' when he decided to visit me for the first time at Bishop's College School. He had flown over to try to launch *Double Your Money* in Canada – unsuccessfully, as it would turn out. I was granted time out of class for his visit, and he was already quite drunk when he arrived to pick me up.

Walking to his hired car, we passed a small, school building. Squinting through the blinding light of the sun on the snow, Father saw that it was a library named in memory of Peter Holt, a wartime volunteer from a prominent family in Montreal. Hughie was good friends with Holt's mother, Babi – one of the elderly ladies he so admired during his lifetime. He immediately embarked on a garbled tirade: 'Peter Holt . . . killed in the war, poor bastard. But *I* wasn't killed. My father saw to that, didn't he? No fucking Spitfire for *his* boy . . . But Peter Holt, *he* was no fucking coward.'

There would be other times when Father would show me his pain and guilt over his 'cowardice' in agreeing to leave England after the declaration of war. I later met Babi Holt and flashed back, with a shiver, to the day of Father's visit.

We went to the neighbouring town of Sherbrooke for lunch at the New Sherbrooke Hotel, where Father ordered more to drink. In an effort to further alienate me from my sister and mother, he made vile allegations about their personal and sex lives. There was not a grain of truth in these statements, but to hear such comments from my father was horrific if not unusual. He loved to set the cat among the pigeons – or, as he described it, 'put pepper in the baby's milk'. He did what he could to cause trouble between me and Linda, telling me, 'Your sister says terrible things about you . . .' without explaining what, allegedly, they were.

Our lunch that day ended up with Hughie throwing a loud and disgusting temper tantrum and overturning our table. In shock, I ran out of the dining room to the cloakroom. I threw on my coat, struggled to get into my boots, and thought only of escape. I had to pass the restaurant again to reach the front entrance. What if Father came lunging out to grab me? Sheer panic overwhelmed me . . . and I saw myself from above. I was out of my body, looking down. And then I ran, straight out and across the snowy, icy street. A passing taxi had to swerve to avoid hitting me. I felt the side of the car, or maybe it was the rush of air it caused. I could easily have been killed.

The cab driver stopped, very shaken, and asked if I needed help. I saw Father running out of the hotel towards the vehicle. Again, panic! I scrambled into the back seat of the taxi and urged the driver, 'Please take me away from that man . . . please take me back to school!' And then Father's hand was opening the door, and he was saying to the bewildered driver, 'This boy is my son and . . .' I protested that I had never seen him before: *'Please take me to BCS!'*

The poor taxi driver eventually told Father that he was taking me to BCS and that if any argument ensued, he would call the police. We drove in silence all the way to the school steps. The driver saw me safely inside, and he drove Father back to Sherbrooke to collect his hired car.

Two other BCS boys had been on special leave that day, lunching in the same venue. With great kindness, they spoke discreetly to my House Master and to a few, select teachers, suggesting that I might need some kind words and counselling. These I received, to my gratitude. One of the masters phoned Mama to tell her about my ordeal. She was furious, vowing that her estranged husband would never trouble the school again. She also told me, with a typical lack of compassion, how terribly upsetting it had all been for *her*.

Towards the end of that school year, Father was again in town and threatening to pay me a second visit, for the annual Cadet Inspection Parade. Mama told him, emphatically, to stay away. He retorted, 'Christopher is my bloody son and if I want to fucking visit him, I will.' Mama panicked and called the head-master, Mr Pattison, to warn of the potential embarrassment. At the same time, she arranged for my grandfather, Bradley Wilson, to collect me and closet me away in Montreal for a few days until Father had returned to the UK. With this new development, Mr Pattison lost his patience. Unhappy about pupils' absence for whatever reason, he told me in his office that he would ask my parents to remove me from the school if anything of this nature should happen again. I burnt with resentment at my father.

9

The Actress and the Bishop

The hurt and humiliation that my father had caused me at school was still stinging a year later when Mama decided, out of kindness, to tell me his most personal secret. It was 1963 and I was sixteen when she sat me down in the flat in Drummond Street, saying it was time for me to start understanding what had made my father the man he was, to see that he was human too and had been dreadfully hurt as a child. Mama never suggested that this excused his often cruel behaviour, but she felt I might begin to accept that it was not me, Christopher, with whom he had a problem. It was the world in general.

She told me about the night of the chicken sandwiches, when Hughie blundered into his parents' Toronto hotel room and discovered his mother *in flagrante* with a lover. At last I could identify the source of his seemingly irrational fury when he had thrown the Christmas turkey out of the window in Chiltern Court.

Twenty years later, I would witness another eruption of this lifelong fear of fowl. Again, it was Christmas, and I was driving him from Montreal to Toronto in a 'white-out' blizzard to spend the holiday with Linda and her husband Rainer. He suddenly started panicking about the festive food: 'Oh, God – Linda does know that I can't even look at a turkey or a chicken, doesn't she?'

Hughie was a fully paid-up member of the 'Bah, humbug!' brigade. He'd never known the value or excitement of Christmas as a boy, and as an adult away from us, he preferred not to observe it traditionally. By the time I'd gone to Canada, he'd taken to spending the day on his beloved boat, the *Enalios*, moored in Calais harbour, with his housekeeper, Mrs Agnes Carr. His Christmas cards would say, 'Spending Xmas Day on the *Enalios* with Mrs Carr and we will be celebrating the twenty-fifth with a wonderful piece of Scottish beef.'

Food was a touchy subject for Hughie, a symbol of his fears and feelings and a trigger for some of his more spectacular outbursts. Back in Chiltern Court in 1954, when food rationing ended, Mama had decided to bake an angel cake, using a dozen egg-whites. We watched excitedly as she took it out of the oven – but it looked like a cow-pat. It hadn't risen to the occasion. Papa happened to be making a rare visit to the kitchen and we could see his ears flattening back – the sure sign of an explosion, which duly followed. He was incandescent with anger, not at the culinary failure and the wasted eggs but at the very idea of using so many to begin with. The war had left its scars.

* * * * *

Hughie appointed Mrs Agnes Carr as housekeeper in 1963, and he adored her. Mrs Carr was elderly and an undoubted substitute for the only women he had worshipped – his grandmother Alice, and Claire's grandma, Makin. Father had a streak of hatred for younger women, starting with his own mother, then mine, and his string of mistresses, whom he treated badly without exception.

Chiltern Court had never been a real family home, but with Claire, Linda and me away in Canada, Hughie began to turn it into a lair and an office. Mrs Carr told Papa that she would allow for 'bed and breakfast ladies' but not women in residence. A household could have only one mistress and that would be her. Father thought this was marvellous. He could tell Gwen Claremont, for one, that she could not move in with him because of his 'contract with Mrs Carr'.

Gwen would never live at 169, although she wanted to, desperately. Still, she and Hughie carried on with their heavy-drinking sessions, and Father's continued use of Benzedrine saw him heading for disaster. It happened on Saturday, April 3, 1965 when he crashed his Jaguar into a seventeen-ton lorry. He was driving to Reading, in Berkshire, with Doris Barry, his auditioning manager for *Opportunity Knocks* and the sister of ballerina Dame Alicia Markova.

It took 40 minutes to cut him out. At Battle Hospital in Reading, he was found to have concussion, six broken ribs, leg and spinal injuries, and a blood clot between the liver and lungs. The bottom of his right lung had to be collapsed to ease the pain, and he was given a tracheotomy to help him breathe. Poor Doris broke her shoulder and collarbone, and was badly concussed.

Father was later relieved it had taken so long to extract him from the wreckage; he could sober up a little before he arrived at the hospital. Mother said it was astonishing he hadn't killed anyone in his years of driving under the influence, and Vic Hallums blasted, 'That bloody Benzedrine . . . I could sense when he was on it, and I wouldn't let him behind the wheel if I was driving with him.' Doris told me that she would not have accepted the ride if she'd known Hughie had been drinking, and that he had not apologised: 'He never said sorry to anyone for anything in all the years I knew him.'

Father made light of things. He swore that he and Doris were saved by the car's steel chassis frame, making up a jokey, rhyming advertisement for the company, 'If you're going to get pissed and drive, make sure you do it in a Jaguar and stay alive.'

He was also impressed at being operated on by the Queen's surgeon, Sir Arthur Porritt, after being transferred to the King Edward Hospital for Officers, in London. Going for surgery, he cracked to Sir Arthur, 'This is the only time I have entered a theatre without applause . . .' Shortly afterwards, he talked to journalists about his 'agony', which resulted in 15,000 letters, cards and gifts. One old lady sent a bunch of white heather she'd had for more than twenty years.

Recuperating back in Chiltern Court, he gave an interview in which I was said to be 23. Father claimed he had found the will to live after a phone call from me in Canada, asking for help with my fees for medical school. In fact, I was only seventeen, I had not talked to Father about my interest in becoming a doctor one day, and I had never asked him for money for anything.

I *had* called 169 immediately I was told of the accident. I introduced myself to the woman who answered, and in an unfriendly and condescending manner, she refused to accept that I had just heard, and berated me for not ringing sooner. I asked her name. She replied, 'You are speaking to Gwen, your father's lady.' She told me nothing about his condition. When I finally got through to Father, quite a few days later, he was offended that I had not phoned before. Either Gwen had not told him about my call or he'd been too drugged to remember.

Doris Barry later told me of a bizarre conversation with Gwen, who'd told her how lucky she was. Doris answered that she was indeed lucky to be alive, but didn't particularly enjoy being broken up in a hospital bed. Gwen responded, 'You were so fortunate to be with Hughie. You could have been killed together . . .' Doris took this to mean that Gwen would have envied her had she died with Father.

Hughie had sustained some residual scar tissue, but he would know another twenty years of self-abuse with booze and drugs before this damage would catch up with him. Nevertheless, his existing hypochondria worsened. His manager, John Heyman, told me, 'There was nothing wrong with your father that couldn't have been cured if he'd stopped all his pill-popping. His illnesses were exaggerated; he used them to get attention.'

Two months after his accident, still trying to struggle back to health, Hughie was dealt another blow. On June 3, 1965, Dr Laszlo Banszky, his surrogate father, died at his practice in Devonshire Street, and with him went the secret of the gold dust. Ironically, Father's chest had suffered weakening injuries in the car smash. How would he now live without his Latzy?

That same year, Hughie published his autobiography, *Opportunity Knocked*, which I felt was full of inaccuracies and lies. He wrote, 'In 1964, Chris became head boy of his Montreal school in his last year there. I flew over from London for the ceremony . . . there was no prouder parent anywhere that day than Hughie Green.'

I did become one of the ten or so head boys in Lennoxville, 75 miles away from Montreal, but there was no ceremony, Father did not see me that year for any reason, and he was never a proud parent. It was just so much bullshit, designed to make him seem 'normal' and 'caring' to his public. But while his TV popularity was going from strength to strength, his private life was becoming ever more complicated.

He had arranged for Gwen Claremont to become the manager of Monica Rose, his cheeky, Cockney sidekick from *Double Your Money*. This gave Gwen financial stability and Father an acceptable explanation for being seen with her. He could also still appear to be a single and available man. 'Uncle' Vic Hallums often had to do a bit of 'traffic control' when Gwen turned up unexpectedly, sometimes with her mother, while Hughie was otherwise occupied.

Father's relationships were always complicated. There would usually be an overlap between one ending and another beginning, and he would often be involved with several women at the same time. He would continue to see and have sex with his ex-girlfriends. All of these arrangements were on Papa's terms and for his convenience alone, and most of his lovers accepted this and knew about each other.

By 1966, he was beginning to tire of Gwen's demanding personality. She had been his Number One mistress for the best part of seven years, and he had become close to her entire family, but now he was taking steps to distance her from his life. The first was to separate her from Monica Rose.

In May 1966, Gwen served Hughie with a writ, alleging that he induced Monica to break her management contract. She further claimed damages against Father, Monica and her parents, who were also accused of inducing breach of contract. Hughie could not risk going to court in case Gwen might spill secrets about his personal life, and so, it seems, he paid her off – probably during his *Double Your Money* summer season with Monica in Weymouth. There was no further legal action, and Monica quietly changed her management. Gwen, however, would still not accept that Father was finished with her, and she became something of a stalker. She was never far away, and she continued to hope for a future with him.

In December 1966, he met singer and 'soubrette' entertainer Yvonne Marsh when they co-starred in the Christmas panto, *Babes In The Wood*, at the Regal Theatre, Edmonton. They started an affair straight away, and Yvonne would go on to become a three-times winner on *Opportunity Knocks*.

She had an alcoholic husband, assistant film director John Oldknow. Although they had their problems, she had compassion and feelings for him, and they stayed married until his death from cirrhosis of the liver in 1989.

Yvonne was the first serious challenge to Gwen, who viewed Father's other girlfriends as lightweights. Yvonne was different. Aged 33, she was thirteen years younger than Hughie; Gwen had seen her fiftieth birthday come and go. Yvonne was intelligent, forthright, beautiful, long-legged, talented and vivacious. Unlike Gwen, she was also tremendously popular within their show-business circles.

Before long, Yvonne enjoyed the unique distinction of being publicly acknowledged by Father as his mistress. They travelled together openly to Aden, South Yemen, to entertain the troops in the summer of 1967 with Tony Hancock – who, according to 'Uncle' Vic, 'was drunk all the time and unpopular with everybody'.

Despite demoting Gwen, Hughie still slept with her, although less frequently. He was so excited by Yvonne, he told Mama about her when he arrived in Montreal in August for the World's Fair, Expo '67. Claire received his news without jealousy. While wishing them well, she also questioned Hughie's capacity to cherish Yvonne.

That same year, Hughie rather unchivalrously claimed to have been 'picked up' in Dublin Airport by the twice-widowed Lady Olivia Conyngham. Father, impressed by her title, began a long-running affair with her too, conducted largely behind the closed curtains of their apartments. Her photograph stood on Father's bedside table for the rest of his life, so Olivia, while playing second fiddle to Yvonne, was significant to him.

During this period, Papa was also making regular visits to a north London supermarket where he was enjoying a liaison with the owner. The relationship stopped only when her husband was released from prison.

He met another lady on a train. So strong and immediate was their mutual attraction that they hurried off to the toilet to get to know each other better, while 'Uncle' Vic stood guard at the door.

*   *   *   *   *

The dawn of the seventies found Father at the top of his career. The critics were starting to attack him as being corny and insincere, but his ratings for *Opportunity Knocks* remained high in the Top Ten and in 1971 he was invited to host another networked, weekly quiz show – *The Sky's The Limit* – for Yorkshire TV. Coincidentally, the drama series *Upstairs Downstairs* began in the same year, devised by actress Jean Marsh – Yvonne's sister – who also starred in it alongside David Langton, my future stepfather.

Father was exhilarated by his new show, which would continue for more than three years. It was based on the format of *Double Your Money*, which had come to the end of its long run, but instead of cash, contestants won air miles. The more they won, the further they could travel.

The Sky's The Limit saw Father reunited with Monica Rose. The viewers loved little Monica and the other hostess, Audrey Graham, an older singer. Father even invited Yvonne Marsh to make a special appearance.

By now, Hughie had turned the flat in Chiltern Court into a fully functioning office with two secretaries, Cindy Rowe and Liz Turner, who worked in my old bedroom – complete with Father's ever-expanding train set.

Liz remembers her first experience of Hughie: 'I let myself in on the Monday morning, and there was a smell of bacon . . . there were voices coming from the room to the right of the hall, Mr Green's bedroom, and he was in bed eating the bacon and talking to Mrs Carr. I crept through to my office, hoping I was unnoticed.

Things immediately became fairly hectic, toilets flushing, bath taps running, strong smells of Aramis coming from the bathroom, phones ringing frantically. I was never properly introduced to Mr Green. When Cindy arrived, I heard him say, "What's that new girl's name?" . . . For a long time he couldn't remember it and had to ask or just shouted down the corridor.'

Liz – whose duties were to reply to fan mail, type scripts, keep Father's flight guide up to date, run errands and refill her office waterfall – finally confronted Hughie over his rudeness.

'One morning when I let myself in, he was in bed, swearing and carrying on in a terrible manner. . . I heard him say, "That fucking new girl is fucking useless." I listened in to discover that he was creating about a script for *The Sky's The Limit* that I should have typed up, ready for that morning, when he would have been going for the weekly recording.

'At this point, I became angry and stormed into his bedroom. "If you took the bloody time to look," I said, "you'd find your bloody typing on the hall table, all ready to go." Both he and Cindy looked taken aback, as I was not heard to swear in those days. I thought he was an ignorant, unpleasant man.'

Liz returned to her room and Father went out, slamming the door behind him. He came back a couple of days later and literally threw a small, gift-wrapped package onto her desk. It was a bottle of expensive perfume.

'After that, I grew to like him more each day and we became good friends. He was invariably in a bad mood, his language was appalling, he treated everyone like dirt, and he shouted at Mrs Carr so that the poor little woman was running up and down the corridor, muttering to herself. I always tried to keep a low profile and sometimes bore the brunt of a bad mood, but got used to the swearing and soon took little notice. It was his way.

'At other times he could be very funny, and we often shared jokes, especially after his morning bath, when the whole flat smelt warm and lovely of Aramis. He used bath soak, soap, body spray, talcum powder (all over the floor) and after-shave. He liked his morning soak, and he seemed relaxed for a few minutes at least after that.

'He would regularly come in to see me in my office – quite often in his underpants . . . Mrs Carr used to tell him off – "She's only a wee lass, Mr Green, sure, you should be ashamed of yourself!" – but he took no notice.'

Father, since his days as a child star living in hotels, had been known to hold court in bed in the mornings, briefing his staff and visitors. He rarely closed the bathroom door, and he would confer with male colleagues while soaking in the tub. He didn't care how little he was wearing in front of anyone, men or women. Early callers would be astonished to catch sight of Father strolling around the flat in his underpants, looking at his tropical fish in their built-in aquarium in the living room – he knew them all by name – or standing in the middle of his Marklin model railway layout, playing with his trains while Liz Turner typed at her desk.

She told me, 'It was my job to keep the train set in good order. This meant regularly ringing a man in Brighton who came to upgrade and repair it. I also had to make a lot of calls about the fish tank when it needed cleaning out or he wanted new fish.'

Father was obsessed with his toys. They symbolised the boyhood he never had. On one occasion during an interview he was drunk and showing off his train set when he switched the points, causing two trains to collide and derail in a shower of sparks. I was closest to the crash scene, and father's rage at me – for 'causing it' – was explosive and embarrassing. The interview was terminated, and both Father and the reporter left the flat. A few minutes later, the journalist returned with some balloons for me and Linda. Handing me mine, he said, 'I'm so sorry.' I felt terrible shame for my father.

On another occasion, Papa had bought a magnificent, clock-work submarine and taken me into Regent's Park to try it out. After one abortive voyage, Hughie accidentally kicked the motor key into the water, to the amusement of some onlookers. He strode off towards Chiltern Court seething with rage, and on entering 169, told Claire, 'Your fucking cretin of a son lost the key of my submarine and humiliated me.' He then stormed back out of the flat, to the pub.

Liz Turner had been working at Chiltern Court for 'quite a long time' before she realised that Violet lived in the same building, and saw her only once at 169. Father's ladies, however, visited frequently – and his staff were aware of many more, listed in an address book which Hughie called 'the crumpet file'.

'It contained only females' phone numbers,' said Liz. 'There was a lady in every town in the country, I should think. When he had auditions in different locations, he would often ring someone and arrange to see them.'

She said of his flat, 'I had no idea Mrs Green and the children had ever lived there . . . I had always assumed it was a bachelor pad, and even that often just seemed somewhere for Mr Green to sleep. It was an office, a business with a bedroom.'

Father bought everything he had ever wanted – his luxury yacht (the *Enalios*), his private plane, his fast cars, a monkey, his birds, his fish, his train set and a retinue of attendants. The only thing he never had was a home.

Hughie's homes were hotels and dressing rooms, where he would set out his personal treasures – a favourite pipe, a photograph or two, a pair of comfortable shoes, a well-worn sports jacket. There, he would hold conferences about the coming show while he applied his make-up; he was always centre-stage. Hughie's obvious sense of *home* in a dressing room was something his manager John Heyman found sad beyond words.

*   *   *   *   *

My relatives were dying. I was taking my final exams at McGill University's faculty of dentistry when Claire's mother, my loving grandmother Helen, had a fatal heart attack on May 26, 1971. Four days later, my Great-Aunt Gladys suffered exactly the same fate. I failed, marginally, two required courses but was granted permission to rewrite these papers during the summer months. In hindsight, that is what I should have done, but I didn't. I panicked. I was 'running away'.

Great-Uncle Billy died of old age the next year, on August 6. Less than a year later, on May 17, 1973, just as I was accepted as a medical student by Switzerland's University of Lausanne, my grandpa, Bradley Wilson, died from the trauma of a broken hip that was inoperable because his liver was so damaged by alcohol.

In the two years between her parents' deaths, my mother sold or destroyed just about everything that represented 'family' in Montreal.

Claire inherited a couple of million dollars from her mother. She rented a small, one-bedroom apartment on Drummond Street for storing her belongings and left to travel the world. And it was the grand hotels of London – and their proximity to Papa – that she found most alluring. Hughie was delighted to encourage her renewed interest: they were unfinished business for each other. His personal life was a mess. He wanted to wipe the slate clean and start again with Claire – and her attractive bank account. Hughie's wealth was being swallowed up by his luxuries, his ongoing staff expenses and Violet's upkeep. His mother, however, was not going to last forever, and Hughie would then be free, without her opposition, to reclaim his wife.

Linda and I were trying, meanwhile, to carve out our own lives. Linda, a dazzling Montreal debutante, had gone on to marry and divorce a Jordanian diplomat called Waleed Sadi. He was serving on the United Nations Security Council in New York at the time of their marriage, which produced a daughter, Delia.

My sister had met the man who would become her present husband when they were stuck together in a lift in the Drummond Street apartment building. Rainer Plentl, an Austrian, was working for the Imperial Bank of Commerce. They married in the spring of 1971, and I gave Linda away in Father's absence.

Inevitably, they would soon leave Montreal since, like Mama, Linda found it boring. Rainer's many promotions would see them shuttling between London, Paris and Toronto, before they finally settled in England.

I was dreaming of rebuilding the family fortunes in Montreal to make my parents, and Linda, proud of me. I would prove I was not my father's 'cretin in Canada'.

My love life had been looking up too. It was understood, if not spoken, that I would eventually marry my girlfriend, Sue Banks.

Grandma Wilson had expressed her wish – to Mama, Linda and me – that Sue and I would together take over the country retreat at Ivry, which I loved so dearly.

Unfortunately, she didn't put this in writing. Three days after we buried Helen, Mama sold that wonderful house for a song to one of Linda's friends, Howard Hall, telling me that he would put some 'poop and pizzas' into it. Effectively, she gave the property away rather than let me take and look after it. A few years later, Howard sold it for a very substantial profit. To me, the value of Ivry could never be measured in money.

Claire also burnt family photos and mementos. She was rubbing out our identity, slowly but surely, in a relentless campaign that had begun, for me, when I did not receive my legacy from Major Green.

It was 1973 and I was at an all-time low. I hadn't had the heart to re-sit my dental school exams, although I had taken a couple of supplementary courses in biochemistry to strengthen my CV. I was desperately embarrassed and ashamed in front of Sue that my mother had sold our future at Ivry. I felt castrated, certain that I had failed miserably. My relatives were dying around me. I was not meant to have a happy family life. I had to get away from everything, and that included Sue, so I decided to take up my offer of a place in the University of Lausanne. Mama was thrilled. She promised to pay for my course and an apartment in Montreal for my use in vacation time.

Makin had left me her engagement ring to present to my chosen bride when the time came. After I had gone to Lausanne, Mama put that ring on Sue's finger and told her she was my fiancée. I knew nothing about it until it was announced that Sue was following me to Switzerland. I was furious with Mama. I'd planned to return to Montreal after a year so that Sue and I could together decide on our future. If she was willing, I'd put the ring on her finger myself.

Now Sue was in Switzerland, struggling to settle into the European lifestyle, and Mama had not kept her promise about my monthly living allowance, only dishing out irregular and infrequent payments. Even worse, she had not rented an apartment for me in Montreal, nor did she allow me to use her flat while she was away. So I was stranded in Lausanne, bewildered and off-track, and would remain there for nearly four years. Sue went home to Montreal after a few months, and met and married someone else.

*   *   *   *   *

The Sky's The Limit was in its third year when producer Peter Holmans was replaced by none other than Jess Yates. Father had remained friendly with Jess after impregnating his wife, and had appeared on Jess' *Stars on Sunday* in 1971 to sing the religious 'I Come Here to Stay' and 'I'd Be There'.

Jess had long been separated from Elaine and fourteen-year-old Paula, who were living in Majorca. Still, in August 1973, the *Sunday People* ran a story headlined, 'The Secret Sorrow of Jess Yates'. Below a photograph of Jess and Elaine an emotional caption read, 'They must live apart for weeks for love of their daughter.'

It was stated that since suffering double pneumonia and a collapsed lung six years earlier, Paula had become prone to illness in the cold, wet, English winters, and had been advised by her doctor that a warmer climate would benefit her chest. Paula had a different explanation: they moved to the sunny Mediterranean island after her mother read a captivating poem by Robert Graves, who lived there.

Jess, living near Leeds, where he was Yorkshire TV's head of children's programmes and organ-playing anchor man for *Stars on Sunday*, was nevertheless said to be heartbroken that he could only see his family occasionally. Father took such an interest in this article that he cut it out and pasted it into a scrapbook.

Then, only weeks later, Jess arrived to produce *The Sky's The Limit*, and the trouble began. Jess decided to make the show sexier, much to the resistance of Hughie, whose success had always been based on clean, family fun. Jess sacked Monica Rose and Audrey Graham because they weren't glamorous enough and replaced them with scantily-clad 'stewardesses'. He also tried to

make the set more exciting, whereas Hughie disliked props and
visuals as they diverted attention from the game and, crucially, the
contestants. Nevertheless, Jess brought in a brash new look and a
rocket-ship, which would be wheeled onstage so that people could
get in it and 'blast off'. Father also 'blasted off' – at Jess.

The straw that broke the camel's back was Jess's suggestion
that Father change his tie for filming. No one told my father what
to wear, and the ensuing screaming match was spectacular. Jess
could not understand Father's hostility towards him. But he failed
to realise that *The Sky's The Limit* was Hughie's show. Jess's job
was to produce what Father had created – not change it.

He could not have guessed at the other factor in Father's anger.
Jess's very presence was a constant reminder of a horrifying
sequence of events – the birth of Paula, the hate mail from his
parents and the shocking death of Major Green on the mezzanine
floor. Elaine Yates had been Father's conspirator and the mother
of Paula; the innocent Jess, rather than Elaine, became the
whipping boy for everything that had ensued.

But Hughie was probably right about *The Sky's The Limit*. Its
consistently high ratings dipped and Father blamed Jess. He
would take a merciless revenge . . .

Hughie again slept with Jess's estranged wife, Elaine, in London
in the early part of 1974. He also, allegedly, had an intimate
moment with Jess's latest and secret girlfriend, Anita Kay.
Ironically, Jess had sent Anita to see Hughie at 169 to audition for
a stewardess's job on *The Sky's The Limit*. The generously
endowed Anita had once performed nude in a revue called
Pyjama Tops.

Hughie told me about her during one of his business trips to
Switzerland. We were lunching in Geneva when he informed me
that she had 'just turned up' at Chiltern Court. During the
'audition', Father claimed that he asked to see her huge breasts,
whereupon she pulled up her sweater and allowed Hughie to
fondle them. He then photographed her nude. When I asked if she
got the job, he replied, 'Oh, no, she didn't – but she told me a lot
of *interesting things*.'

It was unusual for Papa to discuss such things with me, and it made me uneasy. I had this disconcerting mental image of a woman with an enormous bust having her photo taken, stark naked, in the living room of 169 while telling Father 'interesting things'. I wondered if it had been Mrs Carr's day off . . .

Anita, it seems, had confided everything to Hughie Green about her relationship with Jess Yates, the man who, Father told me, was 'breaking my balls' and 'ruining the show'.

On another trip to Switzerland, Papa talked to me about a second big-busted lady he was seeing. Mentioning no names, he said that she was sexy, very intelligent and an author of 'dirty books'. Elaine!

He was preoccupied with her, Anita and Jess during these Swiss visits of early 1974 – and it was then that he first mentioned Noel Botham, a large and bombastic tabloid journalist. Botham had shown up one day at the front door of 169, pursuing a story that Father had been seducing female contestants on *Opportunity Knocks*. Hughie found this highly amusing. He invited Botham into the flat where he told him, 'There is no truth to that, but please do print it. I will, of course, sue the living hell out of you and your rag, and win.'

He found Botham an entertaining character who was skilled at digging up stories on anyone and had lots of gossip to share. He had a leading reputation in this murky world, and he earned enough to buy his own trendy Soho pub, the French House. Father, while not taking him too seriously, enjoyed the odd drinking session with Botham, and he invited him onto the *Enalios* two or three times – much to the horror of Mrs Carr, who disliked him violently.

Hughie's chauffeur John has since confirmed to me that he loaded the *Enalios* with booze for Hughie's sailing trips with Botham. And he has told Linda that he was in the driving seat of the car while his two passengers sat in the back, discussing the exclusive news story that would expose and destroy Jess Yates.

Mama never kept her promises to come to Switzerland. Once, I drove to Geneva Airport to meet her, but she wasn't on the flight.

She'd suddenly changed her mind because Switzerland was 'such a boring place'.

Papa's visits were usually pleasant. I was flattered that he was showing me some attention, even though his primary reason for being in Geneva was to do financial business. On a couple of occasions, he stayed with me for a few days. We both enjoyed the fine food and wines. We sailed across Lake Geneva to the French side and went to the casino, and we drove up into the Alps overlooking Lausanne.

However, on the last of his stop-overs, he was unusually tense and constantly telephoning England. I didn't realise it then, but he had an ulterior motive for staying with me. To my sadness and disgust, I was providing him with an alibi. Father wanted to be abroad when Botham's 'Jess and Anita' story broke in the *News of the World*. Then he couldn't be accused of colluding in it – or so he thought.

The story exploded on Sunday, July 7, 1974 with the headline: 'My Great Love For Jess Yates By Actress Anita'. Father flew back immediately to London, his 'few days of relaxation' suddenly over. He told me about the startling newspaper revelations, but did not mention Botham's involvement, or his own.

Tabloid stories about the actress and 'The Bishop' (Jess's nickname) raged on for days, to the amazement of the teenage Paula Yates. She couldn't understand the fuss, given that her parents had separated many years earlier, and she later berated the press for ignoring Jess's reputation as 'a highly respected, charming, funny man'.

Paula was under the impression that two female journalists had coaxed the story out of Anita Kay by plying her with drinks. That wasn't what happened, according to my information. Anita had been appearing in a seaside, summer show in Clacton, Essex, with comedian Harry Worth when Noel Botham arrived to interview her. Flattered that he was there, supposedly, to talk about her acting career, she saw no danger when he asked about her relationship with Jess. She also, apparently, didn't question how this journalist knew so much about Jess and herself and she blabbed it all out. When she told Jess what she had said, he reportedly told a friend, 'I'm finished.' And he was.

Viewers all over the country complained about the hypocrisy of the *Stars on Sunday* presenter, and he was taken off air for the next and final week of its run. *The Sky's The Limit* had also just reached the end of its season. It was then axed, a victim of falling ratings and Yorkshire programme controller Paul Fox's exasperation with the battling egos of Hughie and Jess as well as his personal dislike for the show.

Immediately after his naming and shaming, Jess was sent home from work, leaving in a car boot to avoid the press, with some sources suggesting that Fox had fired him for incompetence and not because of the scandal.

Hughie, meanwhile, was coming under suspicion of being the source. He was known to socialise with Noel Botham, and his disagreements with Jess were legendary in television circles. In a front-page story in the *Sun* on July 11, Anita said that Hughie had a strong hatred for Jess, and it was suggested that the three-year affair may have come to light because of the arguments over *The Sky's The Limit*. Hughie admitted that he had fought against Jess's attempts to 'jazz up' the format, but lied, 'I don't hate Jess. I feel sorry for him . . .'

Botham protested that Hughie had nothing to do with the original story; he had been out of the country. The information had come from a reader, who had spotted Jess and Anita on holiday together. *News of the World* staff reportedly did not remember any reader's letter.

Jess remained on paid leave for a year. When his contract with Yorkshire TV ran out, it was not renewed and he only ever appeared on television again on the odd talk show and as a guest on the *Celebrity Squares* quiz.

Resigned to living on benefits, and then his pension, Jess divorced Elaine and remained with Anita for another six years until they separated, allegedly, because of her wish for children. In addition, she was said to have felt guilty over her part in Jess's downfall, while stressing that he never blamed her for it.

In the last four years of his life, approaching 70, Jess found a new companion, the nineteen-year-old Serena Daroubakhsh. She was the daughter of one of his old girlfriends, the former Miss

Rhyl, with whom he had enjoyed a brief romance between meeting and setting up home with Paula's mother, Elaine. Jess told Paula that there was nothing improper about the relationship with Serena. But when Jess died from a stroke in April 1993, she sold her story to a newspaper and, to Paula's dismay, demanded his house.

To his dying day, Jess believed Hughie had ended his career and wanted nothing more than to piss on Father's grave. He must have thought Hughie had wanted to punish him for steering *The Sky's The Limit* into oblivion, which was partly true. But he had no idea about Hughie and Elaine, or Paula, or Major Green and the mezzanine floor. Jess represented all of this to Hughie, he unwittingly brought it back, and for that he would suffer.

Jess had been trashed by a long-time friend, but he died not knowing why.

Within a week of Yates's fall from grace, Father was feeling the pressure. 'Why I Might Quit' screamed the *Daily Mirror* on July 13, 1974 in a feature detailing Hughie's 'worst year in showbiz'. Talking about his battles with Yorkshire TV and his conviction that Jess had wrecked a perfectly good show, he described his feelings: 'Let's get out, let's sell my boat and go and live somewhere peacefully.'

This may have had a lot to do with his feelings for Claire. Violet had been diagnosed with cancer, so the way would soon be clear for a reunion. Previously, Hughie had looked to a future in which he would sail away to warmer waters on board his dear *Enalios*. Mama hated boats. That he was thinking of parting with it clearly indicates that he intended to start a new life with Claire.

That opportunity did indeed arise, but Hughie would blow it big-time. The secret of Paula would see to that.

10

A Second Honeymoon

Hughie's dance card was busy. He was juggling the affections of Yvonne Marsh, Gwen Claremont, Lady Olivia Conyngham, Elaine Yates and occasional girlfriend Aileen Blaskey, all gorgeous and spirited. Actress June Laverick – co-star of the sixties' hit TV series *The Dickie Henderson Show* – had also entered the picture.

And then there was Claire, back in his world with the promise of salvation. He desperately wanted to be with her again, especially after the recent, tumultuous events in his life. He could clean up his act and escape to a fresh and straightforward domesticity with his wife – and her money.

Mama had been visiting London, and Hughie, more frequently. Her relatives in Canada had died, Violet had only a few months to live, Linda was married, and I had been stranded in Switzerland. Towards the end of 1974, Claire decided to give Father another chance. Linda called to tell me that our parents were returning to Canada for a second honeymoon, prior to a permanent reconciliation. Neither Mama nor Papa had bothered to mention this to me, but I wasn't surprised at the news.

I knew that a deep bond existed between them, dating back to their shared, teenage confidences on the decks of the *Empress of Britain*. They had parted without tying up their loose ends, and each exerted a powerful and inexplicable hold over the other.

Still, I could not fathom Claire's motives: she knew that Father could not live lovingly or faithfully with any woman. Hughie, I'm sure, convinced himself that it was possible, but he was deluding himself horribly. He would have behaved for a while, but he would never have been able to give up his ladies. He didn't get the chance to try.

Arriving triumphantly in Canada with Claire, he made a big mistake. Perhaps feeling that they should start again with a clean slate, it seems that he told her everything about his affair with Elaine Yates, the birth of Paula, and the baby's direct connection to the hate mail and the death of Major Green. Mama was outraged, incensed, revolted, crushed. For fifteen years, she had agonised over the dark secret clearly known by her father-in-law, the sender of the anonymous letters. In her periodic conversations about that unforgettable October morning on the mezzanine floor, she had made no reference to any baby. She had, rather, fretted that the Major had somehow found out about her lovers, but had eventually managed to reassure herself that the secret centred on Hughie's affair with Gwen Claremont.

Neither theory stands up to examination. Had Major Green discovered Claire's infidelities, he would simply have leaked the information to the press, or to Hughie himself. That would have been enough to get rid of Claire, without any damage to Father's career. The mail had started arriving in May 1959, just after Paula's birth – when Hughie was still several months away from seducing Gwen Claremont.

After the trip to Canada, Claire immediately severed the cord that bound her to Hughie. They barely spoke again; they certainly never shared any further confidences. Yet, afterwards, Mama would subject me to some desperate tirades. I didn't understand them at the time, but they tied up the Major's death, a 'poor little girl in Wales' and the final break with Hughie.

Claire had almost certainly come to realise on her romantic holiday with Father that the fallout from the mezzanine floor had not departed with Major Green. She had finally learned about Paula, and there was every possibility that the truth behind her birth could explode into an enormous scandal at any moment.

Claire had no idea how many friends or lovers of Hughie were privy to the secret, but she was surely terrified that, courtesy of one of them, it would one day rear its head.

Mama was sitting on a timebomb, she heard it ticking, and her 'second honeymoon' was over as suddenly as it began. At that very point, the nature of her 'unfinished business' with Hughie changed dramatically; where once she was unfeasibly loyal and drawn to him through their age-old alliance, she now detested him and would spend her lifetime seeking revenge.

Symbolically, she later sailed into Cherbourg harbour, where she had first met Father as a young girl, and threw the jewellery he had given her out of the porthole of her cabin, down into the water. She would be forever haunted by his revelation, and even on her death bed, would be rambling still about 'that poor little girl in Wales'.

*   *   *   *   *

Violet was failing fast with stomach cancer, which had spread to her liver, but she did not, apparently, realise her condition was terminal. Hughie sat at her bedside during her last days at London's Wellington Hospital, opposite Lord's cricket ground, and reported that she had her hair washed and combed daily. On February 13, 1975, she died, aged eighty, with her make-up on.

No one was devastated by her passing. Father had little to say about it privately, although he told the press that he had become a believer in euthanasia after witnessing her suffering. Mama told people, 'The bitch has died,' and I had no tears to shed for a grandmother who had shown me such cruelty.

Interestingly, she left money in her will to an unknown gentleman and his sons.

Father went to Scotland to scatter Violet's ashes, according to her wishes. Having lost his licence for drunken driving, he was chauffeured there by June Laverick. He had met June in 1974 in the north of England, socialising after a show. She was unaware of Hughie's Number One girlfriend, Yvonne, although Yvonne knew about her, and at this time, June represented no great threat. Only later would she become a central figure in his life.

Papa was really only thinking about Claire. For various reasons, he was still expecting their reunion to go ahead. According to Hughie, he was walking up the designated hill in Scotland with his mother's remains, and June, when he was suddenly confronted with a scrum of newspaper reporters, asking him to comment on the fact that Claire was suing him for divorce. He had had absolutely no warning of this, and he later, repeatedly, complained to me, 'How could your mother have been so cruel? Did she think it was right for me to hear about it from the press, while I was saying goodbye to my mother?'

Twenty-two years later, I would be sitting on a plane, flying to Scotland to spread Hughie's ashes, just as he had done for Violet. Linda was sitting next to me, absorbed in Paula Yates' autobiography, and the person on my left was June Laverick. I asked her about that day when she and father were accosted so rudely by the press. She replied, 'Christopher, my darling, you know how your father always liked a good story. I was with him every minute of that day, and we never saw anyone from the press.'

Still, the papers did manage to obtain a comment from Hughie. The *Daily Express* placed him in Scotland when he said that he and his wife had previously held back on divorcing 'for the sake of the children'. Father added, laughably, 'They were only in their teens at the time and we saw no sense in ruining their lives as well as our own.'

Mama, by then, had briefly returned to Canada, where she refused to take any calls from her soon-to-be ex-husband. With Hughie profoundly shocked over his impending divorce, his various lady friends were jockeying for position. Within days, Lady Olivia Conyngham was telling the newspapers, 'I love Hughie Green.' The 49-year-old Olivia revealed that she had been seeing Father for years, while admitting, 'I suppose he loves me in his own fashion.'

Hughie was horrified – Lady Olivia had misunderstood the rules of his game to a reckless degree, and I heard him call her a 'stupid fucking cow' – but he responded with typical charm for the public, 'Isn't it nice of her to say that she loves me?' He later told the *Daily Mirror* that they were good friends, although not seriously involved, and then added, outrageously, 'I have no attachments at the present time.'

On November 23, 1975, another 'good friend' to whom he had 'no attachments' would be revealed in the press. June Laverick, who had given up acting eleven years earlier to run a hotel, was reported by the *Sunday People* to have walked out on her husband, mechanical engineer Charles Cooke, after buying a new house with him in Redcar, Yorkshire. Claiming to have moved to London to return to show business, June had been spotted at *Opportunity Knocks* rehearsals, and was linked to Father.

*   *   *   *   *

Linda called me in Lausanne at the end of April 1975 to announce that Mama was getting married. I had never heard of the bridegroom, David Langton, or the British period-drama series *Upstairs Downstairs* in which he played the leading role of Lord Bellamy. I was under the impression that Mama and Papa were rebuilding their marriage, for better or for worse, after a wonderful trip to Canada. No one had thought to tell me about the divorce proceedings that had been so widely reported in Britain two months earlier.

Later, I discovered that Mother had started seeing David Langton before her reunion holiday with Hughie. David – really Basil Langton-Dodds – was divorced, but living with a mistress who was dying of cancer at her home in Eaton Place, London SW1. David had offered no commitment to Claire and she had decided that her future lay, after all, with Papa. When he then, apparently, made his devastating confessions about Paula, the hate mail and the death of the Major, Claire could not revive her marriage. She avoided Hughie when they returned from Canada to their separate destinations in London.

She wanted a relationship. She couldn't live in hotels forever, she couldn't keep paying for her female friends to accompany her on her travels round the world, and she had no interest in retiring to Montreal. She hid away, trying to work out what to do next.

Hughie was not stupid. I'm sure he knew he had upset Mama by finally telling the truth to her in Canada, but he failed to appreciate the strength of her reaction. She had not called off their plans in any face-to-face confrontation; she had simply disappeared for a while, leaving him still hopeful.

David Langton then proposed to Claire and she accepted immediately. She wasn't that eager to marry him, but she was flattered by the interest of such a famous and attractive suitor, and he offered the stability she was looking for at the time. Now, according to Linda, Mama wanted me to come to London with all haste to give her away at her marriage to a man I didn't know, and she had booked a room for me at the Ritz. Furthermore, Father knew nothing about the wedding, at Claire's insistence.

Mother later claimed to have been terrified that Hughie would 'fly into a rage and hurt David's beautiful face'. To me, the whole thing looked like a set-up to humiliate Father, and I told Linda that I would get in my car and drive to London the next morning on the condition that Hughie was informed first. Receiving that assurance, I made the journey, checked into the Ritz and met the man who was about to become my stepfather.

We had dinner in the large, ornate dining room. Mama looked elegant and beautiful, and David was tremendously handsome. I extended my hand, to shake his. He ignored it, and leaned back in his chair, commentating theatrically, 'My, my, he looks more like a continental playboy than a struggling medical student.'

I didn't know what to make of this amazing, introductory remark, and things didn't improve over dinner. When the meal was over, I had had more than enough of David Langton. He was boorish, snobby and pompous. He was also vain and unreasonably ill-at-ease. It was obvious he didn't want anyone being close to Claire except himself.

Father was not taking it well. I saw him about a week after the day that Audrey Claire Green, aged 53, had married David Langton. He was desperately hurt and angry. Mama had broken our bargain; she had not told Hughie about the wedding.

He was alerted by the press demanding his comments before the big occasion. Not wanting to look as though he had been left in the dark, he declared, 'Claire could never understand people in show business and never wanted to be part of the show-business life that is me. I wish her only the best with her new husband.'

Quite unaware that Claire's new husband was himself a TV celebrity, Hughie's statement – printed beneath a large picture of David Langton – made him look a total idiot. He was equally upset when he saw me on the front pages of the papers, leaving Caxton Hall register office, Westminster, on May 3, 1975 with the new Mr and Mrs Langton. He believed that I had conspired to keep the secret from him.

I could not understand my mama's behaviour. She was many things, she could be vacuous and selfish, and I'm sure that a part of her was enjoying this ultimate put-down of Hughie, but she was not the heartless, conniving bitch that the escapade would suggest. I said, 'You are taking quite a revenge against Father,' and her tearful response confused me: 'Christopher, it wasn't really like that, but I don't wish to talk about it.' I persisted, 'Are you sure about marrying David?' 'Not really,' she admitted. 'But what else am I going to do?'

Hughie was making it his business to find out all he could about David Langton, certain that he had married Claire for her money and only ever referring to him as 'that ponce'. He would have been delighted to discover that while David's age appeared as 57 on the marriage certificate, he was actually six years older – a 'mistake' that became apparent when he died.

*   *   *   *   *

The previously unstoppable Hughie Green machine was slowing down, and there was nothing Father could do. At the beginning of 1976 he could sense trouble ahead in his career, even though he was very busy. He was setting up a satellite link-up between the UK and Australia for *Opportunity Knocks*, and he was also organising a special show for its four-hundredth anniversary on February 23.

It was watched by millions, and the guest stars included some of the 2,000 acts, chosen from 120,000 hopefuls, that Hughie had brought to the screen since the show began – Frank Carson, Peters and Lee, and Bobby Crush among them. It was also the four-hundreth appearance for Father's band leader Bob Sharples, who had written the signature tune.

On April 28, Father presented a one-off TV special called *Hughie's Full House*, which charted the transformation of the old variety theatres into bingo halls. Hughie played nine parts in the production, which also included his Number One mistress Yvonne Marsh, Beryl Reid, Bernard Breslaw, Pat Coombs and former Miss World Eva Reuber-Staier.

Yet, only the next month, he was doing battle with Thames Television, which was now making and downgrading *Opportunity Knocks*. 'Hughie In Fury Over Cuts' screamed the *Sunday People* of May 2, 1976, reporting that it had been reduced from 39 shows per season to 26. Yet *New Faces*, a rival talent showcase, was getting twice the airtime.

Hughie, in many ways, had been his own worst enemy. His forceful and confrontational personality, his obsession with control, had alienated just about everybody he worked with. While audiences responded warmly to his on-air camaraderie, his colleagues had respect for his talent, but not always for the man. Many loathed him. And as he was the first to admit, a generation of newer, younger entertainers was following in his footsteps.

Controller Jeremy Isaacs axed *Opportunity Knocks* in 1978, and Father offered the show – still a Top Ten ratings success – to the BBC, despite their acrimonious history. The BBC took it – but they didn't take him. They put Bob Monkhouse in his spot and fobbed Father off with a royalty.

He had already devised ideas for two new game shows, but it was too late: no one wanted to work with Father. He made a five-minute appearance in a movie – 1978's *What's Up Superdoc* – and toured theatres with June Laverick in a comedy play called *Ace In The Hole*. But he was finished in television. The doors closed behind him and at the age of 55, Hughie Green was on the outside looking in at the medium he had helped to create.

*   *   *   *   *

Back in Switzerland after the wedding, I would not see my mother again for many years. In 1976, I decided to quit Lausanne. At 28, after three-and-a-half wasted years, I was going nowhere fast. More years of study lay ahead, but I was burning out. I was lonely, I missed my friends in Montreal – especially Nannie who was alive and well – I had no support network, and I was constantly worried about money. Father refused to help me, stating that he needed everything he had to cover the mooring costs for his boat, the *Enalios*.

I should never have gone to Switzerland in the first place. I packed my bags and, with what cash I had left, moved back to Montreal. There, I discovered that most of my friends had dispersed to other provinces of Canada due to the prevailing politics, which were moving to separate and establish Quebec as a sovereign French country.

I rented a small alcove flat only two minutes' walk from the grandeur of my family's former home on Peel Street. Mama then sent me a cheque for $5,000. I received it gratefully while understanding it was 'conscience money'.

Half-heartedly, I took the American Medical Board exams, since I had had an offer of help in my career from a London doctor, Dr Phillip Zorab, and I passed – but my grades were not good enough to get me into another medical school. I felt defeated; I had wasted more of my life. Pharmaceutical houses offered me jobs selling drugs to doctors, and I used Mama's cash to set up in business with a friend, selling gifts around the world via telex orders. The idea was ahead of its time but failed through lack of further capital. Soon, I had sold my car, my Leica camera, everything I owned just to be able to pay the rent.

Then I fell into air transport, securing a job with an American company called CF Airfreight. After a few years, I achieved an enviable record, selling major accounts in Montreal, and I enjoyed it very much. At last I started to have a life of my own, away from the influence of my family.

In 1978, I had begun a relationship with a new love, Jane. We met on a plane. Jane was in 'civvies', but she was actually an Air Canada stewardess travelling as a passenger. Jane was a natural, willowy blonde, with a lively personality. I wrote her number on a cigarette packet, and later called her for a date – which went on for eight years.

Linda met Jane and pronounced that I 'could do better'. She then told Father that I was with 'a totally unsuitable young lady,' and he, without meeting Jane, condemned both her and me. But I didn't care. Left alone to live life in my own way, I was happy. Then, in 1982, a brief but traumatic incident shattered my new contentment, and, of course, it was caused by my family.

I was working at a freight company called Livingston International when my former brother-in-law, Waleed Sadi, visiting Montreal, called to say hello. We were exchanging some polite chit-chat when he suddenly said, 'And I hear that you're a daddy.' Taken aback, I told him that I wasn't married. 'That's why Linda was so upset,' he retorted.

I rang Linda immediately, demanding to know what she had said to her first husband. She sheepishly told me that she had heard I had fathered a child, but refused to tell me the source of her information. Taking the rest of the day off work, I went home to make frantic phone calls. I could not believe that any of the three girls who could possibly have conceived my baby would not have told me. As it turned out, none had.

The trail eventually led to Papa, who was expecting my call. He simply said, 'Chris, I have taken care of it.' He would say nothing more. Linda's source had mixed up the identity of the child's father – who was Hughie, not Christopher Green. Father's personal assistant Pam Jagger later told me that this child was one of three little girls, not including Paula, for whom he was making regular financial payments.

I returned to my comparatively uneventful life, buckled down to work and split up with Jane in 1986, just because we had become incompatible. I went on to set up my own small company, CE Transport Services Inc in 1987, specialising in air transport of goods to and from the United States. Today, we have expanded to both Canadian domestic and international business.

As for Linda – I was deeply hurt that she had not dignified me with a sisterly phone call to ask about the alleged child, or sympathise with my plight, but still thought fit to tell others all about it. I never did receive an apology, and it would be years before we communicated properly again.

*   *   *   *   *

Father had been having his problems in Chiltern Court. The phone had not been ringing with job opportunities after 1978, and at some point after the *Hughie's Full House* special, he had lost his favourite mistress. Hughie and Yvonne Marsh had had a personal and terrible disagreement. Father was so enraged that he had driven through the night to confront her in Wales, where she was appearing in a play. Finding her backstage the next day, just as she was about to begin the matinee, he exploded into a drunken and abusive tirade which began with the words, 'You fucking cunt . . .' and then blurted out their most intimate secrets in front of everyone present. Yvonne never forgave him; she instantly ended their relationship.

Father would tell me this story often, always with immense sorrow that he had so insulted and embarrassed her. In his limited capacity to love, Yvonne – after Claire – was the woman for whom he felt the most affection. To the end of his life, he would regret their estrangement.

Gwen Claremont, meanwhile, continued her pursuit of Father, although she was unable to improve her position in the pecking order, even after Yvonne's departure. By the turn of the eighties, she was in the grip of a recurring depression and was plagued by financial problems.

She arrived at Chiltern Court in June 1981, asking Hughie for help towards her rent arrears, for which she was, apparently, being taken to court. Father said that he couldn't bail her out because he was no longer earning anything and had considerable overheads. His boat, the *Enalios*, and his illegitimate children were costing him a lot of money.

On Tuesday, June 16, 1981, Gwen had her dog put down, telling the vet it was because she had cancer. That same night, or early the next day, she wrote a suicide note, addressed to the police, and left it in her Kensington flat. It said, 'There is no way I can live any longer. To be ill with cancer, and getting older, I have no alternative. Please don't ask my sister to identify me – she could not stand it. I have a deformed right wrist from a break which was not re-set.'

She added, 'I am going to burn myself behind the theatre in Holland Park, facing the North Lawn. I am not crazy, just without hope – life becomes cruel. G.C. Claremont.'

Early in the morning of June 17, Gwen poured two gallons of petrol over herself and struck a light. Two bricklayers working at the theatre saw the blaze and dashed over, with one reporting that she screamed, 'Leave me alone, the dog died yesterday and I want to die.' A passing nurse tried to give emergency aid, but the 65-year-old Gwen died from 100 per cent burns soon after arriving at Queen Mary's Hospital, Roehampton. The post-mortem found no indication of cancer. Her own doctor had had no knowledge of any such illness.

Father, who had previously cared greatly for Gwen and her family, visited her flat. The keyholder, her sister Pat – Hughie's earlier lover – obviously let him in. He later told me that Gwen had 'left things' that would have 'finished' him if they had been made public. By this comment, I understood that he had been left a personal note.

He felt horribly guilty. He had treated Gwen very badly over most of their 22 years together, while she had hung onto her sad, hopeless dream of a future with Hughie. At the same time, Father had not asked Gwen to destroy a perfectly healthy dog and douse herself with petrol in Holland Park. She had problems beyond him, but he blamed himself for her suicide, as he had for the Major's death. If revenge is what she had wanted over Father, then she achieved it. She knew that by so agonisingly and disfiguringly killing herself, she would give him nightmares. Years later, moments before his last breath, he confided in me his fear of meeting Gwen in the great hereafter.

With Yvonne and then Gwen gone, Hughie's love life became more manageable – if only slightly. He began a romantic entanglement with his long-serving assistant Pam Jagger. Pam had been widowed in her early twenties when her husband Jack was shot down over Germany, but over the years at 169 she had come to love my father. When they finally began a relationship, he trusted her discretion and loyalty above anyone else's.

At the same time, June Laverick was on the rise, and her years as Papa's devoted companion were rewarded in 1988 when he moved her into Chiltern Court. Obviously, this would not have been possible while Mrs Agnes Carr, his housekeeper and First Mate on the *Enalios*, was running the household. She was really in charge of everything, on land and sea, and both had been devastated when financial circumstances forced Father to sell the boat in the mid-eighties.

Mrs Carr had laid down her own terms and conditions of employment, including her ban on any of Hughie's girlfriends living in 169. In 1987, she became ill. The next year, she broke her hip, and after 25 years with Father, returned to her daughter Margaret in Scotland. Hughie was lost without her. He would phone her from London wanting to know where to find even the most basic household items.

Right up to her death from cancer in 1994, he would visit her in Scotland. She had always been his staunch friend, defender and confidante, another much-loved woman in the mould of his Grandmother Alice, or Makin. Crushed when she died, he would deliver a tender eulogy at a special memorial service held in Ramsgate. Throwing a large wreath into the water, he would be soaked by a crashing wave which, it was generally agreed, was Mrs Carr saying 'Hello'. Her ashes would later be spread at sea.

Mrs Carr's retirement left Father helpless. He didn't know how to boil a pan of water, but he could no longer afford to take on staff. And so June Laverick became the lady of the house. She would remain there for several years – but she was almost immediately challenged by a new arrival in Hughie's life.

Father's band-leader Bob Sharples died on September 8, 1987. Bob had been one of the few friends to keep up with Hughie after his fall from grace in television. He had never particularly liked Bob's wife, Christina, but when his old friend died, Hughie – and June Laverick – supported her emotionally and practically, in particular helping to arrange the funeral.

Incorrigible, even at the grand old age of 67, Father also offered physical sympathy: he took Christina as a mistress. Pam Jagger could only watch from her dependable and dignified position on the sidelines as Christina slugged it out with June for prime position in Father's affections. For his part, he played each off against the other in an unhappy triangle which persisted until the day he died.

*   *   *   *   *

In 1988, Hughie embarked on an ill-advised but typically high-minded legal battle which would swallow up his declining capital. He became aware that a television show called *Opportunity Knocks* had been screened on New Zealand TV in the seventies, replicating his own creation. He went to New Zealand to demand suitable financial remuneration, but the broadcasting company refused, insisting that no legal, copyright protection existed for TV formats.

Returning indignantly to the UK, Father decided to sue. Pam Jagger begged him to guard his remaining money and forget about a potentially ruinous court case. But even Pam, whose judgement he trusted implicitly, could not persuade him to back down. Father told me that he was the victim of a blatant theft, and therefore had a duty to fight for himself and others who might, one day, be similarly afflicted.

He lost the case in 1989 in a verdict upheld by the New Zealand Court of Appeal. It was questioned by contemporaries and academics – just as the BBC decision, many years earlier, had been deemed unfair by most knowledgeable parties.

The famous action – Green v Broadcasting Corp of NZ (1989) – did, however, result directly in the setting up of a subscription organisation called FRAPA, formed in April 2002. The Format Recognition and Protection Association campaigns for the international recognition of TV-show formats and provides a mediation and arbitration process for members.

FRAPA administration manager Joanna Lyle says that Hughie's landmark case inspired the establishment of the organization, although he didn't live to see it. His health deteriorated in direct proportion to his losing battle with New Zealand.

*   *   *   *   *

Years passed, and David moved Claire first to Chipping Campden, an historic town in the Cotswolds, and then to Stratford-upon-Avon, Warwickshire. There, away from city life, he had her all to himself.

On April 25, 1994, I picked up the phone in my office in Pointe Claire, Canada, to hear Mama's voice. David was dead, he was, literally, on the floor of their living room, and she wanted me to come and see her – after many years of banishment. As usual, I reflexively said yes. She didn't want me at the funeral – David's boys disliked me as much as David had – and so I flew into London Heathrow on May 23, to be met by Linda's eldest daughter, Delia, whom Claire and I both adored. She had been invited along for the week of my stay, presumably to act as a 'buffer'. We drove all the way up to Stratford and Mama's home at 17 Avonbank Paddocks.

She looked marvellous, but she had aged. I felt a lump in my throat: I would never get those years back with her. She was visibly moved at seeing me, but there was no hugging, no tears, just an uncomfortable hesitance.

We spent the week doing touristy things, and we did have fun, but the past returned to cast its occasional shadows. I was personally hurt to discover that David and Claire had made several visits to Canada without even calling me. Mama had seen my ex-love Sue Banks in Toronto and had learned of the death of her mother, of whom I was very fond, but had not had the kindness to let me know.

Delia, meanwhile, found out to her astonishment that she had a great-aunt she never knew about – Mama's sister Pam – who was living in a chronic-care nursing home an hour's drive away. As we looked out over the River Avon from our restaurant table, Delia and I were both upset at Claire's refusal to arrange a visit to my Aunt Pam.

The week progressed and I realised intuitively that Mama wanted to say something important but was holding back, and it was unresolved as I left for London. There, before returning to Pointe Claire, I spent a remarkably pleasant week with Father and Christina Sharples, now his favourite companion. We had met when they came out to Canada two years earlier, and I had liked her then.

On that occasion, Father had intended to travel on to Fort Lauderdale to visit his best friend Art Teulon, but had fallen ill with breathing problems and had to be admitted to the Lachine General Hospital in Montreal. One doctor, looking at Papa's 'travelling medication bag', said to me, 'Your father is a legalised junkie. He should throw most of these pills away.'

I remember driving past Mull Hall with Christina while Hughie reminisced about the Major's old friend Colonel MacLean, who had 'married well'. He remarked that he too had 'married well', with Claire, and Christina had responded, 'Yes, Hughie, you have told me that a thousand times.' I bitterly resented the fact that he could be so disrespectful of our mother in front of Christina.

Hughie was finally well enough to return to London, but he never flew again.

I worried about Mama. She didn't drive, and she was isolated in Stratford. She had expressed her bitterness towards David for insisting that they moved there, and I kept in touch by telephone. She spent Christmas with Linda's family in Mayfield. I wanted to wish her a happy new year, but could not get a reply from her home until January 2, 1995. Then, she slurred her words alarmingly, she was unusually aggressive, and I became certain she had suffered a stroke. Panicked, I called my father.

Hughie tried to tell me that Claire had developed an alcohol problem. But I knew she had never been a drinker, and had shown no such tendencies of having become one seven months earlier.

Father refused to give me Linda's number, and I screamed down the telephone, 'Give me her fucking number or I will have your fucking head on a plate!' And he did.

I told my sister to get in the car with Rainer immediately and drive to Mama. She did not have a drinking problem; she was dangerously ill. While I waited for the first available flight to London, Linda and Rainer rescued Claire and rushed her to London's Middlesex Hospital.

Mama had been diagnosed with breast cancer prior to David's death. She had told no one, and had refused treatment for what was, then, an operable condition. Now the cancer had spread to her brain and all hope had gone. Linda, having courageously faced breast cancer herself, was distraught, deeply hurt, that Claire had kept this terrible secret from her – 'We could have faced it together.'

Arriving in London, I was present when Mama, this time at the Cromwell Hospital, again refused medical treatment. It was her wish; we couldn't argue. We had to face the fact that our mother no longer wanted to live. David's son Andy Langton and his wife Carol very kindly welcomed her into their large and lovely home off the Fulham Road in Chelsea.

Hughie, who had invited me to stay with him on this visit, was contrite for having called his ailing ex-wife a drunk, but he typically shifted the blame to Linda, who had misinterpreted the cause of Mama's speech deficiencies during the Christmas holiday. Hughie slammed Linda for saying 'cruel things about Claire drinking' – which speaks volumes about Hughie's personal honour and his relationship with Linda.

Papa desperately wanted to see Claire, but she would not allow it, and she stated firmly that she did not want him at her funeral. After years of silence, my parents then started arguing over the phone. Father became increasingly frustrated, and upped his consumption of booze and pills. I was the yo-yo, crossing London between them daily.

On the evening of Sunday, January 22, my mother and I sipped scotch in an alcove off the living room at the Langtons' home. It was warm and cosy, but she was determined to tell me something and was clearly formulating her thoughts when Andy Langton and a friend unwittingly blundered into the moment of intimacy.

Alone again with me, Mama's composure had gone. She was agitated, and speaking distinctly but disjointedly, she ordered, 'Don't do that . . . you look just like your father.' She had evidently seen some facial expression that reminded her of Hughie – I do bear a great resemblance to him, and that had undoubtedly been one of Claire's problems with me.

She had brain cancer. Her speech was affected, and she was desperately ill, but she was not ranting, her mind was focused, and she was wrestling to tell me something I had to know. Suddenly, she said it.

'Christopher, you must leave him.'

'Mama, please, you're very upset. Who must I leave?'

'You must leave Hughie. The Major died, and that poor little girl . . . you must leave him, he is wicked.'

Without understanding the relevance of what she was struggling to tell me, I tried to be reasonable: 'Mama, it is late in the day for all of us. He is old and what is done is done. I cannot just leave him now.'

'You must leave him. The Major's death, and that poor little girl in Wales. . . There will be a terrible scandal. You have to leave him.'

'Mama, please calm down. What little girl in Wales? What scandal? Why are we back on the mezzanine floor?'

Mama stood up abruptly, and I followed suit. She wordlessly extended her hand to me, I took it, and she then started tugging me. I followed as she led me to the front door, let go of my hands to fumble with the lock, and, finally, heaving the door open, started screaming, 'Get out! Leave! Get out!'

I stepped into a deluge of cold, driving rain, reeling with shock and embarrassment, and almost on autopilot, I hailed a taxi back to Chiltern Court. The Major? A scandal? A little girl in Wales? I tried to tell myself that Mama was hallucinating through illness, but she had seemed so insistent, so convinced by what she was saying, I didn't know what to think.

I let myself into 169 and found Father and Christina on the sofa in the living room, watching the news. Papa scowled and raised his left hand to signal silence. I crossed the room as unobtrusively as possible, and was rewarded with a stream of abuse. Hughie, who had clearly been drinking, spoiling for a fight, started yelling, 'Can't you fucking see that I'm trying to watch the bloody television?'

I went out to the kitchen, poured a drink and lit a cigarette. Then I heard Father bellowing again. He was standing down the corridor outside the living-room door, lambasting me for 'paying all your attention to Mama and not to me,' which, of course, was petty, irrational and unfeeling.

Days later, I would realise that Mama and Papa had spoken on the phone again and had opened up the Pandora's Box of their shared past.

Father stormed into the kitchen and went into his age-old, terrifying rant, 'I'm going out now and I don't know when I'm coming back. I could die in the gutter and no one would give a fuck.' But I was 48 years old, no longer a cowering little boy, and I found it pathetic. I stared him straight in the eye, and he skulked back to the living room.

In my bedroom, the train set had long since been packed into crates on the floor. I jammed my belongings into my suitcase. I could take no more of the madness. Papa was slumped in a chair with his head down in the living room, with Christina standing by his side, and I thanked him for my stay. It was 10.30 p.m. in Baker Street, and the rain was still torrential. I made for the Sherlock Holmes Hotel and was lucky enough to get the last room.

11

The Boatman and the River Styx

Mama looked beaten and sad the next day, and she apologised to me for her outburst without trying to explain it. I told her that, of course, it was just one of those unfortunate little things and to forget it. Rather than forget it, though, she would bring the subject up again.

The day after that – January 24, 1995 – she moved into a small apartment in St George's Nursing Home in St George's Square, Westminster. Hughie and Christina had most graciously found a place for her there when I asked them for help. Linda and I had checked it out and then gone to Stratford-upon-Avon to collect some of Claire's furniture, clothing and personal items to make her rooms more familiar and comfortable.

Mama had wanted her privacy, even though she was very grateful to Andy and Carol Langton for their hospitality. I checked into the Moat House Hotel in Sloane Square to be closer to her, and a couple of days later, I took her for lunch at the nearby Oriel restaurant.

We talked about her financial situation. Linda and I, at her request, had just acquired power of attorney for her from David's former solicitor, Ian Bray. Mother was alarmed that her savings had dwindled dramatically and worried that she would not have enough to be able to see her days out at St George's. She said to me, 'You have power of attorney. You can see that there is nothing left. David screwed me, didn't he?' I said, 'No, Mother, David didn't screw you at all. There is plenty of money to pay for St George's.'

The reality was very different. Neither Linda nor I had any idea what had happened to her money; we still don't. But we made emergency plans to pay for her care should she miraculously go into remission.

In this context, at lunch, Mama told me that she had not been 'altogether happy' with David. From that, she moved straight to the topic of the Major's death. She was becoming oblivious to her surroundings in this trendy, crowded restaurant, and she was growing agitated in her intensity and determination to communicate with me.

I felt like the boatman crossing the River Styx.

'I know you and Linda think I was cruel to your father when I married David, but I couldn't go back to him after the Major . . . could I?'

She was clearly saying that her intentions to reunite with Father in 1974 had been sincere, but something to do with the Major's death had prevented that from happening, and marrying David was the only immediate option. Mama was back on the mezzanine floor, a pleasant lunch was fast becoming a 'heavy' one, and I had to stop the scene which would surely ensue if she carried on. My mother was ill and everything seemed complex, surreal. By telling her I was getting the bill, I managed to distract her from whatever dark thoughts were submerging her yet again. It was the last time she would broach the subject.

At her insistence, I returned to Montreal on January 29 and Linda flew to Buenos Aires, where Rainer was. We knew that we were leaving Mama in safe hands. The owner and matron of St George's, Mrs Elizabeth Kerins-McManus, is a wonderfully supportive person. As it turned out, coincidentally, Mama had already met Elizabeth at John Harding's hairdressing salon, and they had often chatted under the driers.

Just a little over two weeks later, I received a call from Carol Langton in London. She told me that Mama was not doing well, and advised me to come back. I spoke to Linda in Buenos Aires, and we were both in the air, bound for Heathrow, the next day.

I arrived on February 17 and booked into the Moat House Hotel, which became home for the next 32 days. Linda and I assigned a doctor to Mama at the home. He assured us that if she needed morphine at the end, then he, unlike some doctors, had no qualms about administering it. That was her expressed wish; she did not want to become vegetative.

We told our mother that we had flown in to celebrate her birthday, on February 20, and we took her to her favourite restaurant, La Fontana, on the Pimlico Road. We were joined by her best friend Wendy, from all those years ago in Chiltern Court, and a couple of her other friends.

She never left the home again. It was a harrowing time. She was by then calling me 'Hughie' practically every time she addressed me, and she often appeared to be more psychologically than physically pained.

Around the beginning of March, she went into a comatose state, and by March 8, the time had arrived for us to honour her wishes. The morphine-administrating apparatus was discreetly installed beneath her bed, and the venous drip attached to her arm.

I sat with Mama on March 9, and Linda did the next day while I took time out with my old friend Karin to visit the elephants at our beloved London Zoo. Karin called her mother, Wendy, from a pay phone there around 5 p.m. and handed the phone to me. Wendy told me that Mama had died. Claire had once predicted, 'Your hypochondriac father, always on his death bed, will outlive me.' Her prophecy had come to pass.

I went back immediately to St George's and found Linda, Rainer and their children, my nieces, there. Linda asked if I would like a lock of Mama's beautiful, white hair. I said no. I told Mama, 'Thank you for having given me life,' and I turned and walked away. I was heartbroken that I could not have been more to her.

The funeral was on Saturday, March 18 at St Dunstan's, Mayfield. 'Uncle' Vic, his wife Linda and one of his daughters, Pauline, were among the mourners. Father was absent, at Mama's

request. He sent magnificent flowers with a simple, attached note
that read, 'From Papa, my love.' He was bereft. With Claire went
any last hope, no matter how tiny, that he could go back to the
woman who knew Peel Street, and Makin, and could make
everything all right again.

As the reception ended at the Middle House Inn, I looked out
of the window onto Mayfield High Street and I ached to go home.
I turned to see Linda, Rainer and Father Grant Holmes, who had
conducted the service. Father Grant told me, 'Christopher, I
believe you should know that your mother sought absolution for
her treatment of you in life.' This was intended as a kindness, but
I was horrified and shocked, and then felt dreadfully resentful.
Mama's 'treatment of me' was just between the two of us, or so I
had thought.

Some time later, Wendy took me aside to tell me that, although
she had been Mama's closest friend, she nevertheless believed
that my mother had ruined my life. Again, I was dismayed. I had
always honoured my Mama through thick and thin, and I had
never blamed anyone for my fortunes in life. I felt my blessings
had been far greater than those of my parents. And I had hoped
that the cold spot Mama had in her heart for me was our own,
private business.

*   *   *   *   *

Pam Jagger was the Secretary of Father's company, G&M Air
Interests, but she resigned in May 1995, explaining that she was
too old to carry on. Roy Phillips, Bob Sharples' former accountant
and a good friend of Christina's, succeeded her. Pam also
resigned as executrix of Father's will, and Christina and Roy
Phillips took over the role.

Linda and I were then more concerned with sorting out
Mama's affairs and estate. We drove to Stratford in September
1995 to deal with her personal property and the sale of the house.
We were in total harmony at this time. We had never discussed
our periods of non-communication. Linda, since childhood, had
always had her own life and friends, and she didn't share any

happy family news about her daughters, my nieces. She never made any attempt to 'let me in' except in times of crisis. Nevertheless, I always hoped that when we were 'on' again, we would remain that way.

There was a lot of adversity ahead that September. We were worried about Father's welfare. His breathing problems were now real, no longer imaginary. He was financially insecure, and Linda was unhappy about Christina's increasing influence on him. Christina's power base was very strong by then. As Father became sicker and weaker and more fearful of being left on his own, she effectively took charge.

Linda was very fond of June Laverick, who shared her love of children, had a mind of her own, and never interfered in the troubled relationship that existed between Hughie and Linda. Christina, on the other hand, would promote Hughie's frequent criticisms of his daughter.

Both Linda and I would have welcomed June as a stepmother. But Father, stirring things up in his usual manner, began to speak critically about June: she was not the 'wonderful companion' he had always told us that she was, and he had asked her to leave 169 because she had been 'drinking too much', which was rich coming from Hughie. June had always enjoyed a drink, but if she had been overdoing it, it was understandable.

Christina, Linda and I realised, had been 'cutting June's grass' to set herself up as Father's Number One lady, and Pam Jagger and Yvonne Marsh were only two of the many people who described her as 'manipulative', while Liz Turner thought her 'a bit unfriendly'.

But while Father was trying to bias Linda and me against June – whom we loved – he *also* continued to care deeply for her, he went to considerable expense to move her into a small flat, and he would keep on seeing her until his dying day. Yet, he complained to us that Christina had stopped him from seeing June!

The truth was that he needed both women. He adored June's looks and personality, but he prized Christina's practicality and administrative skills. He had created a love triangle, and it was typical that rather than try to run it smoothly, he deliberately caused chaos within it, and then dragged Linda and me into the whole mess.

Linda, through loyalty to June, found herself pitted against Christina, who also told me, with great hostility, that I could not be friends with both herself and June. Of course, I would get it from June's end, too. I was hopelessly stuck in the middle, unwilling to take sides. I chided Father, feeling more than a little like Saffy, the daughter from *Absolutely Fabulous*, that at his age, it was madness to be carrying on like this with two women. He sighed, 'Chris, what am I going to bloody do? They are *both* driving me out of my fucking mind,' and we laughed. But he never saw June and Christina as individual people with feelings. They were serving him, the star, in different ways; they became a 'composite person'.

Linda and I believed that, in an ideal world, Christina should have left Hughie and June alone after her husband Bob Sharples' funeral. Still, I treated Papa and Christina to a trip to Paris on the Eurostar on September 20. We were like kids on a big, joyous outing. It was unusual occasions such as this that made for the terrible sadness with which I would later reflect on the past. Why were such days so rare?

A week later, Linda's eldest daughter by Rainer – also called Christina – celebrated her twenty-first birthday. The family marked the occasion with a party at the fashionable Hurlingham Club, and they had invited me but not Father. This made me very uncomfortable. I appealed to Linda, and she had relented with an invitation to Hughie and Christina Sharples. I do believe they actually enjoyed themselves, but I was sad to realise, yet again, that there was no real warmth in it for Papa. However, it had been worth a try.

*   *   *   *   *

Returning to Canada, I had no idea that I was about to meet the love of my life. It was January 1996, and I had some years before taken to lunching in a darkly lit and cosy restaurant/bar called La Kachette. I reserved the same booth so often that my friend and fellow-regular Dave Gales had placed a small brass plaque there, reading 'The Green Room'.

I was introduced to Lynne Davies by a mutual acquaintance called John. She regularly ate there with her workmates, and we clicked immediately. Lynne and her two older brothers had been born and brought up in Montreal in a family that was as happy as mine had been dysfunctional. Marrying a teacher, Lynne had had three daughters – Kristin, Keely and Kady – and had left her job with Delta Airlines to look after them at home before the family moved to New Brunswick. When Kady, the youngest, was three, Lynne had taken up a managerial post for Northwest Airlink.

Within a couple of years, her marriage was failing, and the airline went bankrupt. Unemployed and going through a divorce, with three children to look after, she sold her antiques, borrowed some money from her parents and moved back to Montreal, where she found another job. Within two weeks of meeting Lynne, I had asked her to come and work with me as a sales rep for CE Transport. She agreed.

We grew closer, and started spending time together at weekends, although I was very hesitant to tell her more than the briefest details about my family. I didn't want to expose her to the painful aspects of my past. I hadn't come to terms with it myself; to try to explain it to someone else would have been impossible.

Still trying to finalise the sale of Mama's house in Stratford-upon-Avon, I flew back to London in May 1996. Linda and I took a week off and drove to St Ives in Cornwall for a mini-holiday. It was a truly magical time, the best week together of our lives, just being brother and sister. We enjoyed the sunshine and the view of the sea and the harbour from the Pedn-Olva Hotel, set up on the rocks. We watched a basking shark in the shallows of Porthminster Beach, we delighted in the seal sanctuary on the beautiful Helford River, we rode the ferry across the river, and we were so relaxed and comfortable that we even rang Father from a pay phone at Land's End, just to tell him we were thinking of him. He was delighted.

We talked very frankly, never mean-spiritedly, about Father's well-being, Christina's growing hold over him, and June

Laverick. Linda had come round to the idea that Papa was lucky to have Christina around, and as long as June received the inheritance that Father had always promised, we were happy about whatever Christina would receive. Linda said, 'Christopher, who would believe it? Here we are worrying about Father when he never worried about us!'

An enormous story in the British press at the time was the divorce, on May 10, 1996, of a celebrity couple called Bob Geldof and Paula Yates. It meant nothing to us; we paid little attention.

By the time I went back to Montreal, Mama's estate had been finalised, I'd had a lovely time with Linda – and Papa and Christina – and there was hope that Linda might also find some measure of peace and reconciliation with Father.

It would not be long before I was back in London. Father was diagnosed with cancer of the oesophagus in August 1996, and I wanted to offer him the same support that we had given Mother. It was a disastrous trip.

The shock and upset that Linda and I were feeling over his condition were of little concern to Hughie. He was again the ogre of my childhood memories, and he cruelly misled us about his treatment and prognosis.

Father wanted surgery. He had an operable tumour – the cancer had not spread – but the specialists were worried that, because of his chest condition, he might not survive an anaesthetic. He was now reaping the rewards of the lung damage he suffered in his 1965 car accident, his years of pipe-smoking, his drinking, and his abuse of prescribed drugs, especially Benzedrine – and his lifelong stresses. His chest infections had become chronic.

A series of tests was carried out at the Royal Brompton Hospital to establish his suitability for an operation. On one visit, Father pointed to a spot outside the door and said to me, 'Look, that is where the press used to crowd around getting pictures of me when I had to be admitted before, and now – not a bloody person in sight. No, they couldn't give the old horse a lump of sugar, could they?'

Linda and I were on tenterhooks about his test results. Yet, after one important consultation, we visited his private ward to find

Hughie and Christina laughing and giggling about the surgeon, and how he reminded them of General Patton.

Christina then insisted that she had laid down the law to the doctors, 'I said that Hughie would be operated on over my dead body, and I told him that I had power of attorney and would sue them if they did operate and something went wrong.'

Linda and I were both frantic with worry. All we knew was that Father wanted surgery, Christina seemed to be opposing his wishes for an operation, and we were no clearer about his medical assessments.

After his death, reading through Father's medical records, I could see that the hospital procedures were thorough and straightforward. He was advised that 'quite a lot' of his chest problems were due to 'tightness from anxiety'. He had been stressed over the court case that he had lost against New Zealand Television and he was worried sick, literally, over the fact that he had also lost his money fighting it.

Furthermore, an entry for August 20 states that, 'it was concluded that Mr Green was not suitable for surgery and that the aftermath would almost certainly prove fatal.' However, this simple, medical fact was not shared with Linda and me at the time.

He went on to have chemotherapy, but not the psychiatric treatment that had been recommended years earlier, according to his notes for 1991. Then, an eminent Harley Street psychiatrist wrote that there were 'a number of seemingly insoluble stresses affecting him' and that he 'would benefit from continuing, supportive therapy'. Father had pulled away from this, telling me that he could not face '*that* pain'.

Father played games with Linda and me over his medical condition. He could have told us factually that he was not healthy enough for an operation, but he didn't. And that state of affairs confounded us, particularly regarding Christina's role. What did she know that she was choosing not to share with us about our own father? This confusion served no kind purpose for any of us, and Papa was the conscious instigator of our bewilderment.

At the same time, he had started to worry that Christina was about to leave him. The very thought of it reduced him to a nervous wreck, which was both perplexing and unprecedented. Christina's distinction among all of Papa's women is that he was truly terrified of her and what she could do. The tables had turned: no other woman had ever wielded such power over Hughie Green.

At first, he claimed that he feared she was becoming bored by him because he was too weak to travel. There must have been some truth in that because one of his bequests to her was £5,000 for a holiday.

Linda and I were invited to 169 on August 25 and, on arrival, were subjected to an explosive outburst in which he accused us of being 'rude to Christina'. It was a classic tirade; he was trembling, enraged beyond reason. 'If Christina walks out of that door because of your bloody rudeness, then *what am I going to do*?' he yelled, furiously.

Asked directly what she had said to Father to trigger such a tantrum, first she said she didn't wish to talk about it. But I pressed her, and she replied, inanely, 'I told him that you hadn't made me feel like family.' Linda looked incredulous. I stared at Father with a controlled disgust. Crap is crap, and Christina's childish and meaningless statement was just that. Linda and I were really just whipping persons that day for whatever was between Hughie and Christina.

Father then pointed a shaking finger at me and addressing Linda, screamed, 'And your fucking idiot brother there . . .' He then launched into a rant in which he cursed me up and down for not having noticed that a set of his X-rays was missing from a sealed envelope that we picked up from one of his physicians en route to the Royal Brompton Hospital. The doctor's receptionist had sealed the envelope without putting the X-rays inside. Neither Christina nor I had been asked to verify the contents, but she let Father tear me to shreds for my 'misdemeanour' and said nothing in my defence. It was at that moment that my feelings for Christina began to change. She had caused a great deal of mischief that day.

My sister and I retreated to the Sherlock Holmes Hotel. I had already decided to fly back to Montreal the next day. I had had enough. We agreed that we didn't want to be dragged any further into Father's bizarre relationship with Christina. And where June fitted into it all was anyone's guess. We said goodbye, and Linda set off back to Mayfield.

Sealing our new closeness, Linda came to visit me in Canada in November that year. After everything that had happened between us in the past, Linda actually wished to spend time with me. I was ecstatic. We made an almost sacred visit to Peel Street, we drove to Ivry, and we spent a night in a fabulous resort hotel in the Laurentian mountains.

Lynne warmed to Linda straight away, and so did Kristin, Keely and Kady. Linda demonstrably enjoyed them too, and we had a memorable Thanksgiving dinner together at Lynne's.

A lot of early snow had fallen and the mountains looked gorgeous. I drove Linda into the countryside to see some old sights, and we went too far along a tiny little road that was still piled high with snow. Just as we were about to tackle an especially formidable-looking slope, Linda enquired, 'Have you asked Lynne to marry you?' My reply was, 'No, why would she want to marry me?'

My car slipped into the ditch. We were stuck, and Linda chose that moment to tell me that I was a complete fool, that Lynne was the best thing ever to happen to me and that I was an idiot not to realise that she was in love with me. Then, she dropped the mega-ton bomb: 'And I can see right through you. You are deeply in love with her, and just too scared to propose.' A snow plough appeared just then, we were liberated, and I realised Linda had been right. I did later ask Lynne to marry me.

At first she said no. She couldn't understand how a single man with no responsibilities could want to be married to a woman with three children. She didn't realise, because I hadn't told her, that all I ever wanted was a family and a home. The third time I asked, she said yes. By February 1997, only a year after we had met, Lynne and I were looking for a house and planning a spring wedding.

I couldn't contain my excitement, so I phoned 169 – having established an uneasy truce after my last catastrophic visit. Christina answered the phone. When I told her my news, she said, 'Just wait until you tell your father that one. He will think you've gone mad. Why would you want to saddle yourself with all that baggage? I would think this through carefully.'

A few days later, I told Papa. He asked, 'Chris, is she a nice person?' I replied, 'Yes, and I love her.' He then amazed me by saying, 'Thank God! I have been so very concerned that you would be lonely later in life. I cannot wait to meet her and welcome her into the family. You have made your old man very happy, bless you.'

Christina, upon hearing Father's feelings, was delighted also, and 'baggage' was never mentioned again. I dared to hope that we were all coming together at last; that we were approaching some sort of normality.

* * * * *

Hughie, in his last years, made repeated pilgrimages to The Orchard in Meopham, Kent – the magnificent mansion where as a tiny child, he had been brought up by 'the staff' while his parents lived it up in London.

He was beginning to take a hard look at his mortality. Gwen had taken her own life, his older relatives had died and so had Mrs Carr. Bob Sharples' death was one of an increasing number from the original circle of entertainers with whom he had ploughed a furrow in television. He had lost his boat, his money and his court case against New Zealand TV. He was unofficially banned from television, and his flying days were behind him. He didn't have a lot to look forward to – and so he looked back.

That he looked back to Meopham was significant: it was the one place he never mentioned to me. I had never heard of The Orchard until after he died, and at that point, I went to see it for myself. He had, however, taken a friend, Gwynneth Majendie and, later, Christina, to visit the house a number of times, and he would stop off at a local tavern, the Leather Bottle, and wash it all down with a lot of brandy.

There were no living witnesses to his young days in Meopham; without fear of contradiction, he could convince himself that he had enjoyed an idyllic childhood there. He was in denial, in a fantasy. My presence, or even my knowledge of his first home, would have driven an uncomfortable sliver of reality into his rose-tinted reminiscences. I had been in Baker Street; I had been on the mezzanine floor. I knew the realities of his parents' cruelties, and how they had embarrassed him.

He never told me of his true upbringing, of what his childhood had really been about; that would have made him 'weak', or worse, a 'freak'. He couldn't face the pain and shame of the truth.

He was nostalgic for a past that never was. He was also lonely and he wanted someone to relive with him his love of Canada, the people and the places that had genuinely been important to him there. That partner was me. Together we had revisited the MacLeans' grand estate, Mull Hall, and we had made nostalgic trips to Peel Street and Ivry. Hughie wanted me because there was no one else. Linda knew as well as I did that he was not going to change his ways, but ultimately she viewed him as an unrepentant and wilful scoundrel, a monster, whereas I saw the sad creation of his parents, a man who had been rendered incapable of any generous emotion.

I had made up my mind that he would never hurt me again, but equally, I would never turn my back on him. I could understand my father, even if I couldn't forgive him. In his final years, we could begin to joke about our old relationship, perhaps uncomfortably. I would teasingly call him 'Daddykins' – he had never been a 'Daddykins' to me – and Christina Sharples would have no idea why we both laughed so heartily.

When Hughie's condition deteriorated further, he called me back from Canada. For the first and not the last time, Lynne and I postponed our wedding, but I didn't take her with me to England. I was still afraid to let her see the reality of my 'other world'. I was still protecting her. Before I left, I made sure that my presence was genuinely wanted, and that I would not be involved in any personal issues between Hughie and Christina. Both gave their solemn reassurances, and I flew to London to be at his side.

Father was not going to pull through. He was staying in the Royal Marsden, the cancer hospital in the Fulham Road – a place he had lived in dread of ever entering, having visited his friend, comedian and actor Michael Bentine, while he was there dying of prostate cancer.

I arrived on April 23, 1997 and hurried straight to the hospital. Christina was agitated, and told me that I would have to wait for a little while before seeing him since he had some 'private business' to sort out. I would discover later that on that date, in his hospital bed, on morphine, he signed a new will.

Linda wanted to make her peace with Hughie before he died. She visited the Royal Marsden and sat in a small lounge about twenty feet away from his private ward, but he adamantly refused to see her. I had to tell Linda, and I felt both sorry for her and proud of her. It had never been easy between them.

Later, her youngest daughter Marina wrote to Hughie, protesting at his treatment of Linda and imploring him to see her. He was furious, describing Marina's touching letter as 'disgusting and disrespectful'.

Equally astonishing was the survival of Father's triangle, which he was directing as sneakily as ever. June had certain visiting hours, while Christina's were at other times. One night, something went wrong with his traffic control: June rang his room while Christina and I were there. Christina answered, Father took the phone and he handed it to me. June, upset, said, 'Oh, so you are with *them*.'

Father's treatment had been ineffective, but Christina and I agreed with the doctors not to tell him he was about to die. He wanted to go home to Chiltern Court, and we told him that since his treatment had not 'fully reduced' the tumour, he could stay at 169 for a couple of weeks and would then be readmitted to the hospital for stronger treatment.

He wanted only one companion at the flat, and that was me. I wasn't thrilled to hear this, since 169 was not a 'controlled environment' and if things were to deteriorate during that May Bank Holiday period, there were no doctors, nurses or procedures at hand to save the day. Father was adamant, however, that it should be the two of us alone, and I could not find it in myself to refuse him.

We went into the living room. He looked out across Baker Street and asked me to get him a German beer. I was turning to go and fetch it when he called my name. He stared at me with an almost confused look on his face, and then continued in a flat monotone, 'I've had a wonderful life.' There was an aching pause. He added, 'Haven't I?' Another chilling silence. I asked, 'Time for the lager?'

I felt a lump in my throat and I consciously wished him the mercy of death as I set off down the corridor on my errand. Whatever was going through his mind seemed far more agonising than his physical pain. Do we not all fear that in our parting moment, we might regret what our life has been? My father did not have a wonderful life. There had been no miraculous interventions along the way.

That evening, he sat up in bed to watch the General Election returns on TV. Around 2 a.m., I went into his room to give him his latest medications. His light was on, and he had moved himself from the bed to the chair beside it. He wanted to talk. I sat on the bed while he spoke at length of Yvonne Marsh. Yet again, he told me how he had wrecked it with her, that he regretted it and that he loved her.

He turned to Gwen Claremont, who had committed suicide, 'Oh, God, the death she had. And if they had found her letter to me in her flat, I would've been ruined.' He added, 'I wonder if she is still angry at me?'

That led directly to June Laverick. He said he was terrified that June might do what Gwen had done. He cared deeply for her. As the monologue wandered on, he was visibly tiring. I asked if there was anything he wanted to tell me.

'No,' he replied. 'I know what you mean, old son, I do understand, and I have taken care of everything.' I wasn't satisfied. I had expected that he might talk to me directly, for the first time, about my half-brother Barry Hands, or about 'my' love child in Switzerland who was actually his, or about Claire, or about the Major and the 'silly thing' that he did, or about his sorrow for all the family happiness that could have been.

I pressed on, 'Papa, please tell me, are there any surprises ahead that I should know about?'

'Chris, I *assure* you that there will be no surprises. I have taken care of it *all*.'

I believed him then, and I still believe now that he thought he had tied up his loose ends.

Noel Botham has stated, on the record, that Hughie never intended to tell Paula he was her father, since he believed that it was her mother's place alone to do so, if she saw fit. After 38 years, Father knew that Elaine was not going to blow the whistle. However, he was wrongly convinced that Botham would keep the secret too.

I stood up to leave his room, but he asked me to sit down again. 'You are a good boy,' he said, and then, with a gentle wave of his hand, dismissed me. Only hours later, around 7 a.m. on the morning of May 2, I heard Father calling for me. I went running into his bedroom, and knew immediately that the worst was happening. I called Graham Rogers, my emergency contact at the Marsden, and told him that Father was haemorrhaging but still alive, and I needed help. I then phoned Christina and told her to hurry to 169.

We sped across London in the ambulance, with its siren blaring and blue light flashing. Christina was sitting in the front; I was in a seat across from Papa's stretcher bed. As we approached the hospital, he said to me, 'Chris, tell that wonderful lad who is driving that he could have taken a shorter route.' He had been able to see where we were going through a side window reflected in a mirror above my head. His body had failed him, but his mind remained clear to the end.

Linda had already made plans to go to Austria with Rainer, whose own father was unwell. Mindful of what had happened on her previous visit to the Royal Marsden, she decided not to come to Father, so Christina and I took shifts as we kept up a continuous death watch.

It was family history repeating itself. On May 17, 1973, I had driven from my Grandfather Wilson's bedside in the Montreal General Hospital to my Mama's apartment, a few minutes away on Drummond Street, to tell her that her father was dying and that

I would take her to see him. She chose not to accompany me back to the hospital; Grandpa Wilson died an hour later. Linda, for reasons that I fully respect, made her painful decision to be in Austria when Father died. I felt sad that, once again, it fell to me to be the 'messenger'.

On Saturday, May 3, 1997, I arrived at the hospital at dawn, and I could see that Father was dying. Somewhere just before 8 a.m., I stepped out of his private room, and a nurse asked if I wanted anything. I asked for a coffee.

There was an open window exactly opposite Papa's door. Two pigeons flew onto the inner sill, and settled there. One hopped down onto the floor and walked straight into his room. I looked in. The bird was strutting around on the floor beside Papa's bed, unruffled by my presence. Then it flapped its wings, up onto the bed. I told the nurse, returning with my coffee, 'There is a pigeon in my father's room.' We both started to laugh. Surprised, she said, 'They sometimes come onto the windowsill, but they never come inside.'

We shooed the bird out of the window, along with its mate, who had stayed on the windowsill. Sipping my coffee in a side room, I suddenly knew that Papa had gone. Two nurses led me into his room, and, indeed, he had flown away. I had no doubt that with the appearance of the pigeon, the Major had come for his boy.

Hughie died from internal bleeding, resulting from cancer, at the age of 77. We called the Associated Press to announce that Hughie had passed away, and by noon, it was all over the media. Back at the flat, the phones were ringing off the hook.

That night, alone in 169, I became a child again. I could not shut my eyes for fear that the front door would open and Father would come in drunk, and I would hear Mama's voice, and Linda would join me in my darkened room, and we would cower under the blanket all over again. Exhausted but sleepless, I walked into my parents' room, stood in the darkness facing their bed, and asked them just one thing: 'Why?' In tears, I sat in the kitchen, waiting for the night to pass.

I knew that to get through what was ahead, I could no longer stay on in Chiltern Court. I would check into the Sherlock Holmes

Hotel, only returning to 169 for a couple of brief, administrative visits. After 47 years, I would be the last Green physically to walk out of the door, but in my head, I still cannot believe I have left for good.

The night after Father's death, I took Christina for dinner at the Hilton Hotel restaurant, Trader Vic's. There, she gave me a copy of Father's will. I put it in my suit pocket to read later that night in my hotel room.

Studying it carefully, I realised that it was a deathbed will, and that unsettled me. It was the first sign that things were going to get complicated – to put it mildly. Hughie's death would unleash unimaginable waves of ghastly behaviour over the following days, as Christina tried to seize control of the funeral. I would become the reluctant traffic controller, struggling to keep Hughie's lady friends apart, and Noel Botham would shock the entire nation as he stood over my father's coffin and delivered a eulogy scripted in hell.

It was only a matter of days before it would all hit the fan. For me, for Linda, and for the unsuspecting Paula Yates, nothing would ever be the same again.

12

Hughie's Love Child: The Secret Explodes

Christina sat in Father's old chair in 169, only 48 hours after he died, and put her feet up on the coffee table. With that single gesture, she was showing me that she had taken charge. She would never have taken 'his chair' or put her feet anywhere near the table if he had been there.

We were meeting with Roy Phillips, her co-executor of Father's will, to discuss his bequests and to talk about the funeral. Hughie had been very impressed with the way that Michael Bentine's son had handled his arrangements. A private, family funeral was followed later by a public commemorative service. My wish was to replicate that. Christina was outraged. She wanted one big, public event befitting an icon of British television.

I had just met Roy for the first time; he backed Christina, stating that two services would be more expensive. I was shot down on both sides. Flipping through the coffin catalogues, Christina picked out her favourite. It was the same as her husband's. My preference was for a darker and more conservative coffin. The funeral directors from L J Butler & Son of Kenton, Harrow, were present by now and, showing me respect as the dead man's son, remarked that my choice was appropriate. So I won that round, but there was tension in the air. Christina wanted this to be *her* funeral, she wanted it to be just like her husband Bob's, and only begrudgingly was I being asked for my input.

We clashed again over the choice of music. Christina wanted the congregation to exit to the strains of Frank Sinatra's 'My Way', because it had sounded 'so beautiful' at Bob's funeral. My father didn't like Sinatra and, specifically, he loathed that song. I was not going to have it playing as we were leaving the chapel. I was also tiring of hearing about Bob's ceremony and, for the first time that morning, lost my temper. I said, 'Christina, we have buried Bob. This is Hughie's funeral. The exiting music is going be something dignified, by Elgar.' Roy supported me.

Christina then announced that it was time for the executors to open the safety deposit box in my parents' bedroom. I started to follow but was asked to leave the room. I doubt that Father would have let Christina dismiss me from that or any other room in 169, but he was no longer in charge, and Christina was. I felt violated.

Christina and I had been through a lot together over the years, and we had enjoyed some fun times, but her attitude was changing. It didn't seem to matter to her that the dead man was my father. I felt that my fifty years of being his son had given me moral rights that no piece of paper could ever confer upon her. At the same time, I believed that Roy Phillips was a decent and honourable fellow. He was loyal to Christina, but did not let that compromise his sense of fair play.

Linda and I were not expecting to inherit anything, but we were surprised. I was bequeathed £10,000, Father's cigar box, his cameras and his trains, although not the wretched Marklin set which still looms large in my nightmares. He also left me expenses money, with explicit instructions that I had to scatter his ashes – half on the Firth of Clyde in Scotland and the remainder with the Major's, on Mount Royal in Montreal.

Scotland was Father's heritage. The family tradition was built upon the Clyde, and as a young lad, he had watched the ocean liners that he loved being built there. It was, he said, 'the river that leads to the ends of the earth'. Later, he regularly sailed Scottish waters on the *Enalios*. He loved it there.

His will gave Linda £2,500, plus the first choice of any two paintings in his flat.

Father left Yvonne Oldknow (Marsh) 'with all of my love, the sum of £2,000'. He also allocated £500 to the RAF, and 'to my best friend Captain A P Teulon, £200 for a good drink'.

Mrs Agnes Carr's daughter, Margaret Pow, received £500, while Pam Jagger and Louise Ogilvie – a beautiful, blonde, American girlfriend who runs her own inn in the States – were invited to pick a painting each and 'Uncle' Vic Hallums was thanked for his unfailing friendship with £100.

Christina Sharples received £5,000 for a holiday and the full, worldwide rights of several TV shows including *Double Your Money*, plus all of Father's stocks, shares and bonds – 'as an acknowledgement of the love, care and devotion Christina has shown me'.

He left June Laverick fifty per cent of the cash realised from the sale of his assets, with Linda and I picking up ten per cent each and Pam Jagger and Christina Sharples sharing the remaining thirty per cent.

The net value of Father's estate came to £276,182 – and eighty per cent of that came from the sale of 169. His last car was a second-hand Honda. It was not a lot to show for a man who had once enjoyed fabulous wealth.

Notably, Yvonne Marsh, the first person mentioned in the will, was the only one for whom Hughie recorded his love. With Christina, he was recognising *her* 'love, care and devotion' – although, gripped by her hatred for June Laverick, Christina seemed annoyed only about the extent of June's inheritance. June was embarrassed by it and immediately said she couldn't possibly accept so much. But Father had taken far more from her than he had ever given back, and Linda and I insisted that she keep every penny.

John Heyman, Papa's former manager, found it quite hilarious that he had been left the worldwide rights to *Opportunity Knocks*. He already owned them, having paid Father for them in monthly instalments.

Christina made a point of telling me that my inheritance of £10,000 was intended as a sweetener, a persuasion to scatter

Papa's ashes as requested. In effect, he was paying me for doing a job which I would unquestioningly have done anyway, and that revolted me.

Father had known I would be unhappy if he did not also include Linda in the will, but he clearly didn't foresee my anger that her inheritance was so much smaller than mine. I offered to split the difference with her but, magnanimously, she wouldn't hear of it, knowing how much I'd spent flying back and forth between Montreal and London.

Another upset was that Linda and I were to receive ten per cent each from the sale of 169, while Pam and Christina had been allocated fifteen per cent; this placed us lower in the pecking order. As Linda rightly said, 'Neither Pam nor Christina had to suffer in that bloody flat, and he dignified neither with an offer of marriage, but he put them both above us.' Had Papa not had such a strong desire for me to spread his ashes, I doubt that Linda and I would have been in his will at all.

I told Christina and Roy Phillips how unhappy I was that Father had signed the will in the Marsden, only days before he died. It was not a flattering document for Linda and me; I think we would both have preferred not to have been included at all. I expressed my views without hostility or innuendo, and I never disputed my father's right to do what he wished with his money, but it was obvious that Christina still didn't like what I was saying. She, unlike June, could not feel my hurt.

The stars were paying tribute. Bruce Forsyth said, 'Hughie will be a great loss to our business. He was a pioneer.' Bernard Manning commented, 'Hughie gave a chance to a lot of people.' Bonnie Langford, one of his *Opportunity Knocks* discoveries, remarked, 'I will always have very fond memories of him . . . we used to call him Uncle Hughie.'

Another of Hughie's discoveries, comic Eddie Large, offered, 'His was the perfect talent show – and I mean that most sincerely!' And comedian Frank Carson, also a graduate of *Opportunity Knocks*, said, 'Hughie was one of the all-time greats, the ultimate professional.'

Comedian Tom O'Connor, yet another protégé, stated, 'The way he presented the acts on television has never been done since and the ones that followed have been pale shadows.'

Nigel Griffiths, Labour MP for Edinburgh South, remembered Hughie as 'a gentleman of the old school . . . a model of manners, a fantastic storyteller and mimic.'

Secretary Liz Turner later gave a somewhat rounder view of her ex-boss: 'He was a relaxed, suntanned, warm and friendly man, a man who won the hearts of millions of viewers and entertained them week after week with consistent professionalism, enthusiasm and stamina, an enigmatic man, a cross, rude, angry man, a sad, vulnerable, lost and sometimes, I am sure, lonely man, a man I admired, respected and miss.'

Liz still recalls how panicked he became when he had to do anything practical for himself, like crossing London, or buying an *A To Z*, and she has pinpointed the moment when he ceased to terrify her: 'One time I had to go down to his car with him in the NCP underground car park on Marylebone Road. When we got there, he said his braces had come undone and could I do them up for him. He was quite embarrassed. I had to put my hand inside his enormous wool coat and hunt for the offending braces. I felt the warmth of his body and, strangely, I can still feel that warmth. I thought of him after that, for some reason, completely differently. He was sometimes difficult but he became an ordinary man who needed other people really quite a lot. Such a small, personal gesture had brought him down to earth, to my level. I didn't have to feel intimidated by him any more.'

Bob Monkhouse, by contrast, allowed for no shades of character when he brutally dismissed Father in the year after his death as 'a giant haemorrhoid', adding, 'Hughie was awful, a tyrant. I think he knew he had minimal talent and that his entire fame was built upon a very, very fragile structure.' He never understood Hughie's appeal and his genuine rapport with his audiences. Indeed, when Monkhouse took over *Opportunity Knocks*, I think he tried to make himself the star instead of the contestants, and, as a result, in my view, destroyed the very essence of its success.

Linda, of course, immortalised our father in the press as a 'monster', a term I abhorred, but it became a standard reference in his future newspaper coverage.

Hughie was not always the 'model of manners' remembered by Nigel Griffiths. When Christina and I went to see Father Peter Harding about Father's funeral service, he asked abruptly, 'Christopher, was your father a nice man?' I said, 'No, Father, it would not be honest for me to describe my father as a particularly "nice man", but I cared for him.' Christina retorted, stridently, 'Hughie was a wonderful, kind and generous man.'

Father Peter, of St Cyprian's Church, near Baker Street, was about fifty, short, slight, and with kind, twinkling eyes, but his manner of questioning was agitated, disjointed and slightly alarming. I would later discover the reason for this. Although he did not say so at the time, he had met Hughie several years earlier when he opened the church's Christmas bazaar. Arriving, Father was clearly the worse for drink, his opening address bristled with homophobic jibes, and his sly references to the ladies at the stalls, selling their pickles and jams and knitwear, were horribly inappropriate. Father Peter told me later that he had not seen the wonderful, generous person whom Christina described to him in May 1997.

The ladies were fishing. They wanted to find out how much I knew about their relationships with Hughie, and they were all obviously anxious about anything connected to them which might be found in 169.

Pam Jagger rang me several times. I already knew from Hughie that she had been one of his lovers, but I spared her feelings and didn't admit this. Yvonne Marsh also phoned in a dither. She was incensed to hear that the 'dreadful' Noel Botham was to speak at the funeral, and she threatened to boycott it, although she relented in the end – and she would see her opinion of Botham vindicated.

Linda and Rainer arrived back from Austria on May 7, 1997. Rainer commented on everything I'd had to deal with, saying that I had done a good job, but Linda was only concerned with funeral details. She didn't want Christina sitting near us or sharing our limousine, and she insisted that only family flowers should be permitted. I was to 'take care of Christina' and, at the same time, 'keep her away from June'. Despite the unhappiness of her final experience with Father, Linda was furious that Christina had taken charge of the funeral, and wanted us to make our presence felt. Yet this simply heaped more pressure on me.

The next day, we travelled miles in a taxi to see Father in his coffin at the funeral home in Harrow. He was in a small, starkly furnished room, and Linda, looking down on him, said, 'If only I could cry and be sorry, but I'm not. He hurt Mummy so much and he hurt so many other people too.' I prayed that Linda would now find some closure. Turning to leave, she looked around that tiny room and sighed, without bitterness, 'And to think this is where the great Hughie Green came to be in his coffin.'

That night – the eve of the funeral – I had expected to have an early dinner with Christina and a discussion of the final arrangements. Instead, she went to see Noel Botham to go through his eulogy. There was no place for me at their meeting.

Friday, May 9, 1997. The service started at 4 p.m. in Golders Green Crematorium, Hoop Lane. The chapel was crammed, and there were photographers hanging off the walls. Father's coffin was placed upon the catafalque and Psalm Thirteen – my choice – was read out. It was then time for Mr Noel Botham to give a eulogy, entitled 'An Appreciation of the Life of Hughie Green'.

His name was called, but a few seconds passed before Father Peter realised that the first speaker had not arrived. He was forced to 'fill in' with a spontaneous address. He began, 'Many people find church graveyards to be spooky,' explaining that this was not necessary since they contain only mortal remains and not the all-important souls. Someone in the congregation objected vocally, and there followed some headlines that were unjust and hurtful: 'Vicar Says Churchyards Are Spooky At Hughie Green's Funeral'.

Father Peter says he can still hear the sound of the door opening at the rear of the chapel and Noel Botham, a very large man, bustling in and through to the pulpit. It was my first-ever glimpse of Botham, who was visibly nervous and sweating. He kept wiping the beads of perspiration from his forehead with a big, chubby hand.

With apologies for 'not having Hughie's immense talents for public speaking', he launched into one of Father's most homophobic stories, about a male housekeeper he had once hired. Botham mimicked Hughie's mincing impersonation of the unfortunate employee, whose departure led to the recruitment of Mrs Carr. But it can't have been nice for Father Peter, who was and still is in a committed, gay relationship.

Botham fixed his gaze upon Christina, who was sitting immediately behind me, and he praised her extravagantly, especially for the 'love, care and devotion' that she had lavished on Hughie. I could hear her coos of delight; Noel had clearly charmed Christina into inviting him to speak in the first place. He then declared himself to be Hughie's best friend, but stopped, wiped his brow again, and corrected himself, 'No, second-best friend.'

Botham continued with the story of how Mrs Carr was hired, interviewing Father about his suitability as an employer rather than the other way round, and how Hughie had treasured her attitude, spirit and shared love for the *Enalios*. I sat up again as Botham wrongly informed the mourners that Father had been excluded from the RAF's 'gentleman's club' in 1939 and had had to go to Canada to get into the war with the RCAF.

Then he remembered Hughie as 'a character'. He was a 'right-wing person' like Noel himself, and was one of the last free-thinking, free-drinking, red-blooded 'real men' with guts. All very macho stuff . . . and he was building to his climax.

'Hughie was accused of having secret affairs with female contestants [on his quiz shows],' said Botham. 'But he didn't need to because he had four very capable mistresses on the go, and a couple more on the side. Hughie knew I was going to say this, and we both laughed about it.'

Botham then announced to the already disbelieving congregation that Hughie had a secret daughter who was a British television celebrity. He added, 'I don't know if this girl even knows that Hughie is her dad, but he used to see her on the TV or in the newspapers and say, "That daughter of mine again".'

I wanted to stand up and scream, 'Enough!' But my knees were quivering. Had I imagined what he had just said? I was confused, numb. I squeezed Linda's arm and she was shaking. I heard people gasping and walking out. Father Peter moved towards Linda and me, and tried to recover the situation by urging quiet for a prayer. But before we could leave that brutally surreal place, we had to endure a hymn, another eulogy from Nigel Griffiths MP and the rest of the standard service.

At last it was over. I strode to the back door behind the altar, looking straight ahead, and as we walked out of the chapel to the accompaniment of 'Nimrod' from Elgar's *Enigma Variations*, my only conscious thought was, 'Thank God, after this black farce, that it isn't Frank Sinatra wailing, "I did it my way . . ."'

I had travelled to Golders Green, directly behind the hearse, in a limousine with Christina, Roy Phillips, 'Uncle' Vic Hallums and his wife, Linda. Following were my sister Linda, her husband Rainer and my four nieces, Delia, Christina, Stephanie and Marina. I wasn't really giving Christina Sharples anything special by inviting her to ride in the first car; I was, rather, being practical by keeping her apart from my sister. And I walked into the chapel with Christina on my arm because unlike the two Lindas, she had no one to accompany her, and I was nothing if not a gentleman – even though she had hurt and angered me in the days leading up to the funeral.

But now I felt that Christina had also betrayed me, along with Noel Botham, so I did not want to sit in a car with her again. Even Father Peter seemed to have realised that they may have been in collusion. Back in the cordoned-off parking lot, away from the throng of press and spectators, I saw two old family friends – Pat Neatrour and her daughter Adele. They drove me to the reception, and they confirmed everything I thought I had seen and heard. I felt sick.

We arrived at the Landmark Hotel in Marylebone Road before most of the guests, who had been buttonholed by the press outside the chapel. A distinguished RAF man standing outside the door of the reception room approached me, saying, 'You must be

Hughie's son – you look very much like him. I am so sorry for what happened. Your father really did not deserve that.'

I looked into the room and in the far, left-hand corner, standing arm-in-arm, holding glasses of wine, laughing and talking animatedly together were Christina Sharples and Noel Botham. I strode towards the gruesome couple, charged with emotion. 'Mr Botham,' I began. 'You have trashed my father's funeral. That was not the time nor the place to say what you said. So may I know who my alleged illegitimate sister is?'

Botham looked at me with a sarcastic smile on his pudgy face, and responded, 'Well, I can see that you don't have your father's fine sense of humour. If he didn't tell you, then why should I?' I raised my voice and screamed at him, 'Get out . . . leave now!' I was within a split second of punching the hateful, leering face that was looking down on me as though I were a piece of dog shit on the pavement.

Christina grabbed my left arm and kept wrenching it as she screamed repeatedly, 'How dare you talk to Noel like that! You apologise immediately!' In a flash, I saw 'Uncle' Vic rushing across the room towards me, saying 'Chris, don't do it,' and that saved me. For the first and last time in my life, I was about to hit a woman.

My sister was wonderful. She controlled her rage and backed me up with an almost superhuman strength and dignity in the face of Botham and then Royston Mayo, an *Opportunity Knocks* director who had dared to try to defend Christina.

Christina left on Botham's arm, but having seen him out to the street, she came back. I immediately demanded, 'Why did you do this?' She replied, viciously, 'Everybody knows [about the love child]. And that's show business!'

I couldn't understand it. I had never caused trouble for Christina, believing we had a friendship of sorts that would continue after Father's death. Even after the hateful day of the funeral, I kept hoping she'd pick up the phone and apologise for her part in what had happened, although she never did.

Contrary to what she said to me at the reception, no living person, I'm convinced, had known about Father's celebrity love child other than Paula's mother, Elaine, and Noel Botham. Christina had only found out from Botham the night before, although she would have died rather than admit it, since her whole *raison d'être* was to be feted as Hughie's Number One lady and chief confidante.

Botham would certainly have been far too smart to divulge Paula's identity to Christina even then. He may have told her that the unnamed child was actually an 'open secret', so that she would approve his eulogy in the naïve belief that others in Hughie's inner circle did know. Christina, Father's 'greatest confidante', would have been desperate to convey that she, of course, 'knew all about it' too.

I'm convinced that Botham flattered Christina as successfully as he had Anita Kay, Jess Yates's young lover, in pursuit of valuable information. Christina was not only the funeral organiser but an executor of Hughie's will, and it was vital for Noel to verify that Elaine – and particularly Paula – were not included in it.

That being the case, he could break an exclusive and explosive story in his eulogy, knowing that the press were present. And he could afford to sit it out while a tabloid war raged around him, bidding ever increasing sums of money for the name of the celebrity. If either Elaine or Paula had received an inheritance, Botham would have had to release the story earlier because others reading the will might have beaten him to it. I challenged Christina via Roy Phillips on this very point, and both vehemently denied that they had shown Father's will to Noel Botham.

The tide of popular opinion was already starting to turn against Christina at the reception. Morna – the daughter of the Major's influential pal Colonel Charles MacLean, and Hughie's lifelong friend – was there with her son Charles Cochand, reassuring me that I had done the right thing by ejecting Botham.

A close friend of Christina's approached me with her daughter, who asked outright, 'Chris, did you know anything about your father having a love child?' I simply said no. She then remarked to Christina, accusingly, 'You said that you and everyone else knew about this, but you didn't tell Christopher.' To her mother's nodded encouragement and Christina's dismay, she concluded, 'Well, in that case, I'm firmly on Christopher's side.'

Then it hit me – there were sides. The bullshit hadn't ended; it was just beginning. 'Camps' came into my life at that moment, and soon I would be thrown into or up against 'Christina's camp', 'Paula's camp', 'Bob Geldof's camp' and any number of other camps. Before it was all over, my 'celebrity half-sister' would be dead, and one of her closest friends would be telling me that discovering Hughie Green was her father was a 'body blow from which she could not recover'.

After basking in the glow of being publicly 'in the know' about the existence of a love child, Christina Sharples, realising she had backed the wrong horse, began back-pedalling frantically. On May 10 and 11, she was said by the *Sun* and the *News of the World* respectively to have backed Botham's allegations. The *News of the World* reported, 'Christina Sharples . . . supported the claim and said the star had confided in other close friends too.' On the same day, however, she was quoted in the *Sunday Mirror* as saying that Botham had 'hijacked' and ruined the service. By May 12, she had completely changed her tune about the daughter, who had by then been named, telling that day's *Express*, 'These are wild allegations made by someone who didn't know Hughie very well.' And on May 13, the *Daily Star* had her stating firmly, 'If Hughie had a love child, I'd have known.' A remarkable turn-around.

John Heyman, Father's former manager, had flown in on Concorde for the funeral, but he couldn't face the reception. Likewise, Yvonne Marsh turned out for the service, but had no stomach for any form of wake. June Laverick was too distraught to attend either occasion.

But once the true horror of the day's events became public, I was inundated with calls from many long-time friends, colleagues and lovers of Hughie, mostly all conveying their sympathy and support. Some remembered his infinite variety, one minute telling corny jokes on TV and the next, giving forth on the state of education in Britain to the Variety Club at the Savoy Hotel.

Hughie and Mrs Carr: soulmates and seafaring companions. Papa's Christmas cards would often say, 'Spending Xmas Day at sea on the Enalios with Mrs Carr — we will be celebrating the 25th with a wonderful piece of Scottish beef.' He was really a very complex and lonely man.

Hughie with his respected and beloved audience.

Hughie with his 'Opportunity Knocks' discoveries. Front row (left to right): Freddie 'Parrot Face' Davies, Lena Zavaroni, Papa, Mary Hopkin and Les Dawson. Standing to the right is father's great friend and orchestra leader, Christina's husband, Bob Sharples. Also pictured are Peters and Lee (top two on left) and Frank Carson (behind Father).

*Defeated, bitter and on the verge of fury: Hughie on the last 'Opportunity Knocks'
show. Papa believed that 'the intellectuals' had conspired to separate him from his
revered 'little people', his audiences. His curtain had finally come down and he would
never work again in the television media he had pioneered.*

ABOVE *A family affair: Hughie with (left to right): Marina, me, Christina, Delia and Linda. My sister's fourth daughter, Stephanie, was also present at the Hurlingham Club, but not pictured.* **BELOW LEFT** *Linda and I to the left and Christina Sharples and Papa to the right at the Hurlingham Club. Naïveté perhaps, but I enjoyed this photo as a reflection of some new-found unity until father's funeral came along and the cat was thrown cruelly amongst the pigeons yet again.* **BELOW RIGHT** *Papa was so proud of having been granted an audience with Prince Philip, another keen aviator, to present him with a copy of Carl Christie's book 'The History Of RAF Ferry Command'. He would die hoping that Prince Edward might see fit to make a TV documentary mini-series based on this glorious Commonwealth saga.*

Paula with her co-presenter Jools Holland in a promo shot from 'The Tube'.

Me and Linda with Paula.

ABOVE *Bob Geldof.* **BELOW** *Michael Hutchence (sitting).*

One person who wrote to me, indignantly, was father's old *Gang Show* friend Joey Hopkinson. He said, 'I can't tell you how shocked I was at that creep telling all that at the funeral. If you believe that, you'll believe pigs can fly . . . If that was true, I most certainly would have known about it. He [Hughie] always confided in me.'

Hughie hadn't been in regular touch with Joey for decades, and no matter how well-intentioned his letter, Joey, like most people in Hughie's life, knew nothing about him. Even those closest to him, Vic Hallums, for instance, or Christina, knew only what he wanted them to know, and that was very little.

Certain reactions to the funeral speech were more enlightening than others. One of Hughie's former ladies – who has been, and shall remain nameless in this book – was quick to reassure me that if there was a love child, then she was not the mother. Indeed, she had terminated a pregnancy by him many years earlier. I did not tell her that I already knew. Father had been rabid with anger when he learnt about it. He thundered to me, 'She killed my child!' which might have sounded somewhat incongruous: he wasn't the world's best advertisement for protected sex, he disliked children and he saw abortion as a matter of personal choice, but he vigorously opposed such a course of action in his own private life. This stemmed, of course, from knowing that his own mother had tried to abort him.

Some of the callers implied vaguely that they had known about Hughie's unidentified 'love child', although their woolly tittle-tattle carried no ring of credibility. Certainly, none knew her name. They were groupies one and all, anxious to be seen to have been in Papa's 'in-crowd' and party to his most intimate business.

Father was by nature too secretive, too clever, to reveal such a personal matter to anyone. He had confided in my mother, Claire, because he had wanted to make a fresh start with her – which had backfired irretrievably. And it's my firm belief that he blurted it out to Noel Botham on one of their sailing trips on the *Enalios* during some alcohol-fuelled conversation about Botham's newspaper exposure of 'the actress and the Bishop' Jess Yates – the man Paula believed to be her father.

Sober, Father would never have made such a potentially ruinous disclosure about himself to a high-profile tabloid journalist like Noel Botham, whose living depended on such inside knowledge and who was later described by a colleague as 'a classic *News of the World* operator'. I am certain that Papa kicked his own ass many times afterwards. It was the biggest mistake of his life.

Botham had claimed at the funeral, 'Hughie knew I was going to say this, and we both laughed about it.' Yet, he had asserted on separate occasions that, in Hughie's view, the only person with the right to tell Paula about her parentage was Elaine, her mother. Botham also, allegedly, went on to claim that Father jovially encouraged him by saying, 'That will put a few quid in your pocket.'

Later still and feeling the heat, Botham seemed to shift his ground, suggesting that Hughie had not actually agreed for the disclosure to be made at his funeral. They had, however, clinked a glass to the idea that Father would eventually go out in a blaze of front-page headlines, courtesy of this precious information. Botham, therefore, was only keeping his word.

Having sat with my father during his last days, I can categorically say that he was not amused or excited about any aspect of his impending death, and he would not have relished his lifelong fear – of being thought a 'peep-show freak on the pier' – becoming a reality at his own funeral. To imagine Papa sitting with anyone shortly before his demise, 'having a good laugh' about his mistresses and love children being exposed within hours of his departure, is not only fanciful, but is also quite absurd. He would have been appalled, too, at the idea of his beloved 'little people' having any reason to think badly of him.

Looking into the abyss, he wanted only to be remembered as a television pioneer and a wonderful aviator. Indeed, he had been invited to Buckingham Palace a couple of years earlier for an audience with Prince Philip, another keen aviator. He had presented the Prince with a book called *Ocean Bridge: The History of RAF Ferry Command*, a serious, historical work by the Canadian Carl A Christie, tracing the growth of aviation as a result of the Second World War. Only days before he died, Father was sitting up in the Royal Marsden Hospital working on a TV documentary adaptation of Christie's book, hoping to persuade Prince Edward to use it as the basis for a documentary mini series. These were certainly not the actions of a man who wished his epitaph to be a dirty snigger and an insulting exposure of the daughter he had sired almost forty years earlier.

Christina, meanwhile, had changed the locks of 169 two days after Hughie died and hadn't given me a key. I had promised Linda that we would spend some private time in the flat, selecting personal, family items to keep. After the funeral, my goodwill with Christina was ruined, and Linda and I never did get to enter the flat again. Christina later gave a pile of personal, Green family documents to the British Film Institute, and I have only recently managed to recover them. It's a matter of great regret to me, also, that I didn't have the chance to take ownership of Violet's hideous, blue Chinese vase and smash it to pieces, as I had dreamed of doing for so many years.

The next day's papers were in a frenzy over Noel Botham's allegations, and most gave it the front page. They were frantic to find out the identity of Hughie's celebrity love child. The tone of the coverage was generally favourable towards Father but, in some articles, grossly unfair to Father Peter Harding, the most decent of human beings. He had, they said, 'lost control of the funeral', and he later suffered a nervous breakdown.

Father Peter vigorously denies that he lost control at the funeral, and I agree. He did not know or choose the two people who were to speak, and he had no right to stop Botham's address unless the speaker was drunk and/or blasphemous. Furthermore, Father Peter saw no signs that Christina – the funeral organiser – was upset by the eulogy or was acting to prevent it continuing; quite the opposite.

Father Peter told me, 'My only thoughts then were for you and Linda. Linda's face was a mask of horror and you appeared to be frozen . . . I was totally shaken myself. I had never heard of such a eulogy ever having been given.'

Botham immediately set about building the suspense over the identity of Father's secret daughter, offering the *Sunday Mirror* nine clues – including one piece of disinformation which stated that 'her "father" is not and never has been a public figure'.

The remaining clues were that the daughter was 33 (in fact, Paula was 38) and looked like Hughie; she was often on the news, sometimes getting into 'spots of bother'; she was a personality, not a singer or actress; she was 'big in every way', and everyone who watched television would know her; she wasn't at the funeral although – almost impossibly – 'six other people who knew her identity' were; her mother was not in showbiz but her name was known to the public; her mother was married when Hughie fell for her; and the celebrity daughter was still alive.

To be the person to break a story of this sensational nature gave Botham's reputation in the tabloid world an enormous boost. And the sale price of the story skyrocketed as the various papers went into battle for the exclusive.

The morning after the funeral, I went to Mayfield to spend the day with Linda and Rainer. Everything was up in the air; we were holding our breath, waiting for the bomb to go off.

A young, good-looking freelance journalist was driving down from London to the channel coast that afternoon to see his girl-friend – so he claimed – and passing close to Mayfield, decided to try finding Linda's farmhouse in the hope of getting a story. We had nothing to add to what we had said at the Landmark Hotel the evening before, because we knew nothing. He left at around five o'clock, soon afterwards calling Linda from a phone box in a country road a couple of miles away, telling her that his car battery had gone flat and needed a boost. Linda and I drove to the spot to help him get restarted.

While we were there, he used the public phone to check in with his office in London. He came out looking nervous and said to Linda, 'I don't know if I should say anything, and I don't want to maybe upset you, but, well . . . there's a rumour going round Fleet Street that Paula Yates is your sister.'

Linda was flabbergasted. She said, 'She is Paula Yates?' He replied, 'Yes, Paula Yates.' Linda put her hands up to her face and moaned, 'Oh, no, I can't believe it . . . not Paula Yates!' And then they both started laughing. There, on this country lane, Linda and this journalist fellow were laughing fit to bust. Linda was almost hysterical. I broke the mood by asking, 'May I be let in on the joke? Who is Paula Yates?' I had never heard of her.

On that same morning, by some strange coincidence, Linda's daughter Delia had phoned and told her: 'I bet you the celebrity sister is Paula Yates.'

Extraordinarily, the journalist, who was on the spot at our very moment of discovery, did not take the opportunity to interview us, and he never wrote up the story. He was in the wrong business, that lad . . .

I didn't believe for a minute that Hughie was the father of the glamorous TV personality who was then briefly described to me. I was in denial. I made no further attempt to confront Noel Botham because I intended to prove him wrong. I did, however, phone Pam Jagger, who was party to more of Hughie's secrets than anybody else. She volunteered to me that Father had been providing for years for three illegitimate daughters, but they did not include Paula – she swore she had heard nothing about her. Pam also revealed that Hughie was 'very proud, but never boastful, about his sexual prowess,' which was irrelevant and more than I needed to know.

I was certain that if Paula were related to Papa, then Pam of all people would have known. His other close friends were equally insistent that they had known nothing about Paula or, indeed, any 'celebrity love child' – and this strengthened my resistance to the so-called scoop.

The next morning, Sunday May 11, the *News of the World* broke the story: 'I'm Secret Dad Of Paula Yates: Hughie Green's Shock Confession', with extensive quotes from Noel Botham, who was laughably described as 'Hughie's lifelong pal'.

Botham said that Father 'fell madly in love with Jess's wife', and added, 'Paula will have no idea about this. But it was his [Hughie's] wish that after he died, I should tell the world. As Hughie said, "It will put the cat among the pigeons."'

He also claimed to have seen Hughie about five weeks before his death: 'He had a drink with me and I said to him, "Are you ever going to tell Paula what you have told me? I'd love to break that story." Hughie said, "Well, you can do that after I'm gone."' Contradictorily, in the same feature, Botham quoted Father's determination that only Elaine had the right to tell Paula the truth about her paternity.

Father, five weeks before he died, was certainly not in any mood for jovial drinking sessions and jokes about Paula and his imminent death. But at least Botham did back down on his original statement that Papa had instructed him to say his piece at the funeral. Botham also alleged in the *News of the World* that Hughie had followed Paula's career with interest and when news of her exploits appeared in the tabloids, he would cluck, mock-sternly, 'That bloody daft daughter of mine again. Look what she's up to now. There are times I'd love to put her across my knee and spank her. Bring her to her senses.'

Father would never have thought or spoken so paternally. I couldn't ever imagine him saying anything to the effect that he would love to put Paula across his knee. On the other hand, I can believe Botham's assertion that Papa was disapproving of Bob Geldof. Botham said, 'Hughie's politics were very right-wing. He looked at Bob Geldof as being one of those long-haired lefties. He didn't like his manners, the bad language he used in public and on the television. He didn't approve of him as a father for his grand-children.' Botham further alleged that Hughie used to grumble, 'She could have done better than this for herself. She's a pretty girl.'

On the same day as the *News of the World* exclusive, the *Sunday Mirror* rather lamely ran with Botham's 'nine clues' to the identity of Hughie's daughter.

How the press found me at the Sherlock Holmes Hotel I have no idea, but they did. I called Linda, who said that she and Margaret, her driver, would come immediately to get me out of London. We had travelled as far as Selfridges when Linda received a call from Rainer in Mayfield on her first mobile phone. He told her, 'My love, they are here.' He was referring to the press. 'A couple of them are up a tree with a camera.'

Botham was safely installed in his Spanish villa by the time the story exploded all over the *News of the World*. He had earlier said of the mystery lady's name, 'No one and no amount of money will prise it from me.' Now, he was denying that he had divulged Paula's name to the *News of the World*, even though he was the only person quoted in the story, no other source was mentioned, and he had swaggered that Hughie had joked with him about earning a 'few quid' out of their secret. He later admitted on a TV chat show that he had pocketed a sum of money from Fleet Street, but refused to specify the amount. An experienced pressman, he nevertheless professed great surprise at the media's reaction to his funeral address.

One person who had not been too impressed with Botham's oratory was Paula Yates. Returning to the UK after a holiday in Bali with her lover Michael Hutchence and their daughter Tiger, she was engulfed by a scrum of photographers and she did not mince her words. Pictured in the *Daily Mirror* issue of May 16, Paula spat from under her sunglasses, 'My immediate reaction is to say it's all rubbish, be outraged on behalf of my dad [Jess] and thank God he isn't alive today to witness this. I can't believe someone would be wicked enough to stand up at a funeral and say these things.

'Can you imagine how upsetting it is to have things like this said about you? It's a disgusting thing for the person responsible to have done, so insulting. Right now, I don't know what to do. DNA testing has been mentioned, but until I know the legal position, I can't make a decision.'

I was quoted in the same article, vowing that Linda and I would give our blood for DNA testing and confessing that I felt 'desperately sorry' for Paula in this outrageous situation. Bob Geldof, Paula's ex-husband, was collared for a comment at her London home when he arrived to take their six-year-old daughter Pixie to school. He retorted, 'It's personal, and I don't comment on things that are personal.' My admiration for that was compounded by the discovery that he had taken out a court order preventing photographers and newspapers from invading the privacy of his three children by Paula: Fifi Trixibelle, Peaches and Pixie.

Paula's mother, Elaine, by now known as Hélène Thornton-Bosment, was at the same time in vigorous denial at her home in the south of France and, according to the same *Mirror* article, threatening to sue Noel Botham. 'It's an absolute lie and a very hurtful one,' she seethed. 'I don't know what motives lie behind this, but it was a terrible thing to say.'

Linda had been convinced from the outset that Father had, indeed, sired a megastar 'love child'. On the night of the funeral, she had told *The Times*, 'I would imagine it's true. Someone doesn't get up in a public place like that and make a statement of that sort without proper knowledge.'

Now, without any scientific proof, Linda was sure that Paula Yates was her sister, and, after her initial shock, she was thrilled. Her overwhelming joy and her desire for a true, family relationship with the dynamic TV personality and writer would lead to a crushing disappointment for her and a permanent estrangement from me, the younger brother who had only ever wanted his sister Linda's love.

13

In Cold Blood

As Margaret drove us along the country road approaching Linda's farmhouse, we saw crowds of reporters surrounding her driveway. We shielded our faces from the telephoto lenses that were trained on us from all directions. The press had no recent, adult photos of us, Hughie's children, and we did not intend to provide them with any. We had refused all such requests at the Landmark Hotel after the funeral.

Now that Paula had been identified, we were both aware that if the paparazzi were able to snap a clear, frontal picture of Linda, her face would appear in some tabloid the next day alongside Paula's with a caption asking the readers, 'Well, what do *you* think? Are they sisters?'

Linda was not sure if the allegations would have yet reached Paula Yates, as she was on holiday in Bali. She didn't wish Paula, on her return to England, to think that we had been involved in any exploitative way with the breaking story. While I was genuinely concerned for Paula, whoever she was, and was sorry that she was soon to be confronted with this controversy, my primary reason for dodging the photographers was to avoid helping Noel Botham or any other journalist from earning yet more column inches out of our situation.

As we finally broke through the throng and continued up the long drive to Linda's farmhouse, it occurred to me that we were having our fifteen minutes of fame, and it was fifteen minutes too many for me. We were overcome with confusion and paranoia.

We really didn't know what was going to happen next. Some reporters had already suggested – to our horror – that we had been in league with Botham at the funeral, plotting to make a ton of money. We were also wondering what Christina Sharples was doing. As the keyholder to 169, she had access to all the private and sensitive materials that had been left there.

Botham had gone to Spain, ostensibly to write a book. Would it be about Hughie Green? And if so, was Christina helping him? Would it be filled with more hateful revelations, or copies of family documents?

As it turned out, no book on Hughie was forthcoming from Botham. He did, however, go on to publish a sensational biography of Princess Margaret within weeks of her death in February 2002, complete with claims that she snorted cocaine in The Rolling Stones' dressing room. *Margaret, The Last Real Princess*, an updated version of his 1993 portrait, outraged the Princess's friends, who condemned Botham for his 'preposterous' allegations and his insensitivity.

Her son, Viscount Linley, was widely reported to have told friends that he intended to seek advice with a view to taking legal action. Although it is not possible to libel a dead person, other avenues were open to him in the courts, including civil action for alleged breach of confidence.

Linda was searching her house at Mayfield for magazines or newspapers containing pictures of Paula Yates, to compare herself to her alleged half-sister. I steadfastly refused to look at any photographs. I did not believe that Paula was related to us, and I was focused on disproving Botham's allegations. The sight of the press pack outside, staking out the house, did nothing to improve my feelings towards him.

It irritated me that Linda was so positive about Hughie fathering Paula. Her feelings about Papa were different from mine. She had not been with him in 169 for that last night when he had assured me emphatically that he had taken care of everything, a promise I had wholly believed. Linda, therefore, did not share my total denial or my all-consuming loathing for Botham.

But Linda was not consciously trying to annoy me; she was fully entitled to her feelings and her expression of them. We got along very well during this period, just as we always had in periods of adversity. And she went out of her way to help me through my other big worry, which was about Lynne.

We had already had to cancel one wedding date because of Father falling ill. The next scheduled date was coming up, and I had a sinking feeling in my heart that we would miss that one too. My insecurities from the past flooded back and I felt terrified, agitated, alone. Would Lynne, from her loving, middle-class, family background ever be able to understand any of this? Would she have second thoughts about my being stepfather to the three most precious people in her life, her daughters Kristin, Keely and Kady? Would I become some sort of dysfunctional idiot in her eyes?

I had not told Lynne anything about myself that could give her any insight into this unfolding mess. Linda and I had never been able to explain to anyone what it was like to be Hughie's children, and so we didn't try. Lynne, my lovely Lynne – how would she see me now? Would she think that this chaos was somehow *me*?

I saw everything out of proportion; I was exhausted in mind and body from the emotional backwash of all that had happened – Father's death, Botham's satanic eulogy, Christina's seeming betrayal, the newspapers now depicting Father as a sexual deviant, and a named 'love child'.

When Linda advised me that I should get on the phone to Lynne in Montreal and ask her to join me in England, I wasn't at all sure that it was a good idea. I hadn't realised that Linda, seeing my agony, had secretly called Lynne. She told Lynne, simply, that I needed her. Lynne was hurting too. She wanted to understand my plight, she felt helpless far away in Canada and she was anxious to be with me in my time of need, but she didn't intend to fly to England without hearing first, from me, that she was welcome.

In a tearful phone call to Lynne, I proffered the invitation, and we arranged her visit. I met her off her flight early in the morning of May 13, 1997 – four days after Father's funeral. On the same day, Noel Botham was telling viewers of a British daytime TV show that he was proud of what he had done for his old friend, Hughie. And although he was still asserting that he hadn't slipped her name to the *News of the World*, he said he would love to meet Paula Yates to tell her just what a rip-roaring son-of-a-gun her biological father had been.

A couple of days later, I picked up Father's ashes from the Golders Green Crematorium in Hoop Lane – the same road where the twelve-year-old Hughie had staged his first benefit concert for the Royal Northern Hospital. Several people – including a priest in Mayfield – suggested that I should 'flush the ashes down the loo after what Hughie did to you', but I disregarded this advice. Instead, I deposited them at St Cyprian's Church. There was a risk that the press would follow me to Scotland while I was trying to scatter them, so I decided to come back at a later date when the hullabaloo had subsided. Father Peter had been taken ill and was in retreat. I handed Hughie's earthly remains to Mark Graddon, Father Peter's life partner.

Lynne and I escaped to Cornwall for a couple of days, returning to Mayfield to challenge Father's will. Lynne, Linda and I turned out to be a great team at this time, compatible and supportive of one another. Linda and I were not questioning the will for our own benefit – indeed, Pam Jagger informed us that we had fared less well in the original document, which she had seen – but we wanted to reinstate June Laverick's entitlement, which we understood was Number 169 itself. We were unhappy at the fact that Papa had suddenly changed his will on his deathbed when his mind could have been clouded by morphine. We had a 'caveat' put upon the will to prevent it from going to probate until we could do a little fact-finding.

In the end, we were advised that taking out litigation to overturn the will would be a long and costly procedure, without any guarantee of a successful outcome. And so we removed the caveat, consoled by the knowledge that June had inherited some if not all of what Father had said he intended her to have. Still, it was disconcerting to see his scrawled signature on the document, written while he was desperately ill and only days away from death.

Having now done everything I needed to do in England for the time being, I flew back to Montreal with Lynne. Halfway across the North Atlantic, she asked me, 'Do you know what day this is?' I replied, 'Yes, our second missed wedding day.' I then asked her, 'Lynne, are you sure you still want to marry me?' She said, 'Yes, I very much do.' I knew then that I was blessed.

*   *   *   *   *

Paula refused to speak to either Linda or me directly. Although we knew that she wanted to establish the truth of her paternity, she would communicate only through go-betweens, which hurt and disturbed Linda more than words can say. It placed enormous emotional stress on me too, since we were dealing with many other ongoing problems connected to Father's death.

Linda had received a phone call from Emma Worth, Paula's agent, manager, publicist and close friend of more than six years. My sister had also heard from an Australian lawyer, Andrew Young, who represented Michael Hutchence – Paula's lover and the superstar singer/frontman of the Aussie rock band INXS.

But by August 1997, we were still in limbo. We were no nearer to making any specific arrangement for the DNA testing, Paula had not spoken a word to us, and we were receiving no definite information from her representatives. We were banging our heads against a brick wall, and I flew back on August 4 to find out why.

I had other reasons to be in England. My first priority was to recover Father's stored ashes from Mark Graddon at St Cyprian's. On the same day, after my overnight flight, I had arranged with Roy Phillips for Linda and me to recover our family effects from Father's flat at 169 Chiltern Court, having had no desire to liaise with Roy's co-executor, Christina Sharples.

We had arrived in a large vehicle, expecting, as agreed with Roy, that we would be picking up all of Father's letters, diaries, photographs, press clippings and other personal items. These were to be packaged and left at noon at the main entrance with a receipt form for our signatures. We anticipated making two or three trips to move it all.

When we arrived, what was waiting for us would have fitted on to the back seat of a Mini. We had received only a fraction of the property we knew to have been in the flat.

Back in Mayfield, we looked through the stuff that Christina had selected for us. In one of Father's diaries, I came to his entry for April 20, Linda's birth date, and saw his remark about Claire's delivery of 'another little bastard' on Adolf Hitler's birthday. There was very little that we chose to keep: it was hardly a legacy for the grandchildren. And so we took it out into a field on Linda's property and burnt it. The personal articles we had hoped to find, especially family photographs, were not there. We wanted to know what had happened to them, and it would take me almost four years to find out.

On February 12, 2001, Mrs Janet Moat, representing the British Film Institute, wrote me a letter confirming that a Mrs Christina Sharples had phoned to offer to the Institute 'some materials relating to the career of Hughie Green'. Mrs Moat knew that Hughie had visited the BFI to view films and TV material and assumed that the donation was with his blessing, although there were no written instructions from Father. It was only when the staff examined the material more closely that they realised how personal much of it was. In her letter, Mrs Moat sympathised, 'It must be very upsetting for you. I am so sorry. What a mess.'

Christina's donation to the Institute amounted to twenty large packing cases of materials – the very stuff we had expected to pick up that midday from 169. I later spent three weeks in London digitally copying the documents and even then, having recorded everything, there are items that I still cannot account for, including Father's big red book, received from Eamonn Andrews after appearing on his show, *This Is Your Life*.

We would also discover later that Christina had given family pictures to various TV companies. She offered one to the BBC, claiming that it portrayed Hughie as an infant. In fact, it was a picture taken of Linda in Montreal. Another photo was handed to Channel 4, who were obliged to pay copyright fees to the photographer, Barry Breckon.

On August 6, I flew to Glasgow with Linda, June Laverick and half of Father's ashes, which we were going to scatter on the Clyde at Wemyss Bay. During the flight, I was filled with misery as I thought about Papa, and I was resentful that Linda could concentrate only on Paula, whose 1995 book, *The Autobiography*, she was avidly reading in her window seat, or so it seemed to me.

At one point, she read aloud that Paula had been born in Wales, and for a split second, something streaked through my mind – my Mama's dying obsession with 'that poor little girl in Wales'. I immediately suppressed the thought – perhaps subconsciously trying to save myself from even more emotional trauma.

But it would return to me, and I would realise the links between Paula, the Major's death, and Mama's failed reunion with Hughie. The story that Claire had been struggling so desperately to tell me would unfold clearly and horrifically in my understanding. It would all make terrible sense.

*   *   *   *   *

On August 9, the *Daily Mail* printed a story about Linda and me, and our lives with Father. We had given an interview – for free – to journalist Anne Shooter, at Linda's instigation. Linda saw this as our chance to 'set the record straight'. I had misgivings, but I played along because I wanted to help Linda get everything off her chest. I hoped, too, that if we stated our urgent desire to get the DNA testing underway, it might motivate Paula to co-operate.

I was becoming totally pissed off that she had still not committed herself to a testing date, although she had been telling the papers that she intended to proceed. She was talking to the press but not to us and that, increasingly, annoyed me. Linda was stressed and miserable with the waiting.

Andrew Young paid a visit to Linda's house, representing Paula, I thought, and it was simply to tell us that she did wish for the DNA tests. It now appears that Andrew, Michael Hutchence's friend and lawyer, was there to check us out and report back to Michael. I guess that Hutchence was being protective of Paula and wanted to find out what sort of people we were. It was a short meeting, and the only remark that I can clearly recall him making was to do with Bob Geldof. He said that he had met 'a lot of tough customers' but he had never come up against a tougher opponent than Bob during the time of his divorce from Paula.

I also spoke with Emma Worth – Paula's then agent – twice on the phone during this time. I told her politely but firmly that Linda and I were not amused by Paula's attitude towards us. We had feelings too. If Paula wanted to know the truth, it could only be by Linda and me accommodating her. So, did she or did she not want our blood for testing?

Emma was sympathetic, displeased with Paula's behaviour. She assured me that Paula fully intended to have the test, but had many other stressful things going on in her life and was 'not altogether herself'. Emma promised that she would talk directly to Paula and sort it all out.

By this time, I really wanted either to piss or get off the pot. Linda and I were fighting battles all around. Father's will could not be probated in case Paula turned out to be related and decided to put a claim on his estate. Christina was playing games with the contents of 169. We still feared that Botham was about to publish a 'bombshell' book. The BBC was about to do a documentary on Father and wished us to participate – which we did not. Linda was trying to 'set the record straight' without knowing how to do it, or even what the truth was. We had only recently put Mama's affairs to rest. We had just spread Father's ashes. I had business responsibilities back in Canada. And last, but not least, I was still trying to marry Lynne.

I didn't need a prima donna, celebrity, alleged half-sister giving me and Linda grief when we had been bending over backwards to accommodate her, with no ulterior motives whatsoever. Linda had suffered from cancer and to the best of our knowledge she was out of the woods, but she didn't need the extra stress. Rainer and I were extremely concerned.

At the same time, Paula did have her plate full. Since her divorce in May 1996, she had been beset by problems. She had been through the courts in a bitter financial battle with Bob Geldof. Their property dispute was settled in June, after what he described as 'three days of complete bloody nightmare in the High Courts of Justice'. Paula's former husband allowed her to move back into their £750,000 marital home in Chelsea – while he set up home with his new girlfriend, French actress Jeanne Marine, in a nearby, one-bedroom mews cottage owned by Hutchence. Bob also got to keep their £1.2 million priory house in Faversham, Kent.

But, pregnant with Hutchence's baby, Paula was struggling with debts estimated at that time to be £100,000. She had been paid £150,000 for her autobiography and another £100,000 for a weekly column in the *Sun*, but she had lost her day job, interviewing celebrities on a bed for Channel 4's early-morning TV show, *The Big Breakfast*. Geldof's company, Planet 24, produced it, and Paula was dropped after leaving Bob. She insisted, however, that it was not her ex-husband but Charlie Parsons, one of his two partners, who sacked her when her love affair with Michael Hutchence began attracting hostile press. She was then forced to continue through the courts to demand more money from Bob Geldof.

Even more trouble hit the beleaguered Paula in September 1996 when a quantity of suspected opium was found hidden under her bed in a 'Smarties' tube in her Chelsea home. Paula and Michael were holidaying with the weeks-old Tiger in Sydney, Australia, when it happened.

Bob Geldof immediately lodged a successful, emergency application with the High Court for custody of his three children with Paula – Fifi Trixibelle, Peaches and Pixie. Until then, they had been in Paula's custody although they had remained in England when she went to Australia.

Mark Stephens, a lawyer acting for Paula and Michael, said of the drugs discovery, 'The news has come as a complete surprise to them both. Paula and Michael have received no contact of any kind from the police and they wish to make no further comment.'

Bob Geldof then entered an application for permanent custody, and he took the children to the family home in Faversham, where they were later joined by their nanny, Anita Debney. Anita had been present at the Chelsea house during the police raid and had been questioned by the police. She was said to have eventually walked out of Paula's employment after the drugs find. It was an unexpected departure, especially since Paula had praised Anita's loyalty in *The Autobiography*.

Also leaving was her then publicist Gerry Agar, after a 'most distressing' telephone conversation with Paula. Gerry, who agreed to give evidence supporting Bob Geldof at the custody hearing, said, 'At the end of the day, it's the children that come first. I have had to make a moral decision which wasn't very pleasant, because it seems as though I'm turning against a friend. Once this is straightened out, of course, I will be there for Paula as a friend, but right now, my main concern is for the kids.' She added, 'I have been asked legal questions about the drugs investigation and had to answer them honestly. I'm going to have to appear in public and say things that are the truth.'

Of Bob Geldof, she said, 'He is truly devoted to his children and has always been fully involved with their upbringing, picking them up from school at least two evenings a week. He has very old-fashioned values.'

Paula left Hutchence and Tiger in Australia as she flew back, via Paris, for the custody battle, stating that the police had still not asked to speak to her and insisting, 'There is an entirely different way of looking at this whole series of events.'

Emma Worth told me, 'Paula was very open about taking recreational drugs in her youth, but in all the time I worked with her, I never, ever knew her to use or saw her use illegal drugs.' Even today, there are friends of Paula who are convinced that the drugs were planted under her bed by enemies who wished to make trouble for her.

The High Court custody hearing, which took place over four days in early October, arrived at a compromise. Paula and Bob issued a joint statement afterwards, 'Two concerned parents came to court to do what each of them believed was right for their children. They have now resolved matters in a way which they both believe to be in the best interests of the children. Bob and Paula have agreed that they will continue to share the care of their children. No further comment can or will be made.'

Despite the savagely divisive nature of the proceedings, there were signs of lingering affection between the couple, with Geldof at one point putting his arm around Paula and kissing her head. However, it would not be the last of their custody clashes.

After the drug bust, the *Sun* suspended Paula's weekly column, but she was not reinstated, even after the police released her without charge. She was, however, contracted to the newspaper while the investigation was carried out, and therefore could not undertake any other journalistic work. Her financial crises began to bite harder.

At the same time, she had taken advances for books that she was not delivering to her publishers. On September 13, 1996 – only days before the police raid – Emma Worth, in her capacity as Paula's literary agent, wrote an angry letter to Paula in which she expressed her infuriation that she had been ignoring her calls and messages for the past two months.

Emma was at that time working two days a week as a consultant for Virgin Books and, for the rest of the time, dealing with her agency work and writing projects of her own. She sternly informed Paula in the letter that two major British publishers – Random House and Little, Brown – were demanding the return of advances totalling £30,000. In addition, HarperCollins were threatening to cancel a commissioned book on beauty tips, which, if they followed through, would mean Paula having to give back another £15,000. The book, *How to Look Like A Goddess When You Feel Like A Dog*, had already been researched by Paula's friend Jo Fairley and Paula was supposed to write it up in her own, inimitably humorous style.

Emma had her letter hand-delivered to Paula's Chelsea house in Redburn Street so that from there it could be faxed to her in Australia. 'I was quite tough with her,' recalled Emma. 'This was the most formal letter I ever wrote to her. After she received it, she did immediately ring me and it was all fine again between us as friends.'

But Paula seemed unlikely to be forthcoming with her manuscripts. For one thing, she had a new-born baby, Tiger, to look after. 'It was lovely that the baby had been born,' said Emma.

'But Paula was always away travelling, and she was meant to be working. She needed the money.'

It was entirely due to dire financial necessity, some of her own making, that Paula first began selling stories to the tabloid newspapers – something she would never previously have considered doing, but for which she would become well-known as time went on.

With all of this as a backdrop, Paula was preparing to go to the High Court to deal with the financial aspects of her divorce settlement with Bob Geldof. Namely, she intended to appeal for more money, and her friends and associates, past and present, had sworn affidavits about her circumstances to be read as evidence for and against her in the hearing.

By the time she was named as Hughie's daughter in May 1997, she was gearing up for the case of Yates v. Geldof later in the year. Sadly for Paula, her gathering troubles would culminate in an unthinkable tragedy in November, and she would plunge into a desperate freefall from which she would not escape.

*   *   *   *   *

Back in Canada on August 11, I spread the other half of my father's ashes over Mount Royal, overlooking Montreal, with sadness that he felt he had to 'bribe' me in his will to do this for him. I had no idea of what was happening in Paula Yates's life. I still barely knew who she was, and I had no intention of finding out. I purely wanted to get the DNA testing over and done with so that we could prove she was not our sister, we could show Noel Botham up for the liar I believed he was, and we could return to our own, uneventful lives, away from the wretched glare of showbiz and celebrity.

In an attempt to reassure Paula that she was not in any danger of exploitation from us, Rainer, through friends, liaised with Mishcon De Reya, a firm of solicitors which had represented Princess Diana. Together, we set up a confidentiality agreement which guaranteed that if the results of the DNA test proved Hughie Green to be Paula's father, then this would never be made public by us. Paula, however, could either use or conceal the information as she saw fit.

Everyone else was screwing Paula for a story and the money it made for them. This would show her that she had nothing to fear from us; we were victims too. As far we were concerned, we were doing something nice and decent. We later discovered that to Paula and her advisers, we were simply naïve.

We found out, years later, that Paula had received the document, and, indeed, had signed it on September 23, 1997 with Andrew Young as a witness. But she never returned it either to us or our solicitors. I also discovered later, from a document involving the *Sun* newspaper, that as far back as June that year, Paula had been actively looking for the highest bidder for her story about the DNA test results and the allegations that Hughie Green was her father.

Paula had also tried frantically to elicit the truth from her mother, Hélène – who would only instruct her to read her forthcoming book. It would turn out to shed no light on the situation.

Come the autumn, we, in our innocence, had still received no response, only silence. There had been no closure for me with Mama's death, and now I could find no closure with Papa's either. Linda and I had started having cross words. I was tired of hearing from her about 'poor Paula' and the stresses of her 'celebrity life'. I was also fed up with shouldering the problems arising from Father's death, and trying at the same time to run my company in Canada and, yes, have some sort of life of my own. Linda was distraught and I was becoming very angry at the disrespect we were being shown. Finally, I had had enough. I decided to try, for the first and last time, to force the issue, and I wrote to Paula, care of Emma Worth.

My letter, dated October 20, 1997, read as follows:

'Dear Paula,

'Mr Noel Botham will soon be appearing in a BBC production about "The Life Of Hughie Green . . . A Brit TV Icon", and, assuredly, your parentage will be brought into question again. This time, however, your inaction to prove the point one way or another will have given this bastard credibility.

'Neither Linda nor I can imagine why you would allow this to be, when, beyond yourself, others are, and will remain, defamed. Certainly this matter was not of your making nor ours. Linda and I have, however, done all possible to consider your feelings by putting in place a confidential DNA testing that, with any luck, will disprove Mr Botham's allegations. Your prolonged lack of positive response and action to avail yourself of this obvious means of ascertaining the truth can only mean, at this late date, that you wish to live with the doubt. Noel Botham will dine again and you, Paula, have set the table for him! And at that table you have insisted on seating some unhappy guests of which Jess must be as saddened as Linda and myself. Are you truly sure that you wish to do this?

'Paula, I ask you to telephone Linda or myself – preferably Linda – so that we may know directly that you do, or do not, wish to have the DNA testing done. We are both hurting and this will next be exacerbated when Botham leers out at the airing of the upcoming BBC production. If you have chosen for all of us to live with this doubt, then that *is your decision*, and we are all tied to it. Our request that you communicate this to us directly is made in the name of common decency. We, too, are paying for the sins of the father every bit as much as yourself.

'For us all, I hope that you pick up the phone. Things of this nature never go away and doubt is a far more insidious demon than knowledge. The latter we can handle, the former handles us.

'Paula, this is our last attempt to right this wrong. If you choose not to communicate now, you will find that Linda and I have tuned out. There is nothing else we can do.

'Regards,

'Christopher Green'

Paula did not respond but Emma Worth, on her behalf, did. She contacted Linda and told her to 'go ahead' and make the arrangements for Linda, Paula and me to be DNA tested. By November 6, Linda had informed me that my 'vampire kit' was en route to Canada addressed to my doctor for the blood sample to be drawn. At no time did we hear from Paula directly. We still didn't know if she wished to sign our legal document giving her privacy and total control over the test result, should it be in favour of Hughie.

Paula would later tell the press that she 'didn't see any need' to communicate with us, since she was convinced that Jess was her biological father, and that Botham's revelations were 'cruel rubbish'. She had felt only her own pain and had not for one minute considered ours.

She was totally oblivious to everything except her own circumstances. It could be argued that she had, by then, started taking drugs – something she had not done since her teenage years. Some sources have ventured that she was unsure of Michael Hutchence and her future with him. She knew that she could never shake off the considerable figure of Bob Geldof, who would always loom large and loud in her life as the father of her first three, adored daughters. He would forever be regarded as a saint by the public while she, by contrast, was increasingly being seen as the wicked ex-wife. She was having major financial problems and she had ruinously fallen out of her professional working patterns.

And while all of this may well explain her preoccupations during the time that we were trying in vain to make contact with her, I am now convinced, along with other close friends of Paula's, that there was one enormous reason for her reluctance to pin a date on the DNA testing: she was scared about what else might show up in her blood.

At the time of the police and the 'Smarties' tube, I'm willing to believe that Paula was not taking drugs. By May 1997, I'm sure that she was, through my later conversations with people who were close to her. Paula knew she had enemies who would, allegedly, go so far as to plant drugs in her flat while she was overseas. How far would those same enemies go to get hold of any blood sample she might give for our simple DNA tests? If her blood should happen to be analysed for anything other than paternity, how could she be sure that those findings would not reach the wrong people?

I'm certain that Paula was paranoid, irrational and terrified that illegal drugs might be found in her bloodstream, and that if this were somehow imparted to anyone, she would end up having to relinquish her shared custody of Fifi, Peaches and Pixie. She would also be sure to lose Tiger.

It's not inconceivable that Paula might have suspected Linda and me of having been head-hunted by these unnamed enemies, hence Andrew Young's fact-finding mission to Mayfield.

*   *   *   *   *

Michael Hutchence was found dead and hanging naked from the door of his room at the Ritz Carlton Hotel in Double Bay, East Sydney, on Saturday, November 22. He was 37 years old. I heard the news from my Sony 'Dream Cube' radio-alarm clock, when it woke me up at 7 a.m., Montreal time. To my everlasting shame, I rolled over in my bed, groaned aloud, and wondered, 'Oh, fuck. What does this mean now?'

I was due to make yet another costly trip to England for the DNA results in a couple of weeks' time. By now, Linda and I had got used to being treated as mere bit-part players in a saga starring Noel Botham, Christina Sharples, Paula Yates, Michael Hutchence and Bob Geldof. Hughie Green had been written into history as a serial womaniser, and his detractors were queueing up to blacken his memory.

I wanted to kick the living shit out of my 'Dream Cube'; it had introduced yet another nightmarish element to our ordeal. I wanted to destroy the messenger which had brought this latest complication. At that moment, I had no sympathy for anybody. I simply dreaded the future. Where was this all going, and when would it ever end? Later, of course, I was deeply sorry for Paula.

I was suddenly wide awake and desperate to talk to Linda. She, by coincidence, was also in Australia – in Perth – accompanying

Rainer on one of his international business trips. Linda had nearly fainted from the shock of Michael's death.

Michael Hutchence had arrived in Australia to prepare for the twentieth anniversary tour of INXS. He spent his last night dining with his father Kell and stepmother Susan, and reportedly enjoyed a couple of drinks with two women at the bar. He carried on drinking beer, champagne, vodka and cocktails in his room until 5 a.m. with an ex-girlfriend, Kym Wilson, the former *Home and Away* actress, and a friend called Andrew Rayment. Kell, Kym and Andrew all told police that Hutchence had been worried about a custody suit taking place in London.

Paula said in a statement that she rang Michael at some point before 5.38 a.m., Sydney time, on November 22. She told him that she would not be bringing her four children to Australia as they had planned, since a custody issue had not been settled and had been adjourned until December 17.

Bob Geldof had refused to allow Paula to take the children to Australia with Tiger for a long, Christmas holiday. Paula said in her statement that Hutchence told her he would beg Geldof to relent, and that he sounded 'desperate'.

Bob Geldof confirmed that he received the second of two calls from Hutchence at about 5.30 a.m., Sydney time. He reported that the INXS singer was 'hectoring and abusive and threatening', and was indeed 'begging' him to let the children come to Australia. However, he did not sound depressed.

Geldof, much later, told interviewer Ray Martin that he vetoed the visit only because he wanted to be with his children fifty per cent of the time, in line with the shared-custody agreement. He also stated that his last call from Hutchence was simply one of 'loads of conversations' they'd had, and that if Michael drove him crazy, it was 'probably mutual'. He denied rumours that he had hung up on Hutchence. Gail Coward, the woman in the next hotel room, heard a male voice shouting and swearing in Hutchence's room at the time of the phone call.

An incensed Hutchence was also said to be frantically worried that the legal action going on in London might lead to him being judged an unfit father to Tiger. A few hours later, shortly after

9.30 a.m., Hutchence started making more phone calls. He rang his manager, Martha Troupe, and left two messages on her answer phone. In the first, he said, 'Marth, Michael here. I fucking had enough.' She rang the hotel immediately, but could get no reply. In the second, only minutes later, his voice sounded slow and deep.

Martha rang the INXS tour manager, John Martin, who reported having received a note from Michael, saying he would not be attending that day's rehearsal – an important one, the last before the tour.

Hutchence also telephoned a woman called Michelle Bennett, said to be another former girlfriend. He left a message on her answerphone in which he sounded 'drunk'. Calling again at 9.45 a.m., he spoke to Michelle in person and began to cry. She told him she'd come straight over to the hotel, but could not rouse him by knocking on his door or by calling the room. She then left a note for him at reception.

His body was discovered just before noon.

The police allegedly found several prescription drugs, including Prozac pills, scattered around the scene, along with photographs of Hutchence, Paula and Tiger, and empty drink bottles. The officers were reluctant to jump to a suicide verdict. There was no note. Furthermore, Hutchence was kneeling on the floor, facing the door. There was a possibility that his death had arisen from auto-erotic asphyxiation – an activity whereby sexual pleasure is derived from suffocation to the point of near-death – although the coroner later ruled this out, stating that there was no forensic evidence to support it. Simply, Hutchence's belt buckle had given way, which caused him to fall downwards.

Paula, until the day she died, refused to accept that Michael deliberately hanged himself. She did not want to believe that he would willingly have left her and Tiger. And she would not have wished even to consider the idea that her problems with Bob Geldof had in any way contributed to Michael's last, desperate act, as the coroner would declare.

Paula jetted out of England to Australia with Tiger, her latest companion Belinda Brewin, and her lawyer Anthony Burton on

November 23. She spent most of the 22-hour flight sobbing, shrieking or lying with her face buried in her arms, causing British Airways to consider ejecting her at the stopover in Bangkok, where she also created a commotion.

Once in Sydney, she was reunited with Michael at the Glebe morgue, memorably commenting that she wanted to cover him with a blanket to warm him up. She then rested at her hotel before meeting Kell Hutchence and Michael's mother, Patricia Glassop, to discuss the funeral arrangements.

On Thursday, November 27, Paula buried Michael in a coffin festooned with purple irises and one yellow tiger lily. Clutching Tiger to her cleavage, she was joined by Hutchence's family, friends, fans and musical luminaries including Australian performers Midnight Oil, Nick Cave and Michael's ex-girlfriend Kylie Minogue as well as British veteran Tom Jones at an Anglican ceremony in St Andrew's Cathedral, Sydney. U2's Bono sent an enormous floral tribute.

Kell Hutchence, talking on Australian television, blamed Bob Geldof for playing a part in his son's death, saying that 'he made their lives miserable'. However, it would be the next year before the New South Wales coroner Derek Hand would declare Hutchence's death to have been a suicide, ruling that he was in a 'severe depressed state'.

Hand's report stated that Michael's depression was 'due to a number of factors, including the relationship with Paula Yates and the pressure of the on-going dispute with Sir Robert Geldof, combined with the effects of the substances that he had ingested at that time'. In addition to the alcoholic drinks, these included cocaine, Prozac and other prescription drugs.

Although I could not anticipate the coroner's verdict, I was thinking about what had happened between Paula, Michael and Bob as I flew 35,000 feet above the North Atlantic on my way to England for our DNA results. I prayed they would be negative. I could not see how a positive outcome would benefit a woman who was already clearly struggling to stay afloat in a sea of personal misery.

14

Our Sister Paula: The Silence and the Qualms

I couldn't help myself. I had only just parked my bags in Linda's spare bedroom in Mayfield, and already I was on the phone to the DNA lab for a progress report.

The procedure was that Paula, Linda and I had to receive the results at the same time, via registered, express mail. I wanted to make sure that they would be sent out immediately, once they were known. I was due back in Montreal a week later to marry Lynne, who had stayed behind to look after the girls. I was determined that it would be third time lucky; I was not prepared to cancel our wedding arrangements again.

The head of the lab advised me that there had been a slight delay, and I appealed to her to do everything possible to move things along, explaining the reason for my urgency. She promised the results the next day. Knowing that it was against the rules for her to enter into any discussions on the phone, I nevertheless chanced my luck, asking if she had any idea what the outcome might be. My heart almost froze when she told me she was almost positive that Paula was our sister, but that we would have to wait another 24 hours for confirmation.

Ending the call, I fibbed to Linda, 'She wouldn't speculate. We'll just have to be patient and wait for tomorrow.'

In my mind's eye, I saw Noel Botham's face leering down at me. I headed rapidly to the garden to have a smoke, and threw up behind a bush. This 'thing' wasn't over: it was just beginning and we had still heard nothing from Paula.

The next day dawned at last. It was Thursday, December 11, 1997, and Linda and I were in the kitchen having toast and coffee for breakfast. I wondered how Paula was feeling. If the unthinkable turned out to be true and we *were* related, would she be able to cope with it – now or ever? It was shocking to realise how much was happening to this girl in such a short and brutal period of time. It bothered me, too, that her children had been caught up in the turbulence, and I felt for them.

I once again rang the diagnostics company. Breaching regulations for the second time while acknowledging the exceptional circumstances of our case, the doctor verbally confirmed to me that Hughie was Paula's father. I looked at Linda and said, 'Sweetheart, we have a sister,' and she went ballistic. Joy, tears, rage at Papa – total hysterics. I was simply numb.

We could not contact anyone until it was all official, although we made an exception for the *Daily Mail*. We had arranged to give them our story, since Paula had failed to return the legal, confidentiality agreement that we had drawn up three months earlier for her benefit. Under the terms we had offered, Linda and I would be barred from speaking to the press or anyone else in the event of a positive result. Paula, on the other hand, could either sell or suppress the information as she wished. With a negative result, we would all have a free hand.

Paula had started out by altering the typed document we'd sent to her, in her own handwriting, after Linda and I had signed it – which rendered it null and void. She had tried to claim the sole rights to the test results, whether they were positive or negative. But it was important to Linda and me, if we turned out *not* to be related to Paula, to be able to come back at the accusers, particularly Noel Botham, who had catapulted us into the tabloid headlines and subjected us to months of anxiety and uncertainty.

I had felt that Paula was being selfish and unkind towards us when we had only been trying to protect her in the eventuality that Hughie was, indeed, her father, and I had the solicitors send her, again, the original document. She then signed it on September 23 – but, for some reason, no one had ever returned it to us or our legal team.

Sitting in Linda's farmhouse, knowing that Paula was our sister, we therefore had no legal obligation to her, but we both still felt a strong, moral responsibility. I had insisted in my negotiations with the *Daily Mail* that if Paula should suddenly return her signed confidentiality document, even up to the last moment, then we would immediately withdraw our story.

With all this in mind, we phoned Anne Shooter, the delightful journalist with whom we had liaised in our previous, free interview for the *Mail*. Again, we had been offered cash for our exclusive, and this time, I had accepted their several thousand pounds with thanks. I didn't stand to profit from the story, and I didn't want to; I would merely cover the expenses of my last two trips to England.

Anne and her superior Rebecca Hardy arrived at Mayfield within a couple of hours. By around 6 p.m. that evening, Linda and I were tense, emotional and still not co-operating with these two very patient journalists. We were worried sick about Paula. Did we have a deal or did we not? Were we about to do her a great injustice by talking to the press? We were terrified of doing the wrong thing.

Anne and Rebecca were remarkably kind towards Linda and me as we sat dithering in Mayfield with tears in our eyes, agonising over the interview. The two writers are sincere and thoroughly decent young people, and I still count Anne and her husband Dan among my good friends today.

Rainer finally made contact with a solicitor, who confirmed that the only document received from Paula's representatives was the one which she had rendered null and void by unlawfully adding an amendment.

At around 7 p.m, the phone rang, and it was handed to me. A voice at the other end said, 'Chris, this is Paula's friend, Belinda Brewin. Paula is in total shock at the news she has just received.' I could hear Paula, hysterical, in the background. Belinda told me that, quite understandably, Paula was too emotional to talk to us at that moment but would contact us later. I revealed that Linda and I had the press with us, and Belinda replied that *they* were about to talk to the *Sun* – an arrangement which I later discovered had been broached in June. No mention was ever made again of the confidentiality document that Linda and I had gone to such trouble and expense to draw up for Paula. Evidently, she didn't care about it one way or the other.

Emma Worth, who had set up the *Sun* coverage, later explained to me why this was so, and agreed that Linda and I had been naïve. She told me, 'Legal documents don't necessarily keep things out of the press . . . it's a double-edged thing. The press are going to get a hold of a story like that no matter what you do, and we thought we might as well control it as much as possible and get some money out of it. Let's not be too prissy about it. Paula needed the money.

'It wasn't as if Paula was thinking, "There's a certain amount in the pot and I want it and I don't want Linda and Christopher to have it." She wouldn't have ever thought like that. We were doing what we had to do, as professionally as possible, in a fairly traumatic situation.

'And although I was her friend, I wasn't there to say, "How do you feel about all of this?" She felt *awful*. My job was to handle the newspapers.'

Anne and Rebecca returned to Mayfield with a photographer the next morning, Friday, and took us to a hotel in Tunbridge Wells where we completed the interview that would appear as an exclusive on Saturday, December 13. On the same day, the *Sun* ran Paula's story. Clearly, she had been too shocked and distraught to tell the showbiz editor, Andy Coulson, very much at all. The article was largely a summation of everything that had gone before, with one new quote attributed to Paula on the front page, 'I thought I was at the darkest point of my life . . . now this.'

In the *Mail*, we talked about our past with Papa. I told of our last night together at 169, when I had believed that he had 'taken care of everything', and therefore refused to believe Paula was our sister, right up until the DNA results. Declaring Hughie a 'monster', Linda talked of his shortcomings as a father and a husband, and lambasted his immorality and capacity for hurting and humiliating others, even from beyond the grave.

She spoke of her hopes and fears about meeting Paula. Linda had already sent flowers to Paula from both of us with a note saying how sorry we were about everything, and that our thoughts were with her. She didn't respond, although she later mentioned the flowers in a newspaper interview. As far as I know, she never thanked Linda either for footing the bill for her DNA testing, or repaid her.

Linda also revealed to *Mail* readers the existence of a half-brother and three unknown half-sisters – a story which was recycled the next day in the *News of the World*, running another front-page exclusive under the startling headline: 'Paula's Dad Hughie Had 1,200 Lovers'.

Again, it was the work of Noel Botham, and the single most interesting sentence started like this, 'Novelist Botham – who first revealed in the *News of the World* that Green was Paula's father . . .' This was the same Noel Botham who had continually denied revealing any such thing, while at the same time supplying reams of information on the affair between Hughie and Paula's mother, and Father's supposed views on Paula herself.

In his latest piece of work, Botham talked at length of the sexual excesses of his 'second best friend', Hughie, who was described as a 'heartless serial seducer'. He claimed that Father took pornographic photographs of all his girlfriends as an 'insurance' against any ideas they might have of revealing his affairs. Outrageously, then, he stated that Linda and I had found the 'sordid library of photos'. There were quotes attributed to me in which I expressed my shock and horror at this discovery – and I had said none of it. Linda and I had never seen any pornographic picture collection at 169.

Finally, Botham was pleased to venture that Paula had 'at last accepted the truth'. He could not have been more wrong. We had so far received one phone call only from Belinda Brewin, on behalf of Paula. There followed another long silence.

*   *   *   *   *

Lynne and I were married on December 17, 1997. By choice, it was a simple and informal civil ceremony, held in the morning at the Palais de Justice in downtown Montreal. Conducting the service was the Justice of the Peace, a fellow called Gaetan whom we had come to know and like very much. We had twice not shown up, but rather than expressing any irritation with us, he was thrilled that we were finally going to be man and wife.

He was a little rusty and couldn't remember the words exactly, so he had to be prompted – rather theatrically – by his second-in-command. Lynne started giggling. She is a terrible giggler, and once she starts, it's almost impossible for her to turn it off. Gaetan started to laugh. Soon everyone was laughing, but it was nice laughter; there was a tremendously warm atmosphere in the room.

Gaetan then took charge, subdued the gathering and asked the big, climactic questions. 'Do you, Christopher . . .?' 'Do you, Lynne . . .?' Our friend Terry had his video camera running, and he captured for posterity the moment when Lynne replied, 'Yes,' turned to me and clearly said, 'You see, I *did* say *yes*.'

Truly, that was the happiest moment of my life.

It was a magical day, and when we arrived home as Mr and Mrs Green, there was even more joy awaiting us. Our sheltie dog, Daisy, who had bolted out into the snow that morning, was sitting on the doorstep, waiting for us to come back.

We went into Christmas wondering what the New Year would bring. It had all gone quiet in England. Behind the scenes, though, Paula's life was changing dramatically. It appeared, for a start, that no matter what her original relationship with the Hutchence family, she now considered herself at war with Michael's parents.

Dark rumours drifted out of Sydney that his mother was accusing Paula of being responsible for the singer's death, although Patricia Glassop has categorically denied this. There were also said to be arguments over Hutchence's ashes. I believe that they were finally divided between Kell, Patricia and Paula, who sewed hers into a pillow that she slept on for the rest of her life.

Returning from Sydney to London on December 1, after the funeral, Paula consulted her lawyers and made her will. Dated

December 22, 1997, it stipulated, 'I wish that my said daughter Tigerlily shall have no access to the parents of Michael Hutchence without the prior approval of my guardians.'

The named guardians were the New York-based Martha Troupe, Michael's manager, and Bill Liebowitz, INXS's attorney. The will was witnessed by Michael's friend and legal eagle, Andrew Young, who recorded an address in Addison Crescent, West Kensington – the house where Belinda Brewin lived. By now they were lovers, and living together when he was in London.

Bob Geldof, at the same time, was unhappy about the shared custody which had been agreed the previous October. Since then, Paula had suffered the double blow of losing Michael Hutchence and gaining a father she never knew she had. She had lost her future and her past, and her best friend Jo Fairley believes that the revelation of her paternity was 'the body blow that she was most unable to recover from, because it shook the foundations of her life'. Emma Worth, however, disagrees. She contends, 'Michael's death was the more shocking, concrete thing.'

Both Jo and Emma are emphatic that Paula's way of dealing with the Hughie Green crisis was to pretend it hadn't happened; that Jess Yates was really her father, as she had believed all her life. And so apart from an early burst of curiosity about her new 'family', she really didn't want to have anything to do with us, because we were a reminder; we disrupted her state of denial.

Her life, as she knew it, had fallen apart on all fronts. She was dreadfully depressed and screwed-up, and surrounded by rumours of drink and drugs problems. She later shuddered, 'When Michael died I was tipped over the edge. I was beyond grief. I went completely mad.' Seeing her deteriorating condition, Bob Geldof acted to secure the primary custody of his three daughters, thus confronting Paula with another court battle, which would come to pass in June 1998 – with controversial consequences.

There had been a changing of the guard in Paula's life. Her nanny, Anita, had left the household, to her great dismay. Gerry Agar, her publicist, had departed too. Jo Fairley remained her best friend, although it's unlikely she knew everything that was going on in Paula's world, particularly the 'darker' side. Emma Worth had been discarded, and Belinda Brewin had stepped in from the sidelines to become a major player as Paula's right-hand woman or 'road warrior'. When the Hughie bombshell had first dropped, all our dealings with Paula had been through Emma. From now on, the go-between would be Belinda.

Emma is still a respected figure in the literary world. Originally, she had been Paula's editor. She then became her agent. As time went on, Emma carried out the duties of a publicist and manager, and enjoyed a strong friendship with Paula. That ended when Emma received a solicitor's letter dated December 5, 1997, stating that Paula wished to terminate Emma's role as her acting agent.

Things had started to go wrong between the two in September 1996, just after Paula, Michael and Tiger had left for their holiday. Emma desperately needed to contact Paula, not only about certain outstanding manuscripts and publishers' demands for the return of advances, but about a new deal for a novel proposed by Virgin.

Emma described the confusion of the period in an affidavit sworn on April 21, 1997, under the Matrimonial Homes Act 1983. Her statement was given in support of Paula's description of her 'financial circumstances', as part of her bid to persuade the court that she needed more money from Bob Geldof.

'I had no knowledge of Geraldine [Gerry] Agar until I tried to obtain Paula's telephone number from her nanny, Anita Debney, the day after Paula had left for Hong Kong and Australia on or about September 12, 1996,' Emma stated. 'The telephone had been engaged all day and when I finally got through to Anita and asked her why she had been so long on the telephone she was extremely agitated and said words to the effect that, "It is all so terrible, I can't describe it, but ring Gerry Agar, Paula's PR manager, because she knows everything."'

Emma, who had herself been carrying out PR activities for Paula, continued, 'I was somewhat surprised that Paula would have employed a new PR manager without having told me, but I needed to speak to Paula and telephoned Gerry Agar for the telephone number. Gerry Agar was extremely excitable and agitated: she told me that she was unable to contact Paula because she did not have her telephone number and then immediately launched into a diatribe about Paula, saying that she had gone mad and was a drug addict (this was given as the excuse for my not being able to contact Paula), never got out of bed and was taking ecstasy and mixing this with her own prescribed drugs as well as opium.

'I was extremely taken aback at this onslaught. I have never, ever seen Paula taking [illegal] drugs of any description. I said to Gerry was she sure she was not mistaken, because in my experience, Paula had never taken anything . . .

'Gerry, however, was insistent – and told me that a former musician and drug addict had got the drugs for Paula.

'The whole episode seemed bizarre. I know Paula well enough to know that if she was in trouble she would speak to me and she is so sensible and concerned about her children that I could not believe she would not contact friends and doctors if there were any problems. I said this to Gerry who told me I was absolutely wrong. What surprised me was that a supposed friend and PR manager of Paula's would take this attitude and reveal it to someone she had never met.

'I still did not have Paula's telephone number and contacted Anita again, who gave me Paula's fax number. I asked Anita about what Gerry had told me and Anita said that it was true and that she and Gerry had found "stuff like wax in a 'Smartie' tube in the bedroom" and asked if I thought it was opium? Anita said that Gerry came around a lot, and told me that Paula intended to employ a new agent when she returned to England.

'Anita also informed me – unprompted and apropos of nothing – that she knew she was going to be sacked because Michael hated her. The whole episode was strange and I was anxious to speak direct with Paula to ascertain exactly what was going on. It seemed that Anita was trying to put a wedge between me and Paula and I was very concerned about what I was being told.'

Emma relaxed after finally hearing back from Paula in a phone call and then receiving a friendly fax sprinkled with kisses, although she remained a little worried and suspicious. She told me, 'Anita did make me think that, for some reason, Paula might have decided to dump me to go off with a new publicist, but in fact, Gerry Agar was another mum whom Paula had met at the children's school, and I think Gerry latched on to her.'

Belinda Brewin was also one of the school mums, according to Emma, 'I first met her [at Paula's home] in Redburn Street. She was helping Paula doing some cleaning. Belinda was making herself very useful. Paula introduced me. She later said, "Why am I plagued by these mums from the school?" and we laughed a bit and I didn't think anything more about her.

'Belinda came on the scene, as far as I am aware, around the time the Noel Botham story was breaking. Without wanting to sound at all snobby, I thought her rather crass. I didn't like her, and I didn't mix with her socially. And then after the drug bust, Anita had gone, and Belinda became the nanny. I was totally concerned for Paula, but I had my own personal problems too at that time. No, Belinda was not actually her *friend*. Absolutely not. Paula referred to her as "this woman I met at the school". I think she was embarrassed by her. But she was suddenly there a lot doing things for Paula.' Which is exactly what Paula herself would tell me when we finally came face to face.

'Paula was not very well by this time, emotionally,' continued Emma. 'It was nothing to do with illegal drugs. It wasn't drink. She was on her anti-depressants – Prozac. I don't know if she abused Prozac. I mean, she didn't appear to be well, but I don't know how many she was meant to take. It seemed to me that the Prozac was having an effect on her.'

Emma told me, on the record, that around this time, she was asked by a firm of solicitors, on behalf of persons unnamed, to testify that Paula was using drugs, 'I've no idea why this solicitor even contacted me. If there was one person who was never going to go against Paula, it was me.'

However, she admitted, 'Yes, during the time that Michael and Paula were constantly away travelling, there was some concern for the baby to do with drugs, but as far as I'm concerned, it was too much Prozac and nothing else. I don't think there was any secret about the concerns – I don't think that I'm being indiscreet. Paula was ill, and later, after Michael's death she became iller, and no one was helping her, least of all herself.

'I think if Michael had lived, he would have dealt with it. He would have taken them out of the UK and that entire change of scene would have helped. I think he would have married her.'

The likelihood of a marriage is still contested by Michael's mother Patricia Glassop and half-sister Tina Hutchence – not because the woman involved was Paula but simply because, in their view, the INXS sex-bomb simply wasn't the marrying kind.

*   *   *   *   *

Towards the end of January 1998, Linda received a telephone call from Belinda. She was ecstatic to hear that Paula wanted to meet her. Linda rang me immediately. She said that Belinda had given her Paula's private number, and she intended to call Paula to arrange a lunch meeting. I hid my misgivings out of respect for Linda's clear euphoria.

The very next day, Linda phoned me again. She had dialled Paula's number and a little voice had answered. Linda explained who she was, and the child was very excited, crying out to Paula, 'Mummy, it's my new Auntie Linda on the phone!' Linda was over the moon that she had been apparently been accepted as a family member, and she arranged to see Paula.

My emotions were churning. On the one hand, my experience of 'knowing Paula' had brought nothing but anxiety so far. I was dismayed at Linda's growing obsession with her as a person and, worse, as a celebrity. Linda had undergone cancer surgery. I was worried that this new development would lead to even more stresses. On the other hand, Linda was overjoyed. How could I deny her that pleasure? Perhaps I was being too protective. Perhaps I had misread everything and had been too harsh in my judgement of Paula's behaviour up to that point. Was I still in denial over Paula and, yes, my own father?

Linda sent me a fax, asking me to write a note for Paula to give to her during their lunch. I couldn't refuse, and I faxed it back on January 29, 1998. It read:

'Dear Paula,

'The Cheshire Cat never had a smile as wide as the one on my face at this moment. I must truly look stupid but couldn't care less! Linda's fax is exuberant. He-He [my childhood nickname for Linda] has a tendency to underline words and phrases when excited with happiness. The "wish" of "I wish you were here" is one that got the triple treatment, and please know that I really do wish I could be with you both. Finally, after all of the crap and corruption of these past lousy three years (and, of course, the nightmares of the last seven months) something positive and real has happened.

'My saving good fortune during this time has been to have had Linda. Common DNA in itself means little if anything. Shared life experiences, good and bad, and mutual circumstances of upbringing mean everything. So much of what Linda and I have recently discussed was communicated without a word. We just knew. Friends, true friends, were wonderful in their counsel and kind words, but they did not live our showbiz lives, nor lived in 169, nor really had any idea as to what the nature of the beast gnawing at us was. Their intentions were priceless but, in truth, I only wanted Linda, Lynne and my own private space. Others, of course, not only knew dear Papa (how many 'best friends' can one have?) but also relished in treating Linda and me like shit. Either way, Linda and I had one another. Paula, I fear that you were more alone than Linda and me during this, your sad and nightmarish time.

'Please know how sorry I am for that. Well beyond any consideration of a DNA bond, the three of us do have much circumstantially in common. I do hope that Linda and yourself enjoy one another. I do hope that, sooner rather than later, all three of us can meet and laugh; really laugh.

'Linda read to me over the telephone the *Daily Mail*'s interview with your mother. I could not have been more surprised.

'I felt no anger, no righteous indignation, no vindictiveness . . . when Linda finished reading, I immediately blurted

out, "Sweetheart, does Paula believe this crap?" and mercifully, she replied, "No." Please God you don't.

'Paula, few people have been as guilty (stupid?) as myself
for catering to, amongst others but primarily, my father's
personality and actions. Up to literally his last moment, I was
still trying to find the good I had never seen before. How
very much happier my life could have been had I just let it all
go years before. And let it all go I now must do. Please do not
let your mother's unhappiness rob you of one more second
of joy in yourself, your beautiful children, your undeniable
accomplishments and all manner of good things that just
might be ahead – of which, I hope, Linda and I may be, for
you, a large part.

'Okay, enough of my psychobabble for now. If not in
person, I will be with you guys in thought tomorrow. Just
order a double Johnny [Johnnie] Walker with a little ice in a
short glass, please.

'Paula, only good wishes to you,
'Christopher.'

The reference to Hélène was to do with a series of interviews in
which she denied having sex with Hughie during the period of
Paula's conception. She admitted that Hughie had visited their
Llandudno hotel for lunch, although she insisted she was already
pregnant by then. She did, she confessed, have a brief affair with
him – when Paula was eight years old.

She told every journalist that she could not understand the
DNA results. She proposed that the samples may have been
mixed up, or tampered with. She suggested, outrageously, that far
from Hughie fathering Paula, Jess must have sired Linda and me,
which would have been a physical impossibility, since we were
both conceived in Canada.

In her most extraordinary interview, Hélène proposed to
Observer journalist Harriet Lane that Jess had perhaps drugged
her evening coffee so as to make way for Hughie Green to sneak
into her bedroom and impregnate her. The small flaw in her
theory, as presented by Lane, was that Paula had already been

born on the night Hélène described; she was said to be sleeping in her cot in the corner.

In answer to Paula's frantic questioning about Hughie after the initial allegations, Hélène had advised her to read her forthcoming book which, Hélène maintained, would explain everything to her. The only book that was forthcoming, published by Virgin shortly before Paula's death in 2000, was *Cat Chat*. It was a whimsical story set in Provence and starring Hélène, her husband and their cat Bebe. No amorous tomcat by the name of Hughie was mentioned in it.

Paula had been rightfully furious with her mother after the DNA result, demanding, 'How could she be so cruel? Why did she let me go through the humiliation of the DNA test when she must have known there was a good chance of it being true?' Their relationship never recovered.

Linda told me that Paula read my letter at their lunch the next day and appeared to be touched by it. Belinda had also been present. My sister, of course, had phoned me a day or two later, thrilled with the rapport she had built up with Paula, but there had been an unfortunate twist.

Linda was panicked and very upset over the fact that a photographer had spotted Paula and snapped them walking out of the trendy restaurant, La Famiglia, in Chelsea. It had been agreed earlier that the lunch would be private, not only for personal reasons but because – as Linda had informed Belinda – there was a clause in our agreement with the *Daily Mail* that no follow-up events or 'sequels' in any other newspaper were permitted for 90 days after the 'DNA' exclusive. Now, by chance, a photo-journalist had snatched a picture before that clause had expired, it appeared in a national tabloid, and Linda was terrified that the *Mail* would take action against her or us. They never did, but it was another stressful incident.

Paula and Belinda theorised to Linda that the child who answered the telephone when Linda first called must have later told Bob Geldof that a meeting was to take place. Bob, then, perhaps tipped off a journalist. This explanation made no sense to me; it left a bad taste in my mouth. Linda was hysterical and I was suspicious again. I felt sure that the situation had had nothing to do with Bob Geldof. Linda wasn't delighted to think it, but she had quite probably been used for a photo opportunity that, presumably, had been to Paula's financial benefit.

Still, they set up another meeting for a Sunday somewhere around the middle of February. This time, Paula brought Belinda to visit Linda in Mayfield. Very early on that morning in Montreal, Lynne and I were fast asleep in bed when the phone rang. It was Linda, telling me that Paula would like to say hello to her brother.

It was the first time I ever spoke to Paula. She sounded nervous and I was half-asleep – hardly the best combination of circumstances when you are talking to your sister for the first time. We exchanged assorted banalities – 'How are you?' 'Looking forward to meeting you!' – without wanting to approach any meaningful discussion. But it was good to hear her voice. It was a nice voice, and that's what I remember most vividly about our brief conversation.

Linda contacted me after Paula and Belinda had returned to London, and she had 'wonderful news'. Belinda was negotiating with *Hello!* or *OK* magazine for a marvellous, glossy, front-page photo-story about all of us meeting for the first time. The angle was going to be the children – all eleven of them – meeting on Linda's beautiful front lawn. There would be Fifi Trixibelle, Peaches, Pixie and Tiger; then Linda's children Delia, Christina, Stephanie and Marina; and of course my stepdaughters, Kristin, Keely and Kady.

They ranged in age from infancy (Tiger) through to early thirties (Delia). It was a lovely, appealing image, and the magazine would certainly pay our plane fares to England for the privilege of being able to capture it. It all sounded great, but yet I was apprehensive. I just wasn't getting into the excitement and that was simply not me. Why was I not happier about things? I should have been welcoming this proposed introduction to my new-found family as something wonderful and positive.

Linda sensed my hesitation, she reassured me that this was simply a fabulous, free trip over with Lynne and the kids, that apart from the commercial considerations, Paula really did want to meet us, and that appearing in *Hello!* or *OK* was definitely something to aspire to. She pleaded with me to participate since without me, Lynne and the children, there would be no story, and we would be letting everyone down. I vowed to take part with full grace and enthusiasm. Obviously, I had been fretting over nothing.

The meeting was tentatively set for the middle of March 1998. Lynne and I then built our plans around that date. Our children were full of excitement about the trip, and their enthusiasm was infectious. My paranoia and foreboding subsided, and for a few days, I began to feel like myself again.

Then Linda called and, without letting me say a word, told me sternly, 'Christopher, you cannot let Paula down, she needs the money desperately and without you coming, they won't do the story.' I didn't understand this, since there was no question of us bowing out. Linda also said that neither *Hello!* nor *OK* would now be doing the story but that the *Sun* – a far cry from either of the glossy, celebrity magazines – had made a great offer and were going to do the exclusive.

I asked Linda what had happened to *Hello!* and *OK*, but there were no real answers. I merely had to say 'yes' to coming over and sign the faxed, contractual agreement for the *Sun* story. I did what I was told.

This was not my show, and I was beginning to feel that my sole role was to cater to the 'celebrity' and my sister, Linda. I felt no bitterness but, rather, a sadness. I could not see happiness ahead. Everything had been too surreal, too clouded by smoke, mirrors and the agendas of others. I could see Hughie Green, the deathbed puppeteer, still pulling the strings.

Paula had not wanted to meet us before the DNA results, and her reasons – her refusal to believe the allegation, and the chaos that her life was in at the time – were at least understandable. Now that Father's paternity had been undeniably established, she still didn't really want to see us – but she had to. As Emma and Jo pointed out, she intended, however, to carry on believing that Jess was her father. She would have had to give up her 'reality' of 38 years simply to gain a couple of siblings, and that probably didn't seem a fair exchange to Paula.

But she must have been intrigued to talk to us, to see what we looked like. And as a celebrity, there was enormous media pressure on her to meet us. It would have been hard for her to justify her reluctance to the great British public, especially since we had told the press how warmly we would welcome her into the family.

She must also have been curious to find out about Hughie, why he had hated Jess Yates so deeply and why he had trashed his career in 1974.

But the most persuasive factor, in my view, was that Paula was desperate for the money she would now earn from the *Sun*. She needed us to make the cash that would fund her trip to Sydney for Tiger's christening. Once there, she would be paid handsomely by *Hello!* for exclusive coverage of the baptism.

Linda and I had come together over Mother's death and I could now see Father's death and its revelations ruining all the bridges we had managed to build. I prayed that I was wrong. But to me, Linda was not seeing Paula and her circumstances for what they were. Much was going on, and nothing was what it appeared to be at face value.

When Linda first told me about Paula Yates, I hadn't been interested in hearing about her. I rather got the impression that Paula was some sort of celebrity presenter who was famous for being famous rather than anything else.

I had known only a little about Bob Geldof. I was vaguely aware that he had had a musical career singing with the new-wave band the Boomtown Rats, although they were never the biggest news in Canada. I had, of course, heard all about his finest moment – his organisation of the Band Aid single, 'Do They Know It's Christmas?', which he co-wrote with Midge Ure, and the international Live Aid extravaganza, which raised a reported £100 million for starving people in Ethiopia.

I remember Papa talking to me about the concerts, which took place at Wembley and Philadelphia on July 13, 1985. He applauded the sentiments of Live Aid without reservation, he was as impressed as I was by the musicians' charitable intent, but he told me he was sad that the money raised would hardly benefit the Ethiopians in the long-term. He felt that the third-world region needed a permanent infrastructure to bring it into line with the modern world.

I had no feelings about Bob Geldof whatsoever. I could never have imagined that I would ever be involved with him. When I realised that our paths looked likely to cross one day, I remember hoping that he took a shower or a bath more often than his legend suggested, and that, in real life, he could get through at least one sentence without using the word 'fuck'.

15

Her Life and Times

When the blood tests turned out to be positive, I immediately became curious about Paula. I wanted to know the things I had resisted hearing about her from Linda. As the day of our proposed family gathering drew nearer, my sister had met Paula twice. In Linda's opinion, Paula was wonderful, Belinda was wonderful and Bob Geldof was a total bastard because Paula and Belinda had said he was, although Linda had not met him.

Despite the headlines over the opium bust, Linda – who strongly disapproved of drugs – had clearly pushed all such allegations to the back of her mind, since Paula had not been charged with any offence. Back in Canada, I was trying hard to overcome my suspicions that Paula's interest in us was anything other than financial. I felt guilty for having such doubts and I dearly wished to learn more about my half-sister in the hope that I could find some grounds for respect and admiration.

I started pulling up material from the Internet, taken from British newspapers, and was disheartened to find that much of it was negative, sensational or both. I attributed this to the celebrity-bashing, tabloid journalism so typical of the UK. After all, I had spent many years reading laughable articles about my father, Hughie Green. I did not want to accept the caricature which was jumping out of my computer screen, that of an ageing rock chick who had messed up her life by leaving 'Saint' Bob Geldof to take up with the wild, rock'n'roll star Michael Hutchence.

Linda assured me that Paula, in real life, was not the person of her public image. I listened to Linda's glowing praise but reserved judgement. I had not been impressed by the reports of Paula's behaviour on the plane to Sydney with Belinda and Tiger, and I was still resentful that she had not come forward to meet us far earlier in the game.

* * * * *

Paula knew from an early age that her parents were not in love. She contended in her colourful if sometimes fanciful auto-biography, published by HarperCollins, that 'along with baby Jesus, it may have been that I was another immaculate conception'. Unfortunately, she lived to discover that her conception had more to do with the proximity of Hughie Green than the Holy Spirit.

Paula grew up in a family that seemed every bit as dysfunctional as our own. She spent her early childhood in the hotel at Llandudno, where Jess Yates, on medication for his fragile psychiatric condition, would spend all day stretched out in a chair and all night keeping his family and guests awake with thundering, Hammond organ recitals.

Paula described her mother as 'a six-foot red-haired love goddess and a member of Mensa'. Elaine, as she was then known, was definitely not cut out to be a hotel manageress, and still hankered after a career in show business. As far back as Paula could remember, she was looked after by nannies but would spend hours lying outside her mother's door, worshipping from a distance. She wasn't potty-trained until she was five.

Moving to a big house in Snowdonia, Jess Yates insulted the appearance of his beautiful wife when he deigned to talk to her at all, drummed it into Paula's head that she was an especially unattractive child, and developed a fixation with taps and plugs. Elaine shouted a lot.

Paula claimed that her father would make her sit in an orange box at the foot of his mighty Hammond so he could be sure that no freak, domestic accident would befall her. She dreamed of escape, and protested at her treatment by refusing to eat properly, a habit that would persist through her adulthood.

She hated her father in those days, although they would later become firm friends, and she idolised her mother, who dressed in impossibly glamorous designer clothes, painted her toenails and sashayed around the house to the strains of contemporary music. Paula was inconsolable when her mother moved to London in search of stardom without her, and at eight, became anorexic and ill with chest infections. Eventually, Elaine tired of her film career, which had included appearances in Fellini's first movies, and returned to Wales.

Paula was sent to boarding school a few miles from her home when she was eleven. She felt like a condemned prisoner in this place where petty rules, punishment, deprivation and suppression of emotion ruled the roost. While for my own reasons I had responded to such a regime in my young life, Paula didn't, and she was relieved when Elaine quickly realised her suffering and removed her, giving the school authorities a typically outrageous reason: that they had both been summoned to the Vatican for an audience with the Pope.

At the beginning of the seventies, Jess Yates moved to Leeds, where he resumed his career, after years of illness, with Yorkshire Television. Paula shortly afterwards moved to Malta with her mother, Elaine, who was trying to make a new life for herself. Often left alone in bed in their flat, Paula was scared and liable to sleepwalk, subconsciously looking for her mother.

Despite all this, Paula enjoyed living abroad, she claimed, and Elaine persisted with her romantic liaisons when she wasn't working on her first novel – the beginning of a new career.

Mother and daughter returned briefly to Wales and then relocated to Palma, Majorca. There, the thirteen-year-old Paula mastered the art of flirting, and had prolonged romances with various boyfriends – none of whom she slept with. And despite her young capacity to captivate any number of male admirers with a combination of witty repartee, shock tactics and a distinctly personal style of dressing, even then, she was a one-man-girl.

This became a pattern as Paula went on to establish herself as one of the most outrageous flirts on British television. Emma Worth later told me, 'She could play a really good temptress, but it was a joke, an acting skill. She would never whore around – oh God, no. She understood men. Since when did a guy walk into a room and fall in love with the nicest, most intelligent woman there who also happened to look boring? No, they tend to go for the buxom blonde, and she was clever enough to think, "I'll be the buxom blonde and they will fall in love with me," and they did.'

For all of her sexual abstinence in Majorca, Paula was at the same time introduced to heroin by one of her boyfriends. She claimed that they snorted the drug together for weeks as they listened to the Velvet Underground and Paula quoted from Shakespeare, but as her O-levels loomed, she retreated to her home to revise and stopped indulging in smack as suddenly as she had started, with no ill effect. There followed an experience with Quaaludes before Paula was sent back to England.

She lived and studied as a boarder in Oxford in 1976 – the year of the long, hot summer, and the birth of punk rock and anarchy in the UK. Paula was just turning sixteen, and it was not long before she met her first real rock star, Talking Heads' Jerry Harrison, who spotted her sunbathing in the meadows near her school, and came over to say hello. She accepted his invitation to see the group playing that night with another pioneering American punk band, the Ramones, and made her first entry into a world that, later, would become her own.

If her O-levels had marked Paula's withdrawal from heroin, then her A-levels recalled her first experience of LSD. Sitting one exam while flying high from the acid in a piece of blotting paper, she nevertheless walked off with all three passes, and was soon afterwards whisked off to live in a Georgian house in Bognor Regis, on the south coast of England, by Elaine, who had returned from Majorca.

One Saturday night in Bognor, the phone rang. It was Jess Yates, who was, according to Paula, 'distraught but trying to be brave'. He had heard that the next day's *News of the World* was running with the story of his affair with a much younger lady

called Anita. Paula stated in her memoirs that Jess was convinced
Hughie Green was to blame for this, and she described Father as
'the genial host of *Opportunity Knocks*'.

She didn't seem too put out. She related, 'The whole story is so
bizarre it's almost like a film plot – two top television executives
tussling furiously over billing or car parking places . . .'

Recalling how journalists pushed little pieces of paper through
every orifice of her home the next day, begging for comments or
interviews from Jess's family, Paula stated firmly, 'My mother's
house was the wrong place to go looking for moral indignation.'

Paula inevitably moved to London, immersed herself in the
burgeoning punk rock scene, and took a job with Thames
Television as a junior press officer, courtesy of a friend of Jess's.
Later, I was told that it was actually Father, behind the scenes,
who had pulled strings to get Paula her job. This has been
accepted as fact in certain circles, although no one connected
Hughie's discreet help at the time with the fact that he was
actually Paula's dad. I can only assume that if this was true, he
was still in contact with Elaine, who had asked for his assistance.

I have resented Father for it ever since, because he had sternly
blocked any acting opportunities that presented themselves to
Linda and me as children. The Major had briefly dallied with the
idea of making me his 'second child star'. He had taught me
ditties and had wanted me to audition for a part in the movie, *A
Kid For Two Farthings*, directed by his friend Carol Reed. It was
Reed who had made *Midshipman Easy*, the thirties film which
had given Hughie his first leading role. The very mention of the
audition had caused an enormous row between Father and the
Major, and Hughie had stamped on the idea immediately.

Linda, however, certainly had tremendous dramatic flair, and
could well have carved out a career in acting. She had attended
the Arts Educational School while we lived in Baker Street, and
had succeeded in an audition for a TV show filmed once a week
in Birmingham.

She had started out co-presenting the show with a young fellow
called Rodney, who, during its run, committed suicide, much to

Linda's shock and sadness. It was later extended from fifteen minutes to half an hour a week, under the title of *Linda's Corner*.

Hughie later claimed to have been 'delighted' by Linda's success in the entertainment world, but he was lying. In reality, he had sneered at her school as 'artsy-fartsy', he hadn't been aware of *Linda's Corner* until quite some time after she had started filming it, and when he did find out, he put a stop to it.

He had stormed to our mother, Claire, 'Are you trying to ruin my career? Have you any idea how bad it would be for my image if the public realised I had a teenage daughter? I have to portray a youthful image to secure contracts and keep on paying for you all!'

The truth was simple: Father hadn't wanted us in his world of TV studios and theatres. That was to be his sole territory where he could come and go with mistresses and whores without fear of bumping into his children.

Paula left her PR job before long, and took to cleaning for wealthy, Chelsea householders. She spent her leisure time in punk clubs, watching gigs and meeting such ground-breaking personalities as the Sex Pistols, Johnny Thunders and the Heartbreakers, legendary NME writer Nick Kent and New York proto-punk Richard Hell, who immortalised the 'Blank Generation' and became Paula's first lover. Hell was a sensitive character behind the ripped-up clothes and spiky haircut, an intellectual and a lover of the great French poets.

Bob Geldof, Paula's next boyfriend, was equally articulate although in a louder, earthier, more practical and often belligerent manner. Prophetically, she was wearing a wedding dress when she met him, aged seventeen, at a record company party being held in Fulham for the Boomtown Rats, who had arrived from Dublin to join the musical revolution with an energetic but melodic take on the 'new wave', informed more by R&B than by the hurtling punk fury of their contemporaries.

Paula, by then, was developing her own, outrageous fashion style incorporating ballgowns and antique nighties, although her bridal appearance cut no ice with Bob Geldof that night. She met him again in Dublin at Christmas, while staying with her mother at a castle in the Irish countryside, and the romance began there and then, with Paula nicknamed 'The Limpet' by Geldof's cronies, due to her determined omnipresence.

Paula, despite the sunny glow that permeates her memoirs, was filled with insecurities arising from her unconventional childhood and was searching for a partner with whom she could build a normal, loving, family home. Bob Geldof may have been looking for much the same thing. He had also been an injured child. His mother had died from a brain haemorrhage when he was still a little boy, leaving him to be brought up by his eldest sister, Cleo, in a big, dark and cheerless house in Dun Laoghaire, near Dublin. His father, working in carpeting and glassware, had to be away for most of the time, travelling.

However, on one occasion when his father *was* at home, he gave the young Bob Geldof an agonising caning for spending his school fees' money on personal treats. From that moment on, he hated his father, years later writing of 'the hurt, the rage, the shame and the bewilderment' he had felt over the incident, although his feelings mellowed when he became a father himself.

His love affair with Paula would last for eighteen years, during which they would become the best-known couple in rock, with a wide circle of friends that included some of the world's most revered musicians.

The Boomtown Rats toured industriously throughout the late seventies and became one of the most popular bands in Europe (and South Africa) with a string of hit albums and singles, famously 'Rat Trap' and the show-stopping 'I Don't Like Mondays', which were both Number One million-sellers. The group would spend a total of 123 weeks in the UK singles chart. Bob Geldof emerged as a major personality and was much sought after as an interviewee on account of his opinionated worldview, his eloquence, his fearlessness and his liking for a good argument.

Paula posed naked for *Penthouse* in 1979 and, encouraged by Geldof, began work as a gossip columnist for the music weekly *Record Mirror*. She embarked on her career as an author with a dramatic, best-selling debut, *Rock Stars In Their Underpants*, which was published by Virgin in 1980 and eulogised by no less than Andy Warhol. She also began contributing monthly to *Cosmopolitan* magazine, and she would continue with her literary endeavours, somehow turning out a book a year while building a high profile on television and embracing motherhood with unbridled enthusiasm.

In 1982, Paula became a household name after being selected to present a new Channel 4 programme, *The Tube*, with the accomplished keyboardist and renowned wit Jools Holland. Going out live for an hour-and-a-half every Friday at teatime, it was an anarchic mixture of music, interviews and mischief from Paula and Jools, who had established an immediate and chaotic chemistry. Nothing so spontaneous, so irreverent and so frequently controversial had been screened before, and *The Tube* has gone down in the annals of rock and TV history as a genuinely pioneering show. It continued for five years, and introduced some exciting, new rock talents to the viewing public.

Still flamboyantly glamorous, Paula became known for a giggly, playful and audacious interviewing technique. If she had not been Mrs Geldof, she would still have found her way into the papers simply on account of the bubble and fizz that belied her sharp intelligence.

During the first series of *The Tube*, Paula discovered she was pregnant with her first child. Bob Geldof, who was in New York, sent her 200 roses, and when Fifi Trixibelle was born, Paula, who had no experience of babies, found a new purpose in life. Stating later in her autobiography that the little girl's birth had changed her world forever and that 'I was never alone again', she talked evangelically about her children, declaring that 'they were, and still are, absolutely central to my existence'. By her actions as well as her words, she proved this many times over as she put her daughters' needs above her own in every aspect of her work and play.

*   *   *   *   *

One day at the Newcastle studios where *The Tube* was filmed, Paula was informed that she was interviewing Michael Hutchence from INXS. She didn't want to do it, because she knew nothing about the band, but changed her mind the minute she saw the 'heartbreakingly beautiful' singer.

'God's gift to women.'

'Sex on legs.'

'The Taj Mahal of crotches.'

Her admiration has been captured in any number of memorable soundbites, but at the time of meeting Michael, her reaction was almost child-like. The day after the interview, she fixed his picture to the door of her fridge and it would stay there for more than a decade, changing occasionally when Bob Geldof would decide to write the word 'cunt' over his forehead, so that she would have to replace the photograph. She later said of Hutchence, 'I knew he was special, not like anyone else I'd met.'

The fateful meeting seemed to pose no great threat to the Geldofs' relationship, which was generally seen to be stable, mutually supportive and more than capable of surviving Paula's occasional burst of fandom. Indeed, Bob Geldof and Paula were together about to enter the realms of rock royalty when in 1984, the Band Aid project was conceived. By now, Geldof's musical career was in decline, with the Boomtown Rats no longer scoring hit records. He was still, however, a forceful and respected personality in the music world.

Paula claimed that she was first to see the TV news reports. Despairingly, she watched the footage of pitiful, starving Ethiopians, and resolved to raise £200 towards their famine relief. In a phone conversation with Bob the next day, before filming began for *The Tube*, he asked if she would recruit the services of Midge Ure – a guest on the show – for a benefit single.

The rest is history. 'Do They Know It's Christmas?' broke all existing records for singles sales, and raised £8 million. Geldof also organised an American single, featuring the cream of US musical talent, and followed on with the Live Aid spectacular on July 13, 1985. Attended by Prince Charles and Princess Diana at the Wembley end, it was an enormously emotional day, eliciting an overwhelming response from the public, who donated generously, and it resulted in Geldof receiving an honorary knighthood from the Queen.

Paula married Bob Geldof in 1986 in a secret ceremony in Las Vegas, and later held a second wedding for friends and family at the church attached to their Kent home, The Priory, with the bride in sensational scarlet and a sixteen-feet train. The guests included David Bowie, George Michael, Chrissie Hynde, Duran Duran, Spandau Ballet, Midge Ure, Kevin Godley and Lulu. Later that year, the groom became Sir Bob.

Paula wrote to Michael Hutchence, and she saw him sporadically over the next number of years. Newspaper reports alleged a hot affair, but Paula denied it. The press had already misconstrued her friendship with Ben Volpeliere Pierrot of Curiosity Killed the Cat, and there were lurid stories of her snorting cocaine with the acclaimed young soul singer Terence Trent D'Arby. Paula was famous for never touching alcohol or cigarettes, and by this time, her previous experiments with drugs were long behind her. She drank tea and ate Fig Rolls at home, and accepted a Diet Coke when out with friends. She insisted that the stories were untrue, but her relationship with the press was certainly turning into a 'free-for-all' on their part.

She became pregnant again, giving birth to Peaches, and a year later, Pixie arrived, with a face like a 'beautiful bun'. Paula relished her role as mother and home-maker, particularly at The Priory where she enjoyed the changing seasons in the Kent countryside and encouraged her children in their various hobbies.

Bob was pursuing a series of solo, musical ventures which drew audiences but produced little reward financially or critically. However, he had bigger things to think about. He had gone into partnership to set up a TV production company, Planet 24. And in 1992, it had an instant hit on its hands with *The Big Breakfast*, an 'alternative' wake-up show presented by Channel 4 every morning. The programme, hosted by a zany, young Chris Evans, was a riotous affair aimed at sixteen to thirty-four year olds, and Paula flirted for England as she chatted to celebrities on the *Big*

Breakfast bed, while Bob occasionally stepped in to interrogate statesmen and weightier guests.

The format was quite the opposite to the serious, softly-softly sofa technique of other breakfast shows. Once again, Paula was at the very centre of a new phenomenon in British broadcasting. Together, the original *Big Breakfast* team snapped, crackled and popped, and they set the standards by which their eventual replacements would stand or fall. Geldof would wisely quit the ship before it lost its momentum and finally sank ten years later.

Emma Worth remembers, 'Paula had to get up at four in the morning to do the show, she was doing books, she was writing for the newspapers, and she loved it all. She was an extremely hard-working girl, and she was very professional about her work.'

Her memories of Paula, personally, during this period are typical, 'She had an incredibly kind heart. She was warm, funny, very clever. She was a brilliant raconteur, and she was sensitive to other people. She just had a magic. She could walk into the room and she just lit it up.

'She was generous towards her girlfriends, always very complimentary, very giving. I never saw that kind of female rivalry thing with her.

'She adored her children. She did paintings with them, and dressing-up games. She was always very involved. Meetings with Paula would always be interrupted with children doing things, and that was great. I would take my son Sebastian to the house, because he was a baby too, and we had this working friendship that was a bit like a mothers' coffee morning. The kids were always around. They were part of the deal.'

As her best friend, journalist Jo Fairley would tell the North American edition of *Vanity Fair*, in February 2001, the extremes of Paula's personality and interests made her both 'the vixen and the earth mother'.

Emma Worth also saw a 'very serious side': 'When I met her in 1990, she and Bob had the three children whom they adored, but I don't think things were easy in her marriage. I think she was going through, slightly, which everyone does, a mid-life crisis. She was a wonderful rock-chick in her time, and then she made a incredibly good mother. Suddenly, she was in her early thirties, and it was, "What's the next stage in my life?"

'I think Bob was aware of that. He was very interested in her work and concerned about it and very keen that she stuck to her timetable. He knew that she needed to feel fulfilled. But I used to feel that he would take over.

'He was quite a dominating and forceful person, he always had an opinion and he liked to debate things. Paula told me very early on that Bob always had to win in an argument. And if he thought he was losing, he would suddenly quote statistics, or a fact, which would be completely made up. Bob felt he was the boss, the man of the house, and he would always express his worries about Paula's work when he was there, but in a concerned way.

'We would say, "Let's wait until he goes out of the room," and then we could relax and talk properly. Paula would tell me that [in her opinion] he was a 'control freak', and my perception of him was exactly that. He liked to be in on the meetings, and he liked to be in charge. He always thought he knew everything.'

Paula later wrote that she was always 'quite scared' of Bob Geldof, and she would do anything to please him and avoid making him angry, because she hated confrontation. But Emma added, 'As far as I could see, their marriage was all right. I'm absolutely sure that there was genuine love between them.'

Paula, for her part, was determined to create the perfect home. 'It was so important that she have this idyllic life,' ventured Emma. 'Even if Bob had been the saint that everyone thought he was, which he wasn't, it all had to crack somehow because she was so concerned about it.'

Paula put it like this: she had spent the whole of her adult life with Bob Geldof and, at the age of 35, had suddenly realised that she was 'no longer willing to be told when I could chat on the phone or redecorate a bedroom'. She added that 'Bob is the most controlling person in the world,' that she was beginning to feel like she was back in her father's orange box, and she wanted to break free.

Two things sparked the split. One was the death of Jess Yates on April 9, 1993 which, as well as being a shock, reminded Paula that life is short; she felt she needed to change hers. The other decisive factor, she said, was that because of their working routines, Paula and Bob were keeping completely different hours, with Bob going to bed only a short while before Paula got up.

But she thought long and hard about making any changes. On Christmas Day 1993, she confided in Jo Fairley, and was aware of the hammering she would receive from the press should she decide to leave Sir Bob Geldof, the public's beloved hero and saint, and one of the most powerful men in the country. It would be more than a year before she finally decided to pack her things.

On October 31, 1994, Paula interviewed Michael Hutchence on the *Big Breakfast* bed, and the chemistry sizzled out of TV screens across the nation as they tangled their legs together in a public declaration of mutual desire.

Finally, at the beginning of 1995, Paula gathered up the children and moved out of the family home, later saying, 'I left because I was tired and unhappy and wanted to change everything before it was too late.' She was emphatic afterwards that she did not leave Bob Geldof for Michael Hutchence, and that her romance with the INXS superstar began only after the separation.

Not all of her friends would confirm that statement. Jo Fairley told *Vanity Fair*, 'I remember when Paula rang to tell me that she was having an affair [with Hutchence].' And Emma Worth said that Paula was faithful to Bob throughout her marriage – 'until Michael'. However, when the divorce finally went through the courts in May 1996, it was surprisingly attributed to Bob Geldof's infidelity with an unknown co-respondent.

Paula publicly stated that she had no idea whether or not Geldof was seeing other women during their times apart. Certainly, he never expressed an interest in any, and she, Paula, would not have dreamt of asking about his rumoured flings.

Emma Worth told me, 'I didn't keep track of Bob, and I have no evidence to prove it, but Paula definitely told me that he had been unfaithful to her, way before Michael was on the scene. I don't know who his lover was. I have no reason to think that Paula would make it up or imagine it, but who knows? There was that side to Paula which was insecure, although she didn't appear at that time to be any more insecure than anyone else.'

Bob Geldof, by all accounts, did not want to make a public statement about the separation, only finally agreeing at Paula's insistence. But they were too late. Their PR agent had to break the news that the press had been following Paula, they had discovered her spending nights at a hotel with Michael Hutchence, and the *News of the World* was about to publish the story.

Geldof was allegedly enraged, snatching Paula's mobile phone from her hand to interrupt a conversation with Hutchence and demand of the shocked Australian singer, 'What's this about you sleeping with my wife?'

The next day, a frantic Geldof took Paula and the children away for a holiday in a last-ditch attempt to get his wife and daughters back. They visited Bono's family in Ireland before travelling on to Jamaica where the scenery was idyllic but Paula felt simply wrung out. After all the soul-searching she had done, she wasn't going to change her mind.

Her mother, Hélène, reportedly sympathised more with Geldof than Paula. Emma said, 'Paula was shocked, very hurt that her mother sided with Bob. She also backed him, I think, over the alleged drug thing. Paula was so upset. Even though she said, "Well, what else can I expect from her?" blood is meant to be thicker than water, even if you are not getting on like a house on fire. I would like to think that my mother would tell me I'd behaved badly but she would still be on my side.

'Paula would talk about her mother quite a lot, but never bitterly or vindictively. It was always couched in humour. Paula wasn't a catty person, but I could always tell that there was no great love lost. They had an odd relationship. Her mother was more of a rival; Paula felt she could never live up to her glamour. She also wanted to make up for her mother's lack of maternal instincts by having a great relationship with her own daughters and writing her babycare books.'

Asked if she thought Paula would have left Geldof had she not previously met Hutchence, Emma said, 'I cannot answer that. I don't know. But I think, yes, she probably would. I think she was afraid to leave Bob.'

In *The Autobiography*, Paula spoke of her pain and sorrow at ending the long relationship, admitting that Bob had considered her the 'perfect wife' and had not noticed her discontent. She declared herself 'utterly proud' of everything they had accomplished together, confirmed their continuing friendship and stressed, 'Even now, I get angry when people say anything negative about Bob. What do they know?' However, there had been reports of great turbulence immediately after the split, with Paula accused of throwing a rock through the window of her husband's London home.

Bob Geldof was heartbroken by the split but remained silent. Only much later – in an article dated September 2002 – did he confess the extent of his torment to interviewer Ray Martin in Majorca. Describing Paula as 'really funny and really beautiful' and recalling her 'grace and light and joy and beauty', Bob admitted that when she left he couldn't get out of bed, felt like killing himself and probably would have, had it not been for the children. In less responsible circumstances, he would have vanished to some dark place and 'howled into the void for two years'. He spoke of a physical pain that was like 'being pounded', and vowed never to marry again because 'I would be scared stiff of it now'.

The loss of his daughters was equally devastating: 'You drag yourself up the stairs and you don't smell the children any more, you don't hear them rustle in their sleep. I mean, that's the thing that just utterly emptied me, you know. I was incapable of anything, any intellectual function, any physical function certainly . . . I mean, you're rejected and discarded. That's what I felt. What you are is just a single, raw and vivid nerve end, so that if you're touched by kindness or anything like that you recoil like the whipped dog . . .'

He added, 'Nothing compensates. None of the beauty of the world, the coffee in the morning, a beautiful woman passing by, a great work of art, the most fantastic song, driving your car on the open road . . . they mean nothing. Life without love is meaningless.'

Paula wasn't having it too easy either. Despite the 'nirvana' and the 'natural and liberating' essence of her new relationship with Michael Hutchence, even she could not have foreseen the unprecedentedly vicious nature of the media's prolonged attack upon her. She was horribly maligned, and wherever she went, with or without Hutchence, she was followed by stalkers with notebooks, recording equipment and cameras. Michael was stunned and dismayed by the relentlessness and the vitriol of the press-people, and on at least one occasion lashed out at photographers with his fists. There was much ado about his previous relationship with supermodel Helena Christiansen, from whom he had recently split.

Some observers suggested that Paula had herself tipped off the newsdesks about at least one hotel liaison with Hutchence. Whatever, she was now, ironically, being hounded and savaged by the very people on whom she would increasingly depend for her living: the press.

They wanted to know, unkindly, why Paula left Saint Bob Geldof for the earthling Michael Hutchence? And why did Hutchence leave one of the world's most beautiful women for Paula Yates? In a scenario which would have horrified her former, motherly self, Paula would find herself having to sleep with the enemy, who had insulted her so grievously, to raise any significant cash of her own. And it would get worse.

For the time being, Paula and Michael stayed locked indoors, enjoying all manner of physical pleasures until the storm died down, although it never really did, and her one great hope for the future would remain unfulfilled, 'That everyone can now be happy. That's my greatest wish for all the people I love.'

*　*　*　*　*

Paula's first act as a 'free' woman was to have a boob job – something she claimed would have horrified Bob Geldof. She was beginning to transform herself into the woman that she wanted to be, and one that she undoubtedly hoped her world-famous rock-star, Michael, would appreciate.

She made a lot of noise about his 'positive' influence; how he talked her into a new and healthy lifestyle, encouraged her to take walks, and impressed upon her the importance of vegetables and carrot juice. Yet there are those among her friends who contend that she absorbed a darker influence from the self-confessed veteran of the sex, drugs and rock'n'rollercoaster.

Hutchence was an intelligent, polite, gentle and chivalrous person in his routine life, and he genuinely liked women. After years on the road, there was every possibility that he would have loved to settle with the ready-made family he had found with Paula. By all accounts, he rose every morning at 7 a.m to take Paula's girls to school.

He was also a sexual adventurer, according to Paula, who reported with characteristic melodrama that they had tackled six different, illegal activities during their first night of intimacy. Before long, she had become pregnant with Tiger, who was born on July 22, 1996.

But there were whispers that in Paula's efforts to be the woman of Michael's dreams – and again feeling the pull of her youthful curiosities – she was once more taking drugs. One source was absolutely certain that the couple took heroin together, although allegations that they smoked it can almost certainly be discounted, since Paula was known to reject the inhalation of any substance.

Close friends also said that in addition to their legitimate use of Prozac, Paula and Michael were receiving prescriptions for Valium and Rohypnol, the debilitating 'date-rape' sedative.

It was the most supreme irony that Bob Geldof's near-obsessive control of his family – the element that Paula most resented – was the one thing she needed more than anything in her life. Without it, she was lost.

As I arrived from Canada with my family, now fully determined to join in the joy and excitement of meeting my new sister, Paula, I could not have begun to guess at the extent of her problems. The woman I would see in Mayfield would be a shadow of the vibrant, fun-loving character she had been before all the troubles began.

16

We Meet at Last!

I could see immediately that it was all pretty bleak stuff, whatever was going on in her head. Paula was clearly devastated to have learned the truth about her parentage, and seemed for the most part remote, resigned. But I'm convinced she did realise that Linda and I were decent people, and I saw nothing 'mean' about her during that long day at Linda's home in Mayfield. I do not believe that the way in which Paula used and manipulated us was cruelly intended. She had other things on her mind, and she was mentally unwell.

Lynne and I had been stunned at Linda's response when we called her from our hotel room in Montreal to say that our flight had been delayed by a day, that we were stressed and upset, and that little Kady was feeling ill. Linda side-stepped the pleasantries and got right to the point: 'You cannot be late for the *Sun* interview. If you are, they will cancel their contract, and then what is Paula going to do? You must get here on time. The interview starts at ten o'clock.'

Of course, Linda had been terrified of anything happening to ruin the 'perfect day' that it had fallen to her to host. Her potential embarrassment in front of Paula, Belinda and the *Sun* seemed to outweigh any concern for her brother's family. Indeed, the youngsters would not enjoy any great consideration or special attention during the day at Mayfield. We had come to England expecting more than anything to celebrate the children, to bring them happily together, and we had understood this to be the basis of the newspaper coverage. Linda, I believe, had been afraid to tell me about this change of plan in case we wouldn't come.

I love Lynne and our girls; I'm desperately proud of them, and I wanted everyone to meet and enjoy them. Kristin was seventeen at the time, Keely was fourteen and Kady was nine. I was especially sorry for them that they were closeted away for most of the day while Paula, Linda and I were given centre stage.

Tiger also spent most of her time upstairs, away from the action, with Belinda playing nanny. To my surprise, Paula did not show off Tiger to anyone, including the *Sun* representatives, or even talk about her beyond the odd reference. There was none of the 'baby chat' I'd expected. Tiger's christening was up ahead and Paula didn't talk to me or, to the best of my knowledge, anyone else about it. My girls were not invited to play with Tiger and, therefore, did not. Normally, they would have. At the same time, there was no sense that Paula was trying to hide or 'protect' the child from us. She was simply having a working day.

When I first saw Tiger, my youngest niece, she melted my heart. At the second her little face appeared around her mother's ankle on Linda's doorstep, I felt immediately attached. I love kids, and she was an absolute doll, with a shy expression that kept breaking into a lovely smile. I had already thought about her a great deal, and because she had so recently lost her father, I felt hugely protective.

She bore a strong resemblance to Michael Hutchence. Yet, when I looked at her, I thought instinctively of her grandfather Hughie Green, and I felt all the more responsible for this innocent little girl.

Tiger was present during two of my private chats with Paula, including the first one in the kitchen where Paula reflexively and unself-consciously breastfed her. Linda and I held different views about Tiger's frequent attachment, at this age, to Paula's breasts. Linda felt it was wonderful that Paula was continuing to feed her daughter well into her second year, beyond what would normally be considered weaning time. She further suggested that the bonding experience was therapeutic and relaxing for Paula.

I thought it was possibly self-indulgent; that Paula might have been fixating more on her own needs and her reputation as an 'earth mother' than on Tiger's continuing requirement for mother's milk. Even more worrying to me later was the idea of Paula breastfeeding her toddler if she had, indeed, been drinking or taking drugs.

Yet, my sister's adoring eyes would see nothing even a little bit odd about Paula and, up to a point, I loved Linda for her blind adoration. But I had already become concerned that such 'blindness' would lead to bumps and bruises, and I would unfortunately be proved right.

As for Tiger, I have two favourite moments locked into my memory. One was her wonderful, introductory appearance at Paula's ankle. In the other, she was in Paula's arms, stretching her tiny, right hand out towards my face and smiling adorably.

When Paula left Mayfield at the end of the day, I hoped that she would make something personal of my farewell to Tiger – 'Now, say goodbye to your Uncle Chris,' or some similarly endearing comment which would support my hopes for an ongoing relationship. She didn't.

Still, my meeting with Paula and Tiger made an emotional impact on me which has not diminished. Rational people might imagine that a few strands of DNA in common with someone shouldn't necessarily mean too much or, really, anything. But those people have not lived my life, or Linda's.

As the morning progressed, I kept thinking about Paula's other daughters. As with Tiger, she said virtually nothing about them, which struck me as odd. I introduced Lynne, Kristin, Keely and Kady into some of our small talk, but Paula didn't show any interest in them.

I could not have known that Bob Geldof was at that time actively trying to secure primary custody of the girls, which would explain Paula's reluctance to talk about her children. Under normal circumstances, they would have been an obvious major topic of conversation.

I mentioned to her during a quiet moment in the sitting room that I was sorry to hear from Belinda that my three other young nieces would not be coming to Mayfield that day. Paula seemed to feel embarrassed, unhappy and compromised. Whereas Lynne was obviously free to take her girls with her anywhere in the world, Paula couldn't bring her children from London to Mayfield on the train for a few hours.

She suddenly stiffened and, speaking stridently and emotionally, burst into a tirade about Bob Geldof. 'Everything he now seems to do hurts me deeply. He uses the children as a weapon against me. I suppose that is typical, really, in a divorce case. It breaks my heart and he knows it does, and the world sees Bob as a saint. With me, he is really just a mean, nasty bastard.'

By talking about her children, I had inadvertently opened up an enormous can of worms for her. Belinda drifted in to say that Tiger was having a nap upstairs, and joined heartily in the conversation, endorsing Paula's sentiments. Belinda snapped, 'Bob is one great guy, he can feed the fucking world, but he doesn't seem to be able to look after all his family.' Paula nodded her head in agreement, and Belinda then left the room as quickly as she had arrived.

The tirade continued, and Paula's words and tone became quite accusatory towards me. 'I know you really think Bob is great. Everyone does. Why should you be any different? You think he is a bloody saint too. Well, he seems to have turned everyone against me. I'm the bloody wicked one in all of this. I'm the bad person.'

At this point, I had to interrupt. I wasn't enjoying the thrust of it at all. I said, 'Paula, apart from Bob doing Live Aid, I really know nothing about him, and, frankly, I have no opinions about him one way or the other.'

Belinda returned to catch the end of this exchange, declaring, 'Yeah, Live Aid was Bob's big thing. You'll be surprised to hear it was really Paula's idea, but everyone gives all the credit to Bob. No one knows the half of it about Bob. They only know what he puts out – "the saint".' With this parting shot, Belinda left the house with Stephanie to go and pick up Lynne and our girls from the hotel.

Paula became much calmer, but continued her diatribe. I think she realised she had been rough on me and was a little embarrassed. She wanted to speak her mind in a more adult and balanced way. She said, evenly, 'You know, my only "crime" against Bob was falling out of love with him, and no one intends falling in or out of love – it just happens. But he cannot accept that I no longer love him.

'I don't believe he will ever stop making trouble for me, even when the children are grown up. His ego is too big to let everything go. It was always Bob's way or no way. Bob is a control freak and I just couldn't take it any more. And now he seems to know my every move. I don't think I can pick my nose without him knowing about it. And then there is always another bloody writ. And nobody can get beyond his image of being a saint. Well, he's a saint with bullet-proof raiment. And most people think I'm a cheap harlot, but I'm not, you know.'

With that, she had vented her feelings about Bob Geldof. But what is etched into my memory is the despairing way in which she told me that he would never let her go; that and the fact that she appeared to fear him. Mercifully, I didn't hear his name again that day from either Paula or Belinda.

I was surprised, uncomfortable and upset to be on the receiving end of the outburst, and I had said nothing in response, only nodding to acknowledge that I was listening. What was I going to say? 'Oh yes, Bob must have been a real sod because you are so marvellous'? I didn't know him, and I was just getting to know Paula in a tiny way. I had come a long way to see her, and I had not expected our conversations to be about her failed marriage.

Perhaps she was testing to see if I was in Bob Geldof's 'camp'. Clearly, there was a war on. But I hadn't asked a single question about Bob Geldof, and I hadn't wanted to hear about him. At this point, if anything, I was feeling a certain sympathy for him, knowing that he had been publicly humiliated by his ex-wife and Michael Hutchence.

* * * * *

Michael Hutchence was off the agenda. No one mentioned his name except for the *Sun* journalist Amanda Cable, who after wrapping up her first interview with Paula, said, 'OK, everything seems to be fine. Now, do you wish to talk about Michael?'

Paula's body jolted. She replied, 'You know that is not a topic.'

It appeared that Belinda had earlier instructed the *Sun* team that there should be no questions about him. However, Michael's father, Kell Hutchence, was fair game for a savaging – out of Amanda's hearing. The verdict on the elder Hutchence was 'all he cares about is money'. This view was reiterated after Paula's death by one of her friends, who related that Kell had used photographs and information involving her family to sell a story to *Hello!* magazine, without asking permission.

At the time of meeting Paula, I had no idea that there was ill feeling between her and Kell; she was hardly going to tell me that she had already rewritten her will to bar Michael's parents from seeing Tiger, except with the permission of her appointed guardians. Indeed, Paula was promoting the appearance of a loving family relationship between herself, Tiger and Kell – in her own financial interests. She would keep up the charade until after the christening, when she would receive her cheque from *Hello!*

Belinda stated that after Michael's death, Kell had requested money from Paula. The rock star had regularly assisted his dad, and Kell had assumed that Paula would have access to some of Michael's money in London and would therefore continue with the cash transfers. Kell, upon hearing that Paula had no such money, was allegedly very upset.

By agreeing with what Belinda was saying, Paula was showing me her real feelings towards Kell. Money had obviously been an enormous and divisive issue from the moment Michael died, and the situation would worsen as all parties tried to discover the whereabouts of his supposedly vast fortune.

Paula also talked about her mother, briefly, when Amanda introduced the subject. I would later read that Paula had outraged Hélène by swearing at her, using the word 'fuck', during one confrontation about the Hughie Green allegation. But at Mayfield, Paula needed no four-letter language to convey her desolation. Not only had her mother declined to tell her the truth before the

DNA testing, she was also continuing to deny, stonily, that which had been proved by science.

We spoke about Hélène again, privately, while Paula was asking about Hughie. She wanted me to know that her mother was a veritable 'loony-toon'. 'She could have told me the truth years ago,' said Paula. 'She could have told me after Jess died. She could at least tell me the truth now. She has only told me that she's writing a book, and that when I read it I will understand. She is completely in another world, and there's really no point in me talking to her again.

'She backed Bob totally when I left him, she was no mother to me then, so what can I expect now? The woman seems totally delusional.'

As she sat beside me on the sofa in Linda's sitting room, asking me about Father's hatred for Jess Yates, about why he had felt it necessary to trash Jess's career, about why Hughie had not told her personally that he was her father, I was affected not so much by her questions but by *how* she was expressing them. Her plaintive tone was heartbreaking. She was hurting very deeply: she had a need to *know*, and I so badly wanted to tell her. By being able to do that, it might somehow make some of her pain go away.

She awoke in me that day an enormous sense of duty to her to find out the truths of what had happened all those years ago. If I could uncover them, they would give both of us understandings, whether we liked them or not.

I flashed back, suddenly, to the mezzanine floor, to Mama's 'poor little girl in Wales', just as I had on the plane the day that Linda read from Paula's autobiography. Again, I suppressed the thought, not ready to confront or explore it. Later, I would cross continents to uncover the secrets of the unholy triad that was Father, the Major and Violet Green.

Had Hughie died without repercussions, had Paula not been 'revealed', had I not gone to Mayfield and listened to her questions, I would have let the past stay where it was: undisturbed and undiscovered.

* * * * *

They were an odd couple, Paula and Belinda, or so it seemed to me. They had clearly staked out areas of mutual need, understanding and agreement: whether by coincidence or design, it also struck me that Paula's policies were echoed by Belinda.

Paula had gone out of her way to tell me at the beginning of the day, 'Belinda isn't my *friend*,' and this was independently confirmed by Emma Worth several years later. I saw that for myself. I noticed no real interaction between the two, no genuine warmth or respect.

It looked to me as though Paula needed a 'road warrior', someone to look after her, to cook, clean, maybe do some shopping or other important errands, and see to Tiger. These were not the sort of duties that Paula's other friends – focused women like Emma Worth and Jo Fairley – had ever carried out for her.

When Paula and Emma had been together, Paula was a working, functioning person with a clear and intelligent mind. However, the relationship between Paula and Belinda produced somewhat unhealthy and symbiotic results. To me, it seemed that Belinda enjoyed the reflected light of the 'celebrity' she tended. If this was so, it spoke badly of both of them, but oddly enough, I felt sorry for the two individuals because to me it appeared that each was obviously being used by the other. But at the end of the day, both Paula and Belinda showed me new and different sides of their personalities.

They were getting ready to leave, and Paula went upstairs to fetch Tiger. Left in the kitchen with Belinda, I asked casually about their forthcoming trip to Australia for the christening. Belinda seemed to ignore the question and decided instead to regale me with the story of their flight to Sydney for Michael Hutchence's funeral.

This was when Paula had shattered the calm of the first-class British Airways cabin with her weeping, wailing and hysterical pronouncements that Bob Geldof had 'killed' Michael by driving him to suicide. Later, Paula would adopt the opposite view, campaigning relentlessly for her belief that Michael died when a solo, sex adventure went tragically wrong. She would insist that the personal things she knew about him made this the only possible explanation.

Those personal things were not in her stunned and befuddled mind while she was flying to Sydney to bury Michael. Stopping over in Bangkok, Paula, Belinda and Tiger were taken to a lounge and told, essentially, to shape up or ship out. A scuffle of some sort then ensued.

Belinda's version was very colourful, and she told it with her characteristically staccato delivery, complete with a slight accent derived from living abroad as a young person – I believe in the Far East – and a compulsion to scatter words like 'Yah' through her sentences.

She related that in an altercation with a minor airport official, she had said something insulting, at the same time giving him a finger gesture, with the result that he had tried to hit her. This allowed Belinda and Paula to take the high moral ground, and after being cautioned to behave, they were allowed to continue the flight to Australia.

Then, in an unforgettable finale, Belinda declared, 'We are going on BA again to Sydney for the christening, and I cannot wait to be in first-class, being outrageously pampered, and when they ask me if I want caviar, Chris, do you know what I'm going to do? Do you?'

I heard myself say, rather lamely, 'No.'

Belinda then came right up to me and said, 'I am going to tell them, "Caviar? Yes, slather it here, slather it up and down and don't stop. I love caviar!"'

I could never have envisaged such a bizarre performance. Thankfully, Paula came back down with Tiger and handed her to Belinda while she adjusted her funky, fun-fur leopard coat. She then took my arm and pulled me into her bosom, theatrically whispering into my ear, 'You are a very sexy man, and I have to remind myself that you are my brother – after all, sisters aren't meant to have such thoughts about their brothers, are they?'

Coming on top of what had just happened with Belinda, I was shell-shocked, not by what Paula said but by the sudden change in her attitude and demeanour. We had certainly built up an empathy and had established a shared sense of the risqué that could have seen us skating over such a remark with amusement in different circumstances.

But Paula had been generally lifeless all day, only becoming truly animated, and then not in a jolly or joking way at all, when posing for the camera and when discussing Bob, Hélène, Kell, Hughie and Jess. And while she had cracked the odd, acid one-liner and laughed heartily at my seaside-postcard humour, she had not made me personally the victim of her attention.

Now, she was all pepped-up, a seductress and a tease. She had absented herself for ten minutes, she had returned as a stranger, and she was flying.

My mind rewound. And then it fast-forwarded through the stranger episodes of the day. There had been tales of Paula being terribly nervous and on her 'best behaviour'. There had been ominously delivered warnings that she shouldn't be offered a drink. There was the story of the 'bad Tandoori'. Cumulatively, this all painted a picture of someone who was on that very morning, suffering from a drink- or drugs-related hangover, who was abstaining from whatever she might have felt like doing for the sake of appearances in front of the *Sun* and her new family, and who had celebrated her relief at the end of the day with a line of cocaine or some similarly uplifting substance.

My sister Paula was on drugs, I was sure. I hadn't wanted to see anything like that, and it alarmed me, particularly in view of the dreadful things that had recently befallen her. If she was using illicit substances, then, assuredly, it wasn't for recreational purposes.

As for Linda, I didn't believe she had noticed anything amiss. Her great concern that day was to ensure that it all went smoothly for everyone involved, and that we all thought Paula was fabulous. She loathes drugs, and would never knowingly have allowed anyone to use them in her house. Even Paula.

I wouldn't have had a lot of time for Paula Yates The Celebrity. From childhood, I had seen little to admire about the superficiality of most people inhabiting show business. The music world had seemed especially shallow to me, although The Beatles, the

Stones, The Moody Blues, Iron Butterfly, Pink Floyd and Dylan had made my life worth living in the sixties, and I still play their records with respectful and loving awe. At the same time, I was never interested in what drugs the musicians were taking, or which partners, of either gender, they were pleasuring in bed.

I was left cold by the rock-star practice, pioneered by Frank Zappa and David Bowie, of giving their children exotic – or plain silly – names: Dweezil Zappa, Moon Unit Zappa and Zowie Bowie. Paula and Bob had bought into this glitzy, bizarre and superficial syndrome, which ensured that their children would receive undue attention, at least in the press. But Paula and Michael had excelled themselves with Heavenly Hiraani Tigerlily. I welcomed the shortform of Tiger.

Before I met her, Paula had given me a much more personal reason to dislike her. Due to her refusal to communicate with us directly during the period of the DNA tests and beyond, I had been struggling not to think of her as a selfish bitch. But my feelings changed that day in Mayfield. I met my *sister*. And while I could see that she had the capacity to be bitchy, she was really a person who was deeply depressed and beset by great emotional problems, which I believed she was seeking to alleviate with alcohol and drugs. I could also see that she was probably not going to get well, as she had predicted, because she had lost hope.

Tragically, no one person or event was on the horizon to imbue her with any such hope, and only 30 months would pass before she would meet with her almost inevitable death. She needed professional, medical help, and for some reason I can't explain, I was certain that she wouldn't get it.

Before going to bed that night, we had a family dinner together in the Middle House Inn. We told Rainer about the events of the day, although not in any great detail. We were all rather subdued, and I was exhausted and suddenly feeling unwell. I excused myself early, and Lynne followed at about 10 p.m. We chatted for a while about what we had each been doing during the day. Then Lynne asked, 'What do you feel?' All I could reply was that I didn't really know, but it wasn't good.

The next day, two things happened. I washed as well as possible in the drips that trickled out from the showerhead, and I started out downstairs to join Lynne and the children in the beautiful back gardens, where breakfast was being served. Linda had brought her children over, and Kristin, Keely and Kady were getting on like a house on fire with her youngest daughter, Marina, who was then fourteen. We had made plans to do all sorts of exciting things in London with the children – go to Madame Tussaud's, perhaps, or to London Zoo. Have a boat ride on the Thames, or look for trendy junk on the Kings Road . . .

Halfway down the steep, back staircase, my legs turned to rubber. I spent the next five days in bed with one of the worst fevers I've ever known. I spent a lot of time looking across the high street to the graveyard where Mama and David were buried and wondering what they thought about everything that had happened.

The other memorable event of Wednesday, March 18 was Linda's phone call to Paula. She rang to check that she had made a safe trip back to London with Tiger and Belinda. Paula answered the telephone and said, distractedly, 'Oh, Linda, some friends just dropped in and I'm up to my elbows in bacon and eggs. I'll call you back later, OK?'

It was the last time that Paula ever spoke to Linda. I can only imagine the hurt my sister felt as the days went by and no return call was forthcoming. Truly, my heart would go out to Linda, who was too sensitive ever to phone again, for fear that her call would not be welcome.

She had been given every reason to believe in a wonderful future that fully involved Paula and her children.

On Sunday, March 22, I managed to struggle out of my sick-bed to accompany Lynne and the children to Linda's farmhouse for a Mother's Day meal after church. We now refer to it as the 'chicken-lunch day'. It was a beautiful morning – the first sunshine we'd seen on our trip. Linda confided that Paula had not yet returned her phone call, but was sure that she would when she had a moment. As we sat around the dining room table, she made an extraordinary announcement. Paula was planning to go to a retreat in Kathmandu and she, Linda, intended to go with her. Without any trace of sarcasm or mockery, I blurted out, 'Linda, *you* in *Kathmandu*?'

The idea of Linda, in her fifties, a mother of four, a conservative and devout church-goer and a respected member of her village community, in Kathmandu with Paula was amazing and very funny. Linda smiled and blushed a bit, but stuck to her guns.

I'm sorry to say that I pushed my amusement a bit too far. 'What are you going to do there?' I laughingly demanded of Linda. 'Climb Everest or just smoke dope in a Buddhist retreat?' Poor Linda saw no further humour in my thoughtless banter, and the atmosphere chilled. I hadn't intended to offend her, and I tried to make amends with some noises of encouragement.

Linda then revealed that she and Paula planned to get together again the next month, when they would organise an Easter-egg hunt for the children in her extensive lawns, complete with the bunny rabbits that were always hopping around there. It was a picture-perfect, fairytale fantasy, and Linda was thrilled.

I was deeply worried that she might not be given the chance to have the relationship she desperately wanted with Paula. However, I had a chat with Caroline, one of the managers at the Middle House Inn, about the possibility of Paula and her children staying there over the Easter break. Caroline, a former fan of Paula's, responded diplomatically but with some unease: she was worried about the potential media interest such a visit would create, and she wasn't sure that Paula would 'fit in' at the inn. Obviously, Paula's reputation had suffered from the drug bust and her antics on the plane to Sydney. She was beginning to be regarded as trouble.

The next day, Monday, Lynne and the children returned to Montreal. We were meant to be flying home together, but my week of illness had prevented me from meeting my brother Barry Hands and his wife Audrey for the first time – and that was something I simply had to do. Linda, who had met them several times before, decided to come with me.

As Lynne, Kristin, Keely and Kady headed towards the airport, Paula, Linda and I were front-page news in the *Sun*. They had started their three-day coverage of our meeting at Mayfield under the banner of 'Paternity Knocks: Paula meets her new family'.

Monday's feature carried a selection of photographs of us together, with comprehensive quotes from Paula about meeting her new brother and sister. On Tuesday, the emphasis was on Linda and her reactions, and on Wednesday, the spotlight focused on me.

I spoke about my refusal to believe Hughie's paternity of Paula until the DNA results were confirmed, I talked of a recurring nightmare I had suffered about meeting Paula, and I expressed my delight at finally spending a day with her. I was also quoted as saying, 'There's one overwhelming emotion that hit me – the desire to look after my kid sister. I never expected I'd feel that way. But Paula's been through so much I knew I had to protect her.'

I concluded that I would love to take Paula to Cornwall. Naïvely, perhaps, but with all of my heart, I would have liked to spend some peaceful days with both of my sisters in the beautiful surroundings of St Ives.

Linda said of her first meeting with Paula, at La Famiglia, 'I desperately hoped she wouldn't think I was too boring or ordinary for her. . . but the chemistry was immediate. We were like two schoolgirls catching up on the gossip. I love her dearly. . .'

She added, 'She was the warmest, funniest, smartest girl I've ever met. She was a real tonic, and I couldn't get enough of her.' That afternoon, Linda related, was 'one of the happiest of my life'.

Paula revealed that she had rejected the paternity allegation from the outset, which is why she never gave *us* a second's thought during the testing period. She went into such 'deep shock' over the result that Jools Holland immediately swept her off to his house where he nursed her through the worst of it.

Paula continued that it took her a long time to 'pluck up the courage' to make contact with Linda. Now, however, she was wildly in love with both of us. Paula said of me, 'He's everything I could hope for in a brother. He's bold, brash, funny and outspoken. Now all three of us are together, we're never going to let each other go.'

This was an important theme with Paula. 'Finding Linda and Chris has given me a little hope again . . . They have given me the strength to carry on . . . Linda and Chris came into my life at exactly the right time. I got a big sister and brother just when I needed them most.'

She then added, 'While Linda is quiet and reserved, he [me] is loud and very funny. Later, he admitted he was terrified of me and said he thought I would hate him because he looked like Hughie Green. I could never hate my own brother. We have talked and talked, and we're doing what we should do – making up for lost time.'

Paula reserved special praise for Linda, saying, 'She has been there for me from the start – an instant big sister. She's sweet and nice, ready with a cup of tea or on the end of a phone. The best thing she's done is to be very normal at a time when everything around me wasn't . . . I knew I would never be alone again.'

Paula talked up a good story; she certainly earned her cheque from the *Sun* that day. The truth, devastating as it may have been for Linda, was that Paula was simply weighed down with misery. She had no interest in seeing either of us again or asking for our help as her life spun completely out of control.

*　*　*　*　*

Linda had arranged for us to get together with Barry and Audrey Hands at the Moat House Hotel in Sloane Square. Barry had contacted my sister after Father's bizarre funeral, saying he wanted to meet and know us. They both kindly came down to London, rather than having me travel north to Birmingham, to accommodate my latest flight plans back to Canada.

I spotted them moments before they walked through the automatic doors into the hotel lobby. To look at Barry was to look at myself, and Father. Something Claire had said many years earlier suddenly leapt into my mind. 'Barry has been raised very differently from you,' she'd told me, firmly. 'You would have nothing in common.'

A slight moment of inner panic ensued, and I mentally pleaded, 'Not now, Mama, please not now,' and then I was embracing Barry. As we hugged, my eyes met Audrey's, and they were moist, happy and relieved. I then looked him in the face and said, 'You wouldn't, by any chance, be my brother Barry, would you?'

'Oh, Christopher, stop it!' giggled Linda, delighted by the warmth of our introduction.

And that set the tone for the rest of our meeting. It was extremely happy and enjoyable. Barry's a builder, Audrey's a school assistant, and they were and are lovely, friendly people – although I still wish my Canadian ears were more tuned to their Birmingham accents. We have since exchanged family photographs and we are in touch to this day, usually by phone.

This encounter was quite unlike the one we'd had a few days earlier with Paula, but one particular emotion struck me on both occasions. Inexplicably, perhaps, it was a feeling not of hate or loathing for my father but of guilt and shame on his behalf.

Barry was born in 1938 after Hughie, as a teenager, had impregnated Vera May Hands while he was appearing in the Birmingham theatre where she worked as an usherette. Hughie's parents, the Major and Violet, had ordered him to ignore her persistent, lovelorn correspondence in the hope that the problem would go away. But it didn't.

Years later, when I was about eleven and living at 169 Chiltern Court, a couple of fellows showed up at our door, saying that they represented Vera May Hands and wanted Father to make a financial settlement for Barry, who by then would have been around twenty. (Barry believes that a settlement was made much earlier, about three years after Vera began her letter campaign, although this would not fit in with the factually known dates of events in our family.)

Mother told us about our half-brother, simply because she feared that with the arrival of these men, there might be some resultant publicity, and she didn't want Linda or me to find out about Barry from kids in the playground. She felt badly for him, but she was not proud of Father's indiscretion, and I doubt that I would have mentioned it otherwise.

I was told afterwards that Father did make a financial settlement with Vera May Hands via a lawyer, that the agreement did not acknowledge what, specifically, the sum was being paid for, and that it did not identify Barry as being his son. It was a one-off payment – understood by Barry to have been a somewhat miserly £500 – and no others were made beyond that. The matter was then considered resolved, never to surface again.

Barry had heard a different version of events from his grandmother, since Vera never talked to him about his father. He explained, 'My mother honestly believed she would spend the rest of her life with him [Hughie]. He promised to take her to Canada. But when the show finished – he was there for three weeks – he dumped her and moved on.'

Hughie didn't speak to me or Linda personally about Barry, although he knew that we had heard about him from our mother. And Mama did tell me that the liaison with Vera May Hands was extremely brief and careless. My own researches into Hughie's itinerary have revealed that Father appeared at the Birmingham Aston Hippodrome for one week, not three, performed at another venue in the city on the next night, and then moved on to Brighton, Bishopstone and Manchester.

It seems unlikely, too, that Hughie would have suggested taking Vera to Canada. He was just seventeen, and even at that age he had no shortage of willing, sexual partners. In the unlikely event that he *had* fallen hopelessly in love during this close but short encounter, he was firmly under the thumb of his parents at the time, and would not have been at liberty to make such an offer.

Hughie, throughout his life, treated women abominably but he was brutally honest. He was never known to lure ladies into bed with false promises. He didn't have to. It seems to me that poor Vera May Hands may well have developed an unrequited attachment to Hughie and, in her loneliness, continued to nurture dreams of a happy ending that was not forthcoming.

Alternatively, she may have decided to protect her parents' feelings, and her own dignity, in the story of her doomed love affair. But whatever the circumstances, I'm privileged to have met Barry and I look forward to seeing him again, with Audrey.

Hughie has three other illegitimate children that we know exist, and they are 'out there'. My travels and my research into the shadows of the past have led me, literally and figuratively, to certain doors. But I have always backed away when it appeared that I was getting too close to my half-sisters. They may be unaware, innocent, and I do not wish to shatter their lives with news they may not have been expecting. I have seen the damage, first-hand, that such revelations caused Paula Yates.

*   *   *   *   *

There are unsubstantiated reports that Paula's friends rushed her into two different rehabilitation centres after Michael's funeral – and before the day in Mayfield. Certainly, she received treatment *after* I met her, both at a southwest-London celebrity retreat called The Priory – a very different proposition to The Priory she had known and loved in Kent – and at a clinic called Clouds in Wiltshire.

It's suggested that Paula suffered a nervous breakdown early in 1998, and that she received bereavement counselling while continuing to swallow Valium tablets by the handful and smuggling alcohol into her room.

If, indeed, she had been in the care of professionals, then they obviously couldn't help her. Within weeks of our strange day together at Linda's farmhouse, Paula was wrestling with her sanity and teetering on the verge of suicide.

17

In Sickness, Not in Health

When we closed the door behind Paula at Mayfield, I believed that she was going away from us and would not look back. Despite my dreams that she would be able to banish her demons, restore her health and have a relationship with Linda and me that would be warm and beneficial for us all, I feared that her problems would overwhelm her. I did not believe that she would have the time or mental energy to be able to look to us for a relationship of any kind.

Linda had had her reservations about Paula before she met her, worrying that her famous sister would find her 'dreadfully dull', given the differences in their lifestyles. Yet, they had seemed to bond very successfully when they got together, they had discovered a mutual interest in collecting religious statues, and they had started to make plans to meet again. Linda was totally sure that she and Paula would become very close and do many things together.

It broke my heart for Linda that she heard nothing at all from Paula after the 'bacon and eggs' phone call, which I had strongly suspected was the beginning of our feared brush-off from Paula. After that, Linda only ever attempted to contact her through Belinda, but didn't succeed. However, she would never accept the possibility that Paula was not interested in us. She was deeply hurt, but she entered into a state of denial, preferring to believe that her sister was merely too busy. She would never give up hope that one day the phone could ring and Paula would be on the other end.

I regretted that we had not met the *real* Paula, before she became disturbed. I believe *that girl* would have treated us very well, and that there would have been a possibility for a meaningful and loving relationship. As it was, we went on to watch our sister falling apart in the pages of the tabloid press, and we talked worriedly about her on the phone almost every day.

In April 1998, the month after we met Paula, she went to Australia for Tiger's christening. It was later reported by the *Sunday Telegraph* that while they were in Australia, Michael's mother, Patricia Glassop, made a phone call to the police to voice her concerns for Tiger's safety. Officers from the station at The Rocks were duly dispatched to Paula's door to check on the child, and it was said that Paula naturally was and would remain 'tremendously upset' by this. Still, she painted on a bright smile and struck cheerful poses with Kell for the profitable christening story which would appear in words and photos in *Hello!*

Shortly after her return to the UK, Paula was admitted to a private clinic, having just announced her intention legally to challenge the Australian coroner's verdict of suicide in Michael's death. She was reported to be receiving treatment at the clinic for severe depression, while other sources indicated she had suffered a complete nervous breakdown.

There were no mentions of any addiction at this time, although as Patricia Glassop and Tina Hutchence, Michael's half-sister, say in their official information website, 'We knew that each time the press reported that she had been checked into The Priory for "grief counselling", it was highly possible that it was something else. The Priory is popular with British celebrities who need detox, rehabilitation or rest.'

The same month saw the start of the fight to find Michael's missing fortune. Patricia and Tina had initially taken legal advice after Michael's death, when they say they were led to believe that his will requested cremation, discovering too late that it contained no such wish. Their enquiries into this had opened up great concerns about Michael's financial affairs and the eventuality that his bequests could not actually be paid out.

Paula and Kell Hutchence – Michael's father – declined to join in the women's action to track the various trust funds that were said to have been set up. It was later suggested that this ongoing, legal campaign added new turmoils to those already existing in Paula's life.

Patricia and Tina have written, 'In reality it was in Paula's best interest to join us in our litigation as Tiger's future depended on it . . . I think she was given poor advice and trusted the wrong people because it didn't make sense when she refused . . .

'We think that Paula was under the impression that we were trying to take something away from her, when in fact we were trying to secure her future along with Tiger's.'

According to Patricia and Tina, Paula was consulting with (and receiving hand-outs from) some of Michael's business associates. The extent and whereabouts of his assets were, however, a mystery. Stating that Michael had been worried about irregularities in his finances before he died, and had even had his American Express card embarrassingly refused in a restaurant, they stated that his money was still 'paying the bills for several people – just not the people who Michael intended it for, in particular his daughter.'

Patricia and Tina maintain that Hutchence left fifty per cent of his estate to Tiger in his will and ten per cent each to Paula, Patricia, Tina, Kell and Michael's brother Rhett. Yet, none of the beneficiaries had received what they believed was their due inheritance, although some 'minor' amounts totalling £500,000 had allegedly been paid out to Paula.

Michael had invested his assets in offshore trust funds to avoid exorbitant taxation. Money generated after his death from sales of his properties and continuing record royalties was deposited in these accounts which, say Patricia and Tina, were owned by Michael but controlled by businessmen in different countries, while sums of money were being shuttled around the world, from the UK to France and Liberia, and from Australia to Hong Kong and the Virgin Islands. They say that all efforts to establish the true worth of Michael's assets and have them distributed to his heirs and heiresses ran up against a brick wall.

Eventually, Patricia and Tina claimed to have gathered 'over-whelming' evidence to launch proceedings against fourteen people, from whom they were demanding the return of Michael's assets to his estate. But the women would eventually be forced to back down and settle out of court after realising that they could not, financially, take on a case that would last for up to six months. They now predict that Tiger will never get her full inheritance, stating, sadly, 'Her father's royalties alone should have secured her future.'

*　　*　　*　　*　　*

In June 1998, Bob Geldof won primary custody of his three daughters. Although there was to be 'shared care', this only applied to school holidays, when the couple would split the residency equally. To all intents and purposes, Paula had lost Fifi, Peaches and Pixie.

Nobody was aware of this at the time. Reporting restrictions had been placed on the hearing to protect the girls, and would not be lifted until October, after a legal application by the *Sun*, at which time it was stated that the reasons for the decision would remain private and that the order was subject to variation at the couple's discretion.

Geldof, meanwhile, began a campaigning, vocal support for fathers' rights. It was reported by the *Sunday Telegraph* that Bob had originally included the name of Tiger on the court custody documents, but had had to withdraw it – an allegation which was not repeated elsewhere at the time.

At the end of June, Paula made what the press reported, with reference to Hutchence, was a 'copycat suicide attempt', in which she tried to hang herself. Other observers felt that it was a desperate cry for help or attention. Whatever the case, and we will never know, Belinda Brewin found Paula in a 'distraught state' at her London home.

Belinda later told writer Steven Daly, for an article appearing in *Vanity Fair*, that she had phoned Paula on the day in question to say she would be visiting in five minutes' time. When she arrived, Paula had a red neck and bloodshot eyes, having apparently tried to hang herself with a luggage strap.

Belinda also informed the interviewer that she had found Paula almost dead in September 1997 – six months before we met her. Paula, her lips turning blue, had ingested a mixture of Valium and two types of liqueur – Malibu and Bailey's Irish Cream.

After the abortive 'hanging', Paula was rushed back into rehabilitation, reportedly for 'grief counselling', and sensational press reports of the incident carried comments from Linda which confirmed that Paula had attempted suicide.

Linda had not given any such verification. The first she had heard about it was when a news reporter called at her home and asked for her reactions. Shocked, she said she was extremely upset at the news and felt Paula was still grieving for Michael. This simple statement appeared in the paper as, 'I feel so sorry for Paula. It's been one tragedy after another. I know she has simply not been able to come to terms with Michael's death – she was so in love with him. She feels unable to think of anything else. I'm sure this is part of the reason she tried to copy the way he took his life.'

Her words had been both misquoted and made up. She was distraught that Paula might think she had actually said this. Linda knew that Paula would be terrified of the authorities taking Tiger away from her on account of the alleged suicide bid, and Linda was frantic for her sister to know that she would not have said anything to hurt her or put her in jeopardy of losing her child.

Linda called Belinda in a panic. It was the first time she had tried to communicate with Paula after being fobbed off with the story of the bacon and eggs. She wanted to speak to Paula in person, but Belinda didn't offer that opportunity. Linda then asked her to tell Paula that she had not spoken to the press in the manner reported. Belinda replied that Paula had seen the publicity and was upset by Linda's comments, but that she would pass on her message. Linda was, once again, very hurt. She called me in Montreal and we had a long chat about it.

Linda mentioned that Belinda herself was in crisis. She had been invited to Australia by Andrew Young, her boyfriend and

Michael's former legal adviser, but with Paula in her current condition, was not sure whether or not she should go.

I needed to express my urgent fears and so, again swallowing my dislike for Belinda, I wrote a letter and faxed it to her on July 1, 1998. I told her, 'Paula desperately needs professional help at this time. This you cannot afford her. Please come to terms with this difficult fact and put those admirable but misplaced feelings of guilt away. Accept Andrew's invitation to go to Australia with the children. Do this in the clear knowledge that you are not the one who can exorcise Paula's demons.

'Whether or not you do decide to go to Australia, for all, this is a sorry tale that apparently has little chance of a happy ending if Paula does not receive, voluntarily or by court order, the medical help she so evidently needs.'

Belinda never acknowledged my letter.

I was becoming greatly concerned about Tiger's welfare and I was, of course, extremely anxious about Paula. On the one hand, I was encouraged that she was receiving treatment, but on the other, I suspected that she was only going into the clinic for a 'cosmetic' stay, and that after a few days, we would see a glossy, magazine cover-story about her 'celebrity rehab'.

A close friend of Paula's later told me that she spoke to one of the doctors who had treated her. In the doctor's opinion, Paula showed no interest in co-operating. She needed to be there to appease the authorities and retain charge of Tiger. Indeed, her friend believes that Paula actually wanted to be thrown out of Clouds clinic. She achieved that very quickly.

Belinda, meanwhile, had made the decision to visit Australia with her children, Montana and Indiana, for three weeks. She had also taken Tiger, now her god-daughter. It was felt that Paula and Tiger would each benefit from the space between them: Paula would hopefully concentrate on her recovery, while Tiger would enjoy a carefree summer vacation in Sydney.

Belinda and the girls 'had a ball' visiting shops and markets, and Tiger was reunited with members of her paternal family. Kell Hutchence, who had recently undergone a heart bypass operation, was quoted by the *Sunday Telegraph* on July 26 as saying, 'She [Tiger] is here to have a little holiday and spend some private time bonding with me and the rest of my family. We'll be going to the park and the zoo and doing all those other lovely things one can do in Sydney.'

Michael's brother, Rhett, saw Tiger's visit as an ideal opportunity to heal the rifts which had torn his family apart. Kell and Patricia had fallen out on the day of their son's funeral in a physical altercation in the limousine taking them away from the service, although Patricia has emphatically denied reports that she punched Kell in the teeth, claiming that her bracelet caught his mouth accidentally while she was trying to clamp her hand over his mouth to stop him talking.

Kell was allegedly now working in his own right to unravel the complications of Michael's financial legacy.

In another family division, Rhett shared Paula's conviction that Michael had died accidentally, while Kell, Patricia and Tina believed that he had taken his own life. In their writings, Patricia and Tina say that Paula had at first shared their opinion, but had shortly afterwards changed her tune on a television interview for which she was paid. It should be pointed out that after her initial shock over Michael's death, Paula stoutly defended the 'accident' theory for the rest of her life.

Rhett said, 'Being the only blood child left between my mother and my father, I've been pulled around like a puppet. There's been a big divide since the day of Michael's funeral. I'm really trying to get them together.'

He spoke delightedly of the growing bond between Tiger and her cousin Zoe, his daughter, and he revealed the closeness of Belinda and Tiger, confessing that he was 'really hurt' when Tiger called her godmother 'Mummy'.

'Belinda thinks of her as her third child,' said Rhett. 'It is Belinda Tiger clings to when she's feeling shy around strangers. I guess that's understandable because of the time they've been forced to spend together after all of Paula's problems.'

He added, 'Still, I have grave concerns for her welfare . . . Tiger's had so much controversy for a little baby, and I just wish she could grow up to be a normal little girl. Paula is missing out on so much, such as Tiger learning new words.'

Rhett's 'grave concerns' were shared by the warring factions of the Hutchence family. All were now taking serious steps to try to secure Tiger's safety. Paula was about to be assaulted by custody problems that, for once, did not emanate from her former husband.

*   *   *   *   *

Paula had responded to her great, personal challenge at Clouds clinic by ignoring the rules and taking a lover, her first since Michael Hutchence. She had become besotted with Kingsley O'Keke, who was being treated for heroin addiction. According to press reports, they had met in a therapy group but were both chucked out of the clinic after being caught in bed together and 'bonking like rabbits' in the grounds of the building.

The UK tabloids had a field day with the story in August, especially when Paula continued seeing the unemployed O'Keke in the outside world. He was, the papers said, a small-time dealer, who had fleeced addicts at his West London flat by supplying them with only half of what they'd paid for. He had been accused of theft and drug offences. Now, apparently, he had moved into Paula's home in Notting Hill, but it would not be long before he was telling the press about their lusty romps, and how Paula slept on a pillow containing Michael's ashes. An anonymous friend of Paula's commented, 'She and Kingsley have become very close very quickly, but nothing will come between her and the children. They are the most important thing for Paula.'

Rhett Hutchence remarked, 'Paula is in what you call early recovery and, in that phase, you're supposed to concentrate on one thing and that is yourself, not a new lover . . . I would like Paula to be happy and I just want Tiger to have a normal life.' He added that Belinda Brewin had 'reached the end of her tether' with Paula over O'Keke. Belinda also told Linda that Kingsley was a 'disgusting' type whom she did not want near Paula.

It would turn out to be a short-lived romance, not much more than six weeks in duration, but it was terrifying for those of us who cared about Paula and her daughters. At this time, we had no idea that Bob Geldof had legally spirited Fifi, Peaches and Pixie away from danger. But Tiger, as the youngest and most helpless child, was the one who concerned us the most.

The phone lines between Montreal and Mayfield glowed red-hot as Linda and I agonised for hours over the situation. What could we do? Paula was trashing her own reputation and any lingering appearance of responsibility as a mother.

It was then that I mentioned to Linda the option I had intimated to Belinda in my letter: Paula could be sectioned; she could be *made* to get well. I didn't understand how anybody in her close circle, including Bob Geldof – the father of her first three children – could watch this terrible disintegration without doing something, anything, to help her.

Lynne and I would have been happy to look after Tiger if her mother would only accept the need for treatment and agree to work with, and not against, the experts. As it turned out, Tiger's Australian relatives were queueing up to offer the same assistance.

Kell Hutchence thundered, in an emotional but unreasonable outburst, that Paula was 'common'. He had already, recently, made a custody bid for Tiger, pledging to look after her temporarily until Paula had made a full return to health, and this I had applauded; I felt sanity had finally prevailed. I believed that with Kell taking decisive action, there was some hope that Paula's story would not end in tragedy. Linda, however, was incensed at the thought of any further separation of Paula and Tiger, and this was where I started seriously to disagree with my sister.

Linda was extremely concerned for both Paula and Tiger, but she was angry at me for backing Kell, whom she branded a 'total bastard'. 'How could he possibly try to take Paula's baby away from her?' she railed. 'How could he be so cruel?'

In my view, Kell had no intention of permanently removing Tiger from Paula. He merely wanted to protect the child while her mother received the psychiatric help she badly needed and withdrew completely from drink and drugs. However, Kell would eventually back off and several months later would offer the hand of peace to Paula. I'm not aware that she ever took it.

Meanwhile, Patricia Glassop had met with Bob Geldof to discuss Tiger's welfare, amid reports that she, too, was seeking custody of the child.

All of this activity was brewing while Tiger was in Australia with Belinda and her daughters. Kell told the *Sunday Telegraph*, 'I would rather not comment in these circumstances. It's all a bit loaded.' Rhett Hutchence tried desperately to quell the tide of media interest, protesting, 'My mother and father have never tried to gain custody of Tiger. Their only concern, my whole family's concern, is for Tiger's wellbeing, that she's OK, that she's being looked after.'

Patricia Glassop and Tina Hutchence were, behind the scenes, making frantic phone calls to England, trying to register their certainty that Tiger was not safe.

They relate, 'We desperately tried. We tried so hard and made such a nuisance of ourselves with the British authorities [Social Services] that Paula's attorney finally got an injunction against us. We were told by Social Services that they no longer had to deal with our calls and letters, as Paula's attorney had formally told them they should ignore Michael's family.

'We even had a meeting with Bob Geldof at the suggestion of our London attorney. As he suggested that Bob is so powerful and he had won custody of his children, maybe he would help.'

But the documents that had secured Bob's success in achieving custody of his own three children were sealed and held in the utmost confidentiality. The women had no means of proving their contention that Paula was no longer capable of looking after herself, never mind Tiger.

Patricia and Tina now complain, 'Tiger was surrounded by many adults, godparents, publicists and attorneys who were more interested in protecting her mother's image than protecting a little child cut off from family. We are still very angry that so many people surrounding Paula, who should have felt responsible for a little child, ignored her plight.'

Unaware of what Patricia and Tina were thinking and feeling, Linda and I were giving voice to similar worries in our phone calls into the autumn of 1998. We discussed Social Services. We were under the impression that they were 'looking into everything', but where *were* they?

Belinda had told Linda that Social Services were coming round to see Paula and that she was going to take on a nanny. Patricia and Tina were also told by Social Services that they would visit Paula and make an assessment. However, since this visit was made by appointment, it was always possible that Paula could straighten herself out for the occasion.

As time went by, there was still no sign of any nanny. If, indeed, one had been hired, or put in place by the authorities, he or she hadn't lasted very long.

'I was aware that Social Services looked into it,' said Emma Worth. 'Knowing Paula, she would probably have fired any appointed nanny.' She continued, 'By the end, Paula WAS on drugs and alcohol, she had done her head in and she wasn't capable of rational thinking. It's very easy to make moral judgements. She did love those children, but she was not wading but drowning. She had obviously reached the point where she had no self-esteem. I don't know what could have been done.'

Social Services seemed to be screwing up big time. Paula was falling between the cracks, probably because it was assumed that as a celebrity and the ex-wife of Bob Geldof, she would have top-flight backing.

At our home in Canada, Lynne and I were outraged by the way in which the British tabloid press were circling Paula like vultures. They presented their coverage like a soap opera, with Paula as the tragic star who could be relied upon at all times to take another sensational fall. They no longer saw her as a person, let alone a woman who was ill. They hounded her like an animal, in the way that they brazenly harass and intrude upon all celebrities, but Paula was too frail to take it any more.

I was horribly convinced that without medical intervention and follow-up support – as opposed to her farcical visits to rehab clinics in which she smuggled alcohol and drugs into her room and initiated sexual liaisons with the likes of Kingsley O'Keke – she was a dead woman walking.

It was far from a happy new year for Paula. On January 22, 1999 – the day that would have been Michael Hutchence's 39th birthday – she was seen staggering around barefoot in a busy supermarket and, on leaving, took the hand of the wrong child and set off along the street. Someone came running after her with Tiger and made her exchange children. Paula was 'confused' and had clearly placed her daughter in great danger.

Linda and I were very angry – angry at Paula, angry at Social Services, angry at the whole situation. It was the first of a string of public appearances in which she was obviously under the influence of alcohol and/or drugs.

In March, she attempted a TV comeback by hosting *An Evening With Jerry Springer* for the UK Living channel in front of a celebrity audience. She had lost all of her authority as a presenter. Fluffing her lines, sniffing and mumbling incoherently, she made such a spectacle of herself that Belinda Brewin told Linda that she doubted Paula would ever work in television again.

Days later, Kell Hutchence called for the death penalty to be imposed for drug dealers.

Come the summer, Paula took Tiger to London's open-air *Party in the Park*. The British singer, DJ and all-round personality Boy George, who saw Paula at the July concert in Hyde Park, later wrote in his column for the *Sunday Express* that he considered her to be a 'wounded soul' who had found in drugs a perfect hiding place, an escape from the death of Michael and the discovery that Hughie Green was her father.

A former heroin addict who sympathised with her plight, George recalled that she was 'clearly unwell and staggering around with Tigerlily in her arms while celebs and punters were pointing, judging and sniggering'. A friend of Paula approached George, smirking, 'Have you seen Paula? She's just fallen over and been sick in the VIP bar.' He responded, 'Well, if you are a real friend you should take her home.'

Things were not much better by the beginning of the next summer: early in June 2000, Paula turned out to attend the premiere of Madonna's film, *The Next Big Thing*, at the Leicester Square Odeon in the West End – ironically, the scene of Father's first big London show many years earlier, when it was called The Alhambra. Swaying and crying, she was filmed by the TV news crews, with the result that her tragic appearance upstaged even Madonna.

There were other stories, too. Paula had collapsed at home while her daughters (with Geldof) were staying with her, and one of the girls had had to dash out into the street to summon help from a passerby. The children were taken away by the police. On another day, Paula was photographed obviously wildly intoxicated, struggling to get into the passenger seat of a car – at somewhere around 8.30 a.m.

To be fair to those around Paula, and as Boy George said, it's almost impossible to prevent an adult from destroying themselves if they themselves do not wish to be helped.

Linda and I felt terrible. We obviously didn't know the full story about what was going on with Paula, but all that we read and heard was alarming and desperately sad.

And I was feeling very confused about Bob Geldof. I had always thought of him as a good person, and had felt supportive of him when I had had to witness the torrents of abuse being heaped upon him by Paula and Belinda in Mayfield. I applauded the fact that he had secured custody of his children – any decent man would have done that in the circumstances. But he must have seen that this woman he had loved for so many years, this wonderful mother with her bright mind and lively personality, was down, out and ill. The media had turned against her. She was barely functioning.

Bob Geldof was a powerful, well-connected and wealthy man, who enjoyed great public esteem and adoration. I wondered why he was not intervening somehow to help the mother of his children; why he was not flexing his enormous clout.

As I saw, it, all that Kell Hutchence could reasonably have expected to do was to secure temporary custody of Tiger in an attempt to persuade Paula to get help and take it seriously. Bob, however, had far more power than Kell, and Bob was in the UK.

I was watching all of this unfolding from Canada, and I was frustrated and dismayed. Belinda was obviously in control over who had access to Paula, who in turn was choosing not to respond to Linda. We couldn't speak directly to our sister. I will always regret that Lynne and I did not get behind Kell Hutchence when he made his bid for Tiger's custody. I don't know what good, if any, this could have done; at least we would have tried.

Other things had been going on in Paula's life. It was reported in February 1999 that Belinda Brewin, on behalf of her god-daughter Tiger, had lodged documents in an Australian court claiming funds for maintenance, education and 'advancement in life' from the estate of Michael Hutchence. Tiger had still received no money and Belinda made it known that Paula had been forced to take out a large mortgage to help meet her expenses.

Lawyers for Michael's estate were insisting that his assets were worth only £720,000 when he died, although Patricia Glassop and Tina Hutchence were sure that he had more like £10 million in various trusts and investment companies around the world.

Linda and I, still phoning each other regularly, worried over Paula's finances and how they would exacerbate her problems, especially since we knew she hadn't been working.

Two months later, there was dramatic news. The legal proceedings brought by Patricia and Tina against fourteen people, including company executives and accountants, had been settled out of court. It had been established as part of the agreement that the total value of Hutchence's estate was only £4 million, and Tiger would receive just half of that. Paula was said to be 'astounded', and insisted that her daughter was entitled to the whole £4 million.

Belinda Brewin angrily attacked the Hutchence family. She was quoted as saying, 'We haven't agreed to anything and we've got our lawyers on to it. There was a mediation in Sydney last week. The family and executors voted that Paula and I were unwelcome to go. We were told that it was only a mediation and that there would be no settlement.

'It was only when we read the newspapers that we heard about the agreement. Paula and the rest of the benefactors should get nothing. It should all go to Tiger.'

What has happened since then is undoubtedly being guarded as a private matter by the Geldof family, which now includes Tiger.

There were more boyfriends. In 1999, Paula enjoyed a two-month fling with the highly respected singer and writer Finlay Quaye, who had built his reputation with an affecting blend of jazz, blues, rock, soul and reggae. Finlay had burst onto the music scene in 1997 with the memorable single, 'Sunday Shining'. His debut album, *Maverick A Strike*, released the same year, racked up a convincing 56 weeks in the UK charts. Finlay was known in the business as an eccentric and his relationship with Paula made great tabloid fodder when it was discovered.

Paula was also linked to the aristocrat Samuel Robinson-Horley. Belinda told Linda, rather contemptuously, that Samuel and his friends liked nothing better than to spend their time playing video games.

Throughout 1999, for all of her inelegant displays, Paula had equal moments of strength and optimism. From time to time, she would be photographed out with Tiger, poised and smiling, beautifully made-up and stylishly dressed. The more sympathetic press would duly note that, 'The dark days are at last behind her,' and that, 'For Tigerlily's sake, Paula has pulled herself back from the brink of despair and vowed to leave the pain behind.'

Belinda Brewin would faithfully promise that Paula was a recovering and reformed character and was looking forward to resuming her career. Not everyone was so sure.

In the late summer of 1999, Paula appeared on a TV documentary with Rhett Hutchence in a joint campaign to discredit the coroner's verdict that Michael had killed himself, discussing evidence previously unheard at the inquiry. Paula also relived her colourful sex life with Michael and talked of his attitude towards fatherhood. *In Excess: The Death of Michael Hutchence*, screened by Channel 4, featured Kell Hutchence too.

He presented the opposite view, that Michael had committed suicide as the victim of his own lifestyle.

By the autumn, there were rumours of a *Tube* revival special reuniting Paula and Jools Holland in their famous roles, but nothing transpired.

The year 2000 brought another trauma for Paula when, in March, an intruder entered her home, threatened her and was subsequently sectioned. However, there was a wonderful result for Paula in June when she won substantial libel damages from the *Mail on Sunday* over false claims that she had tricked Michael Hutchence into getting her pregnant with Tiger.

Paula used her windfall to buy a house in Hastings, an attractive, seaside town on the south coast of England, and she spent most of the summer there, living quietly and uncontroversially. By all accounts, she was well-regarded by her new neighbours who would later recall only her motherliness, domesticity and visits to church.

She returned to London to put on a united front with Bob at a school sports day, only briefly rocking the boat in August by announcing that she would sue Patricia Glassop and Tina Hutchence if they should libel her in their forthcoming biography of Michael, *Just A Man*. She appeared to be very upset about the impending publication, in view of the unhappy nature of her relationship with the Hutchence family.

Away from London, Paula had been cleaning up. Jo Fairley said in *Vanity Fair* that in Hastings, her best friend had broken free of drink and drugs, she was eating vegetables, she was drinking organic juice, and she was fully committed to relaunching her career.

Things were looking up. On September 14, Jo and Paula attended a meeting in London with an agent called Stella Wilson. She signed Paula on the spot and promised to draw up a plan of action to put her back on track professionally.

Celebrating with lunch at London's Groucho Club – a members-only venue in Soho, frequented by people in the media and the music and TV industries – Paula was approached in the ladies' toilet by the notorious rock'n'roll star Courtney Love, whose husband, Nirvana's charismatic leader Kurt Cobain, had also committed suicide. Having wrestled with her own drug problems and suffered the unique disadvantages of being one half of a famous couple, the American hell-raiser recognised a kindred spirit in Paula.

Courtney had outraged and inspired the world in equal measure with her own group, Hole, and had then transformed herself into a Hollywood movie star. She rang Paula later to suggest that they could 'hang'. Paula famously retorted that Courtney's choice of expression left a little to be desired.

Visiting Jo Fairley on Saturday, September 16, Paula revealed that she had fixed up a meeting with Courtney for the following Monday. She also mentioned that she'd bumped into one of the people she'd met in rehab, a 21-year old called Charlotte Korshak, who had been receiving treatment for heroin addiction.

Jo heard alarm bells ringing loudly in her head. At this point, with her health and professional future rapidly improving for the first time in ages, Paula did not need temptations placed in front of her by someone so closely associated with a part of her life that she had only just managed to renounce.

Jo's worst fears seemed to have come to pass when Belinda Brewin turned up to collect one of her daughters at Paula's London home early on that same evening. Belinda told Steven Daly, writing for *Vanity Fair*, that she had become so close to Paula, she was now able to spot instantly which drink or drug she had been using. And she was certain that Paula had taken heroin.

According to Belinda, Paula was aware that she'd been rumbled and apologised for her helpless condition. Belinda then spent two or three hours trying to bring her round.

Paula had been sick; Belinda cleaned it up. She helped her into the bath, washed her, and then walked her around until she was sure that Paula was able to move about independently. When she finally departed, Belinda was happy that while Paula was not in brilliant shape, she was at least well enough to be left on her own. Belinda did not realise that Charlotte Korshak had been in the house for the entire duration of her visit. Charlotte later swore that she had 'absolutely not' supplied drugs to Paula, had not seen her take any drugs that night, and had left her feeling 'fine, in a really good mood, happy'.

We were sleeping when the call came through to our house in Montreal at around 7 a.m. on Sunday, September 17, 2000. Keely answered it, and Lynne got out of bed to take the phone from her. Then she passed it to me, hearing that it was from the UK.

'Sorry to bother you at a time like this,' said the Scottish accent. 'But may I have your reaction to the news?'

'What news?'

'Oh, you don't know . . . ?'

'OK, please, I am awake now. What is this about?'

'Well, your sister is dead.'

'My sister is dead?'

'Yes, I'm so sorry.'

'Which sister is dead?'

'Paula.'

'Oh, dear God . . .'

'You didn't know?'

'No, I didn't know. I'm getting off the telephone now, OK?'

18

Life After Death – Defeat Goes On

Tiger had been alone with her mother's dead body for hours. Jo Fairley started dialling the number at 8 a.m. She wanted to remind Paula to ring Pixie, at Bob Geldof's house, to wish her happy birthday. Finally, Tiger picked up the phone and told Jo that her mother was asleep.

Eventually, Jo went round to Paula's house at St Luke's Mews, Notting Hill. Tiger let her in. Jo later stated, 'I rushed upstairs to tell Paula to wake up and took one look at her and knew she was dead. She was naked, half out of the bed. I touched her and she was very cold.'

Taking Tiger downstairs, Jo called an ambulance.

Lynne and I sat together on our bed. I heard sobbing, and it was ours. Suddenly, our pain turned into panic. Where was Tiger? And why had Linda not called us? We rushed downstairs and turned on the radio, the CNN news channel and the computer. I rang Linda's house. Stephanie answered.

'Oh, Uncle Chrissy, thank God you called. I couldn't find your number. It's all terrible. The press are calling every second, and they are all around the house, and I can't get hold of Mother . . . what are we going to do?'

It was after midday in England. Linda was with Rainer at a birthday party on a boat on the Thames. The guests had had to

switch off their mobile phones while on board the craft, and Linda
was oblivious to what had happened. After disembarking, they
heard the news on their car radio and urgently called Stephanie.
Hearing that their Mayfield house was surrounded by media, they
diverted to a flat they owned in London. From there, Linda called
me; our shock and sorrow were gut-wrenching. I promised that
Lynne and I would fly to England immediately, and asked if she
knew where Tiger was.

She responded, 'I hope you aren't thinking about adopting
her . . .'

I said, 'Well, of course, Lynne and I will offer her a home with
us. She doesn't have one now.' I felt that as Hughie's children,
Linda and I should both come forward and at least make it known
that we would welcome Tiger into our lives.

We heard on the news, to our relief, that Tiger was with Bob
Geldof, and we blessed him for coming to her rescue at that
terribly sad and traumatic time. Within 24 hours, the newspaper
headlines would be screaming of 'Custody Battles Looming
Over Orphaned Tiger'. It never occurred to me for a second that
Bob would be one of those seeking custody of Paula and
Michael's child.

Emma Worth had a female pal staying at her Wiltshire home that
Sunday. They'd been for a pub lunch, and when they returned, the
phone rang. A close friend of Emma's broke the bad news.

'I was only glad it was him and not some journalist. I was glad
my girlfriend was with me. I was terribly shocked. I knew things
had been very difficult for Paula, in and out of rehab, and I had
heard that it wasn't going well in Notting Hill, and on top of all
that, she wasn't working. But I had read about [Paula's move to]
Hastings – "Thank God she's better." And that's why I'd been
thinking the time was right to see her again.' (Paula had called
Emma three weeks earlier and left a message on her answerphone
suggesting they get together.)

'The only reason I didn't call back right away was that I
knew Paula had not been in a good way, and I needed to be very
strong to deal with it. I talked it over with a friend of mine, who

thought it would be a good thing, and then I did feel ready to deal with it. I decided I would ring her back, but I never got the chance.

'I was utterly shocked at how it ended, at how desperate she'd got, and that Tiger found her like that. That would have been Paula's hell. I just thought, "Oh my God, how does anybody get like this?"'

As Jo and Belinda did what they could to help in the aftermath of Paula's death, with Jo clearing up her affairs at the house, floral tributes began piling up outside and Bob Geldof issued a statement, saying, 'We are all so sad. The loss for all the children is insupportable.'

Six months later, he reportedly admitted, 'I haven't forgiven myself for her death. I feel partly responsible because I wasn't there for her. I'm still not over it. I miss her terribly, and it's very hard for me and the kids.'

Later still, he said of both Michael and Paula, 'They just didn't kill themselves . . . in both cases it was accidents, accidents that happened way out on the limb of what you're doing.'

Kell Hutchence described Paula's death as 'very shocking and very tragic'. He added, 'I know that Paula had her ways and often we didn't agree, but God bless her, I never really thought it would come to this. She was a good mother, she loved her kids and I just think it's very, very tragic.'

Asked what their reactions were to Paula's death, Patricia Glassop and Tina Hutchence later wrote, 'We are just lucky that Tiger is alive. She could have ingested anything while alone with her mother's body.'

They also expressed their fury at a court system which allowed for Bob Geldof's custody of the three older girls while permitting the youngest child to remain with Paula in her troubled state. They asked, 'How many people who knew the particulars of the Yates/Geldof case had a hard time sleeping after Tiger was found alone with her deceased mother?'

Linda was different when I called her back half an hour after our first, tearful conversation that Sunday. She no longer wanted

Lynne and me to fly over to her. She had heard there was to be an autopsy, and believed this could delay the funeral.

'And then what are we going to do?' she demanded. 'Sit and look at one another until Paula's body is released?' Her tone was cold, almost hostile. I was absolutely dumbfounded. She then instructed me, 'Just wait. I will let you know what is happening and when to come.'

Before she rang off, Linda told me, 'I spoke to Rainer and he said he wouldn't mind at all offering Tiger a home with us, but I don't think we should – and you and Lynne have enough on your plate too.'

I said to Lynne, 'Linda has dismissed me, again.'

We considered her comments about Tiger. Reasonably, a woman of 56, who had already raised four daughters and who loved travelling with her husband, would not want the commitment of another infant child. Was that it? But if so, why then was she so opposed to our offer? Lynne was thirteen years her junior, our girls were still in the nest and, as parents, we were extending an open welcome to Paula's daughter.

That afternoon, Lynne and I sat down with Kristin, Keely and Kady and discussed the idea of Tiger coming to live with us. They were all for it.

First thing the next morning, Lynne and I went to the passport office. I needed an emergency renewal so we could rush to London at a moment's notice for Paula's funeral. While we were there, Lynne received a call from Linda on her mobile. She passed over the phone, and Linda immediately started barking at me that I had no right to be coming over to sue Bob Geldof for custody. We didn't understand where all this talk of suing was coming from. What new madness was this?

We wanted to be at Paula's funeral, to pay our respects to her and to achieve a measure of closure after everything that had happened. We had, in a way, been living in Paula's shadow since the day we met her. As a blood relative of Tiger, I simply wanted to make it known that we would be delighted to have her with us if all of the 'responsible parties', collectively, decided that to be the best option.

Several hours later, I called Linda back. Extraordinarily, her mood had changed again. She was calm, almost laconic, and made no mention of her earlier tirade. I told her that I would be calling Belinda Brewin to ask for Bob's telephone number. I intended to offer my condolences and establish a human connection with him so that we would not meet him at the funeral as strangers. The topic of Tiger's future was something I expected to talk about at a later date. In conclusion, I told Linda that I intended to speak with Bob personally; I had no wish to discuss Paula's funeral with Belinda Brewin. Linda ended the call by promising that she would keep us informed of all that was going on.

But she was breaking her word even at that moment. It had already been reported in the UK that Tiger had been made a ward of court that day, with her interim care and control committed to Bob Geldof. Kell Hutchence said from his home in Australia, 'As far as the custody of Tiger is concerned, I feel she's in very good hands. Naturally, I'm greatly concerned for my granddaughter's welfare, and I think it's just a matter of letting the dust settle on this whole matter and then working out what is best for Tiger.' He later declared that he would not be seeking custody because of his age and ill-health, adding, 'I only ever tried to get a temporary custody, if you can call it custody, which would just have been looking after Tiger when her mother was not well.' He concluded, 'I think that the responsible parties will sit down and no doubt work out a plan for her future.'

This seemed like the only responsible way forward. As Paula's half-brother, I hoped to be included in those talks.

Meanwhile, Patricia Glassop and Tina Hutchence were consulting lawyers with a view to Tina applying for Tiger's custody. Tina was quoted by *The Times* as saying that it was 'worth fighting for' Tiger, whom she hadn't met recently. 'All I've seen for two years are magazine photos,' she said. 'I just hope we can put everything that has happened behind us and my parents can have a relationship with their granddaughter.'

On the official website run by Patricia and Tina, it stated, 'Tina would have been happy to do whatever it took to make sure her

niece was loved, well taken care of, and had contact with her older
stepsisters, as well as her cousins, who are closer to her age, not
to mention the rest of Michael's family.

'Unfortunately, she did not get that chance as Bob Geldof
filed for custody the day after his ex-wife died. Michael's
family was not notified. Instead, Bob assured Tina that he was
just providing a home for Tiger and her nanny until she arrived
in London.'

Although it was widely reported that Tina had made an official
custody application, their website gives a somewhat different
version of events: 'The law in the United Kingdom is such that
once a person applies for custody of a child, anyone else (even a
blood relative) must ask permission of the first party to "join" the
proceedings – a mere formality. Tina and Patricia were assured
that Bob would not object as it would be embarrassing for him to
publicly object to Michael's family joining the proceedings.
Tina's attorney was wrong, because Tina never got the chance to
apply for her niece.'

Belinda explained that she was rushing out of the door with some
clothes for Tiger but would be back soon and would get Bob's
number for me. I knew she already had his number, but said
nothing. I assumed she wanted time to contact him so that he
would be expecting my call.

She didn't ring back. I called her again and it sounded as though
I had woken her up. She hedged that Bob's number was 'out in the
car', and she would get it for me later. I asked, incredulously why
she didn't have it to hand. She replied, 'Chris, I cannot give Bob's
number out to just anyone.'

It was then clear to me that I was not going to be able to contact
Bob Geldof. Belinda was the eternal go-between, she was not in a
position to decide who could and couldn't speak to him, and I
couldn't blame her if he didn't wish to talk with me. I let it drop.

I believed that I had every right to contact Bob Geldof. I am
Tiger's flesh and blood, and I had been sure that that would be
respected. How wrong I was.

It was Tuesday, September 19 – the third day. I called Linda early in the morning at her London flat and was initially delighted that the phone was answered by my dear old pal Karin. Karin, the daughter of Mama's friend Wendy in Chiltern Court. Karin, who was with me on so many happy, childhood visits to Regent's Park and London Zoo. Karin, who was watching the elephants with me when Mama died. Karin, who immediately started haranguing me when she realised who was on the telephone that day at Linda's.

She told me that I should not fool myself that I could sue Bob Geldof for custody of Tiger. Bob Geldof was a 'saint' in the UK, and if he wanted the child, then he would get her. I was staggered. I realised that Linda must have repeated to Karin her misapprehension that I intended to sue Bob, which just wasn't the case. Worse, Linda had apparently made the same allegation to Belinda Brewin. I never tried to sue anybody. Our offer to help Tiger was made purely out of love and concern, not a legal challenge to anyone.

When she finally let me speak, I told Karin, 'That innocent little girl is my father's grandchild. I have feelings for her. It's too late to do anything for Paula, but I'm not going to sit back and listen to all this crap about custody battles. If I can do something for Tiger, who is my flesh and blood, then I will. If that means giving her a home in Canada with my family, where she can grow up as a normal child, away from all the celebrity associations, then I'm happy to do that. That's all there is to it.

'Now, please let me speak to Linda . . .'

Linda was hysterical when Karin handed over the phone, virtually screaming at me in short, clipped sentences. It was the last time we ever spoke.

'You cannot be so wicked,' she raged. 'You cannot break up Paula's family. You don't know how cruel those people are who are trying to take the child away. I'm trapped here and I can't go back to Mayfield. The press are all around. You cannot sue Geldof for that baby. I just cannot talk about this now. I just cannot explain it to you. Oh, Paula has a will. There, you see. Paula's will will say what she wants.'

It would turn out that Martha Troupe and Bill Liebowitz had been appointed as Tiger's legal guardians in Paula's will – but I would not hear their names mentioned once as the case for her custody progressed.

Lynne and I were bewildered and hurt. Yet again, we were in *Alice In Wonderland*, surrounded by bizarre behaviour and emotional headlines. I wanted to try and get my own voice heard, so I wrote an open letter, dated that same day, to the *Daily Mail*, care of my friend Anne Shooter, in the hope that it would be read by Kell and Bob Geldof and Belinda Brewin.

Part of it said, 'Already headlines are emerging to the effect that custody battles are looming. That they are, if this is correct, is totally disgusting and only serves to perpetuate a climate of bitter feelings that will not let Tiger thrive in her own right.

'I can only hope that Paula has recorded clearly in a will what she wished for Tiger if her passing was premature. Failing this, I appeal to Kell and Bob and Belinda Brewin that at a time in the future, when Paula has been put to rest, all will meet as concerned and responsible adults to privately honour Tiger with our love and unselfish consideration.

'My wife Lynne and I wish to be present at this meeting. Our home in Canada is a happy one with three young girls, two dogs, two cats and all that a little girl could need growing up. If in harmony with those loving this child, we were deemed suitable to raise Tiger, our family joy would be complete and encompass us all.'

My letter wasn't printed.

Lynne and I were booking and cancelling flights to London daily as we waited for Linda's call with the funeral details. We didn't know that she wouldn't phone us again. We certainly didn't know that we would be blocked from attending the funeral.

On Thursday, September 21, Rainer called me at my office sounding troubled, struggling to speak. He ventured, 'What is it that Linda has done to you that she feels worse about it than even Paula's death?' I will never forget those words. He asked, 'Are you coming over for Paula's funeral? Linda has told you about the funeral, hasn't she? Well, she must have told you about the funeral . . . ?'

He gave me no space to answer his questions. I said we were still waiting to hear from Linda. He replied, 'Oh, so you haven't received a telegram?' 'Lynne and I are on constant standby for a flight over for the funeral,' I retorted. 'Life is hell at my end. Linda has not told us anything. Rainer, please tell me what this is all about.'

Rainer then explained that Belinda had been at their London flat for a couple of hours on the morning of the outrageous conversation with Linda and Karin, and that the funeral arrangements had by then been settled. He was surprised to have been allocated a seat, because they were in such short supply. Linda had insisted on his presence.

He had asked Linda why he — and not I — was to accompany her, since the seating was restricted. But she didn't answer, and that's why he was ringing me. He was dismayed that Linda had kept us in the dark. He told me, 'Christopher, I would give you my seat — I don't even wish to go — but they are all strictly reserved for the designated person. The security is tight and there are codes to identify the people attending, so I can't just "give you my ticket".'

I could not believe that Linda was doing this to me. I needed the closure of Paula's funeral. And the thought that Linda could possibly sit in that church without me after all that we'd been through together as our parents' children broke my heart. We had shared the bad times. Increasingly, I had thought, we were looking towards good times ahead as brother and sister.

I made two urgent phone calls to the UK, hoping to find out more and, with any luck, receive a belated telegram. The first was to the church. I believed that the priest would understand my confusion and need, and possibly be able to put things right. There was no reply. I then rang Paula's solicitor, Anthony Burton, in London to ask if he could shed some light on my omission, and he unsympathetically referred to the limited seating. His coldness prompted me, suddenly, to ask if he thought Bob Geldof should be given permanent custody of Tiger. He said, 'Yes, and then she will be with her sisters.' This was somewhat puzzling, given that he had been Paula's solicitor.

Mr Burton continued that Jo Fairley was organising the funeral, and said he would relay to her my request for a seat. I was and still am under the impression that Bob Geldof was the funeral organiser. I heard nothing back. Whatever had transpired between Linda and Belinda that Tuesday morning had sealed my fate: I was an outcast.

The stars turned out in force for the service, held at the church of St Mary Magdalene in Faversham, Kent, on Saturday, September 23, 2000. It was the same church, attached to The Priory, where Paula and Bob had held their second wedding ceremony, and where all three of their daughters had been baptised.

The cortège was led by an undertaker in a black top hat and gloves. Paula's cream-coloured coffin was festooned with pink tiger lilies and surrounded by other beautiful flowers. Inside it, she wore a patterned, Empire-line dress which was one of her favourites – and not the mink bikini of legend. That had reportedly been Jo Fairley's idea, after hearing from Paula that she intended to have a skimpy two-piece made from a fur coat that Jo had given her.

The service was led by the Reverend Ian Black, a family friend. The congregation sang 'Jerusalem' and 'I Vow To Thee My Country', there was a reading of a poem by Keats, and U2 frontman Bono sang *Blue Skies* to Jools Holland's piano accompaniment.

Other mourners included Annie Lennox of Eurythmics, singer Paul Young, actor Rupert Everett, DJ Paul Gambaccini, former model Yasmin Le Bon (wife of Simon), fashion designer Jasper Conran and Australian singer Nick Cave, who had also attended Michael's funeral.

The one famous name which was conspicuous by its absence during the service was that of Michael Hutchence. He was not mentioned, and there was speculation later that he was 'written out of Paula's life' at the behest of Bob Geldof who, some felt, had reclaimed his wife.

Paula was carried out of the church to the strains of her own voice singing 'These Boots Are Made For Walking'.

The cortège then drove solemnly to Charing Crematorium in Ashford, Kent. A spokesman for Chelsea Funeral Directors, which conducted the event, said that Paula's ashes would be interred with the pillow containing those of her soulmate Michael, although he declined to say where.

The Reverend Alan Duke, spokesman for the Diocese of Canterbury, had been insistent that the private funeral was for Paula's family. Yet, only six blood relatives of Paula's were present – Paula's four children, her estranged mother Hélène and my sister Linda – plus one relative by marriage, her former husband Bob Geldof. Susie Hutchence was there too, although her husband Kell had not been well enough to travel. I was surprised to hear that Emma Worth, a former close friend of Paula's and one with whom she had planned to be reunited, had not been invited.

Emma told me, 'I nearly, *nearly* went to the funeral. I wondered what Bob would do if I turned up. It wasn't Paula's day, it was Bob's, and maybe he needed that. I mean, gosh, heaven knows what he has been through. He was going through a very rough period, he was going through *hell* when Paula left him. At the end of the day, it's between Bob and God. For me, of course I wanted to pay my respects to Paula, but I felt I couldn't. It would've been a fiasco if I'd shown up only for Bob to turn me away.'

Linda, meanwhile, was apparently becoming enamoured of people she had previously despised. Within six months of her introduction to Bob Geldof at the funeral, she was telling the *Daily Mirror* that he was, 'one of the most selfless and caring people I have ever met'. She wasn't saying anything like that when Paula was alive.

Linda also changed her mind over Hélène Thornton-Bosment, who reportedly embraced her in the living room at The Priory. Linda was later said by the *Sunday Times Magazine* to have felt 'sympathy and sadness' for Hélène – having previously been one of her biggest detractors.

Then, of course, there was Belinda Brewin, who crossed to Bob's 'camp' after Paula died. I had personally been a party to Belinda's hostility towards Geldof as she stood unequivocally in Paula's corner, defending her against her former husband. As Emma Worth commented, recalling some of the rows between Paula and Bob: 'I would say to Paula, "Bob will calm down." Belinda would have been the one going, "Yeah, what a bastard." When Paula died, there was only one 'camp' left, and that was Bob's.

I was desperately sad that Linda had not had the kindness at least to telephone me and explain that we were not invited to the funeral. There had been no closure from Father's funeral. Now, Paula too was gone, and closure had again been denied to me.

I thought about Papa, and wondered if he was taking any pleasure from Linda's actions. I questioned, sadly, the legacy of my parents, and Hughie's before him. Our dysfunctional family state was continuing without him.

Two days later, a fax arrived from Linda. Addressing me affectionately as 'Dearest Bruv' and signing off with her pet name of He-He, she seemed to be making an effort to calm the troubled waters between us – but the content of her letter only made them more turbulent.

She revealed that Rainer had only just told her about our conversation because she had been so distressed over Paula, he didn't think she could cope with any extra upset at the time.

Linda was under the impression that I was accusing her of stopping me coming to the funeral, and was sorry if I believed such a 'cruel and stupid' thing.

At no time, she said, had she spoken to 'the lawyer'. However, she had, as I requested, expressed my worries about Tiger to Belinda, and she had asked Belinda to tell Bob and any other interested parties that, as a blood relative, I wanted to make the serious offer of a home for the child.

She did not feel it was the right time to introduce such a proposal – 'as I told you at the time'. But she did so anyway because I had insisted.

Linda told me that she was sure there were enough 'problems' surrounding the little girl as it was, with Michael's mother and half-sister 'wanting Tiger'.

Her fax went on to explain that she had not been invited to the funeral in the first place. She had had to 'beg' Belinda for her seat, and 'they' had been 'very abusive' to Belinda, declaring that it was impossible. More than a thousand people had wanted to come to a church holding less than a hundred.

Linda stressed how much she had cared about Paula, and how she would never forgive herself for not having tried to help her.

She apologised for any hurt she might have caused me by refusing to support my offer of a home for Tiger, stating that after seeing her with Bob Geldof and his girls, she was certain that Tiger was where she belonged, with a family who truly loved her.

Linda's fax continued with another apology, about the phone call in which she and Karin had upset me, adding that neither of them could 'pretend or lie' when they were absolutely convinced that Tiger should remain with the Geldofs.

Finally, Linda concluded that she appreciated my concern for the little girl, urging that 'we must all pray' for a happy future for her.

Linda's tone appeared reasonable and quite conciliatory on the face of it, but the fact remains that I had at no time asked her to tell Belinda or Bob anything about our hopes for Tiger. I had simply expressed our desire to offer Tiger a home, and I had said I intended to talk to Bob Geldof privately. That was to have been about Paula's funeral.

My sister had *not* told me, 'I did not feel it was the time to bring yet another player into this tragedy,' as she put it in her fax. She may have known about the custody plans being ventured by Patricia Glassop and Tina Hutchence, but I hadn't. It wasn't in the news in Canada at that point. Linda had said, 'You don't know how cruel those people are who are trying to take this child away . . .' but I had no idea to whom she was referring, and she didn't tell me. All Linda had shrieked, wildly, at me was that, 'I just cannot talk about this now. I just cannot explain it to you.'

She had been emphatic that she didn't want me to have Tiger, preferring to see her with Bob Geldof, a man she had always regarded with contempt.

I still don't know which 'lawyer' she was referring to.

And if Linda had had to 'beg' Belinda to ask Bob for a seat at the funeral, and 'they' were 'very abusive' to Belinda – how then had she managed to obtain not only an invitation for herself but one for Rainer too?

Linda's fax convinced me that she had attained a measure of closure by seeing the girls and Bob together. And Belinda . . . well, she quickly adapted. In September 2001, she would tell the press about Bob and the children, 'He has made them very happy. What does it matter now what went on before? A year on, Tigerlily comes to stay with me once a week and she is absolutely fine. And I had a drink with Fifi the other day and she seems happy too.'

'What does it matter now what went on before?'

To me and to Lynne, it meant everything.

As the custody proceedings dragged on into the autumn of 2000, I contacted Kell Hutchence by telephone. I wanted to know why there had been no family meeting to discuss Tiger's future, as he had proposed more than once after Paula died. He answered simply, 'Because Bob's in charge.'

Kell had undergone major surgery, he had bronchial problems, and he would finally die from lung cancer in 2002. He wasn't well enough to enter into combat with an adversary as determined as Bob Geldof. He had no love for Bob – indeed, he bitterly considered him to be a major factor in the suicide of his beloved son, Michael – but he intended to be dignified in his retreat. At least, that way, he might once again see his granddaughter Tiger, whom he adored.

He was a peacemaker. Kell, publicly and privately, had tried to restore some sort of harmony with Paula after calling off his bid for temporary custody of Tiger at the very moment that the little girl was sitting on an airplane with Belinda and her children, waiting to take off from Australia to return to London, her mother

. . . and Kingsley O'Keke. Kell had also called for an end to the in-fighting which was destroying his own family, although he had personally come to dislike his ex-wife and her daughter Tina.

In my opinion, Kell was the only sane and kind voice in this incredibly messy tragedy, and I emailed him to ask if he would be kind enough to convey to the relevant people my wishes, and Lynne's, to be granted some degree of family contact with Paula's daughters, my blood relatives. On October 13, he replied, 'I will keep you informed of any significant outcomes, as I know you are rightfully concerned for Tiger's welfare and will tell the executors and guardians of your need to have access to not only Tiger but Fifi, Peaches and Pixie. I can't guarantee anything, but I will do my best to bring your interests to the full attention of the parties involved.'

The executors were Belinda Brewin and Colin Diamond, a business colleague of Michael's.

With this, we established an irregular correspondence with Kell that was friendly and chatty while focusing on a changing situation that brought us little comfort. In May 2001, he sympathised, 'I am sorry you have had no luck in penetrating those walls around Tiger. It is a pity.'

Paula died from an overdose of heroin, coroner Paul Knapman reported on November 8, 2000. She had apparently overcome her previous drug problems, she was an 'unsophisticated' user with little tolerance, and the amount she took would not have killed a regular user.

He recorded a verdict of death by non-dependent use of drugs, saying, 'The evidence does not point to this being a deliberate act of suicide. It seems most improbable that she would attempt to kill herself with her daughter in the house. Her behaviour was foolish and incautious.'

The coroner also quashed tabloid rumours that she had been drinking vodka miniatures. There was no alcohol and no other illegal substance in her bloodstream.

He explained, 'The powerful narcotic drug depressed the cells of the brain which basically stopped her breathing.'

Belinda had told the court that Paula hadn't taken illegal drugs for nearly two years, but, on the night she last saw her, 'She was slightly staggering, her eyelids were drooping, she was slightly incoherent.'

Charlotte Korshak, the last adult to see Paula alive, testified that she knew her to take heroin, cocaine, ecstasy and acid 'from time to time'. She had been questioned about Paula's death, but was never accused of any illegal activity in connection with it.

After the finding, Paula's solicitor – Anthony Burton – read a statement on behalf of her friends: 'An inquest tells you how someone died, not how they lived. It gives no clue to the fullness and joy of Paula's life. Her friends will always remember her as loving, affectionate and witty.'

By Christmas, Bob Geldof had won custody of Tiger in a private hearing. Mrs Justice Hogg said the order would be reviewed a year later.

Bob had had a lot going for him. First and foremost, he was the father of Tiger's three half-sisters, and he had been looking after her since Paula's death. He lived in England – courts don't favour a child leaving their jurisdiction if it can be avoided. He was rich and well-connected, and he had the love, support and respect of all of Britain.

Interviewer Ray Martin later asked Geldof, 'What about the suggestion that you've done something noble, you've done something incredibly decent by taking on Tigerlily as well?'

'But that is a no-brainer,' Bob replied. 'That's ridiculous. Anyone would have done exactly the same. It's a little kid who has lost her mum and dad, whose sisters are with me. I mean, please, you know.'

'But even though she was the daughter of your ex-wife and her lover?' pressed Martin.

'What's that got to do with it?' retorted Bob. 'She's a gorgeous, beautiful little spark and the girls adore her, we all adore her. She's a fantastic kid.'

Bob wanted to keep the sisters together, he said, and he was, as always, beyond reproach. To suggest that Tiger could possibly have gone elsewhere would have been akin to heresy. Yet, Patricia and Tina have written that they were 'incredulous' at the court's decision to award her custody to Geldof. While describing him as a 'terrific, caring dad', with whom they enjoyed a 'harmonious' relationship, they contended that since Fifi, Peaches and Pixie had not been living with Paula for some time, they weren't necessarily as close to Tiger as they were to each other, and furthermore, they weren't 'caretakers'. Patricia and Tina also noted that 'as nice a person as Bob may be, he and Michael were anything but friends'.

However, even though they 'miss her very much', they were doing their best to keep in touch with Tiger on a weekly basis. They had been told by Geldof that they could see her at any time, and they 'continue to let her know that she is deeply loved by her father's family'.

Emma Worth said simply, 'The very last person on earth that either Paula or Michael would ever have wanted Tiger to go to would have been Bob, and Belinda must have known that absolutely. In the most positive light, perhaps she decided that Paula had lost her judgment and that Bob actually was the right person.'

After Paula's death, Belinda was quoted widely in the press as saying that 'with all my heart' she believed that Tiger should go with Bob, the man I had once heard her bitterly abusing, along with Paula.

Emma added, 'Bob did feel that Tiger should be with her half-sisters. And as for Kell Hutchence, he was trying to put all the bitterness behind him for the good of the child. I suppose he thought it was the right thing.'

Personally, I believe that a child should remain in the country of the court's jurisdiction and raised with its siblings wherever possible. What we really wanted was to be involved in the decision-making process, as family members. We definitely did wish for the opportunity to have access to the children, and if it was decided that we were the 'best option' for Tiger, then that would have been wonderful. If, on the other hand, the family together had decided that Bob would have been the best bet, or Tina, we would happily have abided by that decision.

Lynne and I had no intentions of breaking up a family, but we saw ourselves as having much to offer. We were neutral, not involved in any of the family feuds. We wanted to give Tiger a home away from the British press. We discussed the degree to which Tiger would have already bonded with her older half-sisters, and how much of a wrench it might be for a four-year-old to move to Canada to live with us and our three girls. We truly believed that she was still young enough to adapt to a new life. But we were offered no say in the decisions affecting Tiger's future. Bob Geldof simply seized control, and that was that.

*   *   *   *   *

Patricia Glassop blamed Paula for Michael's suicide. Little more than a month after Paula's death, Patricia told the BBC that she thought her son would still be alive if he hadn't met her. Claiming that Hutchence 'lost his elegance' after taking up with Paula, she was quoted as telling Nicky Campbell, a presenter on Radio 5 Live, 'He never had problems beforehand. He never had a deep drug problem before Paula.'

Patricia was in London with Tina to promote *Just A Man*, the book that Paula had dreaded. Tina said, 'Michael saw a psychiatrist and said he couldn't handle the in-fighting that was going on between Bob and Paula.' She added, 'Paula had many, many personalities – and I met about six of them.'

Yet, if Paula had expected a critical mauling in *Just A Man*, she could not have guessed at what would be in store for her had she lived to hear Bob Geldof's solo album, *Sex, Age And Death*, released in 2001. Written before Paula's death, it describes the emptiness and pain, the anger and the emasculation Geldof had experienced when she left him and then took up with Michael Hutchence.

The reviews, at least in the UK, were his finest since the days of the Boomtown Rats: 'Geldof's masterpiece' (*Big Issue*); 'his most vivid collection of songs for twenty years' (*The Sunday Times*); 'striking, harrowing, compulsive listening' (*The Times*);

'magnificent' (amazon.co.uk); 'it has a nakedness that almost takes the breath away' (*Daily Telegraph*); 'fantastically raw – had me in tears' (*Independent*); 'a series of extraordinary songs runs the entire gamut of human emotion' (*Uncut*); 'his most powerful collection of songs' (*Hot Press*); 'bleak, spooky and unsettling' (*Evening Standard*).

Geldof himself described his album as 'exhausted and weary'. He said, on his official website, of the album's lyrical content, 'I don't discuss these things literally because I can't. I can't show you my soul. Some things are unsayable but maybe you try to articulate the unspeakable in music. So I have made an unspeakable album.'

In an obvious reference to Michael Hutchence, one lyric reads, 'You got the gold, I got the lead/What the fuck's going on inside your head?/You got a life, you left me for dead/What the fuck's going on in your head?/ You got a life, you left me for dead. So why put a noose around your neck?/What the fuck's going on inside your head?'

Bob Geldof told Ray Martin, 'That line is, "Why would you do that? Why, why would you do that?" How could it get to that?' He added, recalling his carefree, early years with Paula, 'This wild, beautiful girl and this mad Paddy meet when they're kids and they go off on this wild ride together where they just see everything in the world that's there to be seen and then it ended. Isn't that sad? Yeah. And would she have gone off and had great things with Michael? Yeah, and that's sad that that didn't happen. It is, it's all awful, it's all awful, and nothing good came out of it. Nothing. Where's the upside here?'

Defending his right to be explicit, in view of the fact that Tiger would one day hear his words, he said that she already had; and no one could deny the facts of what had happened.

When I first listened to the CD, I felt physically sick. I respect fully Bob's entitlement to say 'the unsayable' in music, but, at the same time, he indulged his own, personal misery with a total lack of sensitivity towards Paula. These would have been cruel words indeed for her to bear, coming at her from her former husband and the father of her three eldest daughters.

Personally, I found the album as 'bleak, spooky and unsettling'
as the *Evening Standard* had suggested. Two images came to
mind: Paula, sitting in a room alone, listening to the memory of
her beloved Michael being battered with the accusatory, 'What
the fuck's going on inside your head?'; and Linda, blithely telling
the press that Bob 'forgave her [Paula] for so much while she was
alive . . .' I felt that Geldof's lyrics contradicted the spirit of
forgiveness with which Linda had so glowingly credited him.

Following on from *Just A Man, Sex, Age And Death* would
have been a massive body slam to Paula, who was in an extremely
fragile, damaged and vulnerable condition after Hutchence's
death. It is clear, from what I have read, that Bob intended
releasing it without regard for Paula being alive or dead and has
no problem with Tiger or the other children hearing it.

*   *   *   *   *

Emma Worth had two things she really wanted to say about Paula.
One was that she valued her children and her privacy above all
else. She only initiated her ill-fated collusion with the tabloid
press when she was rendered unable to work after the controversial 'Smartie' tube discovery at her home, while she was
abroad with Michael.

She hadn't even wanted to write *The Autobiography*, but as
someone who was being vilified – she was being portrayed as 'the
Devil' to Geldof's 'saint', and she was even being compared to
child-killer Rosemary West – she was forced to explain her side
of the marriage breakdown, to take some responsibility for her
reputation: 'The love affair with Michael was completely beyond
their control.'

The other thing was this: 'My strongest recollection of Paula
was of an incredibly kind, generous person who could be difficult,
but was a ground-breaking presenter. She had a way with words,
she was a very talented girl, and she would have gone on to be a
very, very memorable writer. That's what her children should
remember. I just wish I could have helped her more, and I hope
she is at peace now.'

Paula was a victim of Hughie Green, Elaine Smith and Noel Botham. Linda and I were victims of Hughie and Claire, our parents and star-crossed lovers. Hughie was a victim of child exploitation and psychological abuse inflicted by his own parents, Major Green and 'The Violet'.

Yet, despite these patterns of neglect repeating through the generations, I concede that we were in many ways privileged. My family members have enjoyed wealth, health, status, reasonable intelligence and a host of other blessings. And on the day that I spread Father's ashes on the waters of the Clyde, I recognised how much we, collectively, had had going for us and wondered . . . why had there been so little happiness?

Paula's impact upon the life of my family had been inestimable. Her birth dictated momentous events affecting Major Green, Violet, my mother Claire, my father Hughie, Linda and me. Had she not been born secretly to my father, I doubt if I would have been sent to Canada to be raised by my grandparents Wilson.

Meeting Paula was a deeply moving experience for Linda and me. It forced us both to look back, but in different ways. Paula's need to know what really happened was genuinely haunting, and that propelled me towards people, places and discoveries that I would never have known otherwise.

I will always regret that Linda did not accompany me on my journey into our shared past. It might have helped her to come to terms with the fact that our father, Hughie Green, was not in himself a monster, even though he undeniably did some monstrous things to us and to others. This odyssey, I believe, would have shown Linda that our mama was, in her way, as sad and unfulfilled as Papa, who was her fatal attraction.

Both Linda and I have known unconditional love among the many advantages in our lives. I am sorry that things were not better for us in our family, but I appreciate the blessings that I have received along the way. I feel no bitterness or self-pity, only sadness for the waste in what has gone before.

*   *   *   *   *

Linda and I had differing opinions over a documentary – *The Real Hughie Green* – which was being considered by ITN in London before Paula's death and finally aired in August 2001. The BBC had already screened a none-too-complimentary portrait of Father. Now, ITN's researchers were asking for our help. Linda was very enthusiastic, saying – as she had done a number of times before – that she wanted to 'set the record straight' and 'put things right'. I was apprehensive, yet again, that nothing would be clarified in such a venture, that it would merely keep the old wounds open and bleeding. I gently asked how she intended to 'set the record straight'.

Thanks to Noel Botham's eulogy from hell, Papa's reputation was in ruins, and I felt that any further destruction of him as some sort of insincere and monstrous freak was really not in order. Linda replied that it might well be our last chance to 'get our story out there'. I wondered if she would be willing to talk about the mezzanine floor and the day the Major died. She retaliated, 'Oh, no, we wouldn't talk about things like that, and why should we? I don't really know anything about it.'

I was interested in helping to portray Hughie Green as a complex, innovative and talented personality who was the flawed product of his own, extraordinary upbringing. I was not prepared to contribute to what I believed might be a one-dimensional portrait of 'the beast', and I withdrew when I was refused any editorial rights.

The documentary did turn out to be, as I had feared, and as *The Times* described it, a 'hatchet-job'. Linda played a leading role. With tears rolling down her cheeks she, as Hughie's daughter, validated his demonisation as a demented, insincere, greasy, talentless, cruel and wicked womaniser. Watching a video of the production, I felt great sadness, again, for Linda's obvious pain. I pray that by learning of the things that made Hughie Green the person he was, she will take the first steps towards her healing.

*   *   *   *   *

Paula's death was not necessary. I believe there should be guilt that nothing was done to help her. Not Paula the effervescent celebrity, the ex-wife of Bob Geldof and the lover of INXS superstar Michael Hutchence. Just Paula, a human being who was ill and a mother of four children who needed her, and loved her, as much as she loved and needed them. Paula, someone with problems who did try to cry for help while we all looked on. Didn't we?

Bob Geldof asked, 'Where's the upside here?' Wherever it is, it isn't in the past. We are not going to get Paula back. The only possible upside is in leaving our personal angers and hurts behind us and doing what we can to save the next 'Paula', who is certainly out there now.

I think of her and I can see her standing in the doorway of Linda's house at Mayfield, with little Tiger holding onto her ankle. I hear Linda saying to me, 'Chris, please, be very, very gentle with her,' and my heart breaks all over again, because nothing was gentle for her.

> 'To the living, we owe respect.
> To the dead, we owe the truth.'
> – Voltaire

Index